PC Confidential

Secure Your PC and Privacy from Snoops, Spies, Spouses, Supervisors, and Credit Card Thieves

Michael A. Banks

SYBEX®

San Francisco • Paris • Düsseldorf • Soest • London

Associate Publisher: Roger Stewart
Contracts and Licensing Manager: Kristine O'Callaghan
Acquisitions & Developmental Editor: Diane Lowery
Editor: Linda Good
Technical Editor: Michelle Poole
Production Editors: Jennifer Durning, Teresa Trego
Book Designer: Maureen Forys, Happenstance Type-O-Rama
Interior Art Designer: Chris Gillespie
Graphic Illustrator: Tony Jonick
Electronic Publishing Specialist: Maureen Forys, Happenstance Type-O-Rama
Proofreaders: Carrie Bradley, Molly Glover, Elizabeth Campbell
Indexer: Ted Laux
CD Technician: Keith McNeil
CD Coordinator: Kara Schwartz
Cover Design: Daniel Ziegler Design
Cover Illustration: Daniel Ziegler Design

Library of Congress Card Number: 00-101175
ISBN: 0-7821-2747-9

Manufactured in the United States of America

10 9 8 7 6 5 4 3 2 1

....

This book is dedicated to Debbie,
with much love and affection.

Acknowledgments

This book is the result of many years of working with computers and the people who use them. Writing it also involved the help, support, and goodwill of a number of fine folks.

First, to Roger Stewart and Gary Masters of Sybex Books, a hearty thank you for your enthusiasm about this project. Special thanks are due to my developmental editor, Diane Lowery, for her effort in making this come out right, and to Linda Good, my editor, and Michelle Poole, my technical editor, for the fast and accurate edits. Thanks also to Maureen Forys, the electronic publishing specialist who also created the book's sharp design; Jennifer Durning and Teresa Trego, the book's production editors, for handling the choreography in production; Margaret Rowlands, marketing design manager, for coordinating with Dan Ziegler Design to come up with a great cover; and Nathan Whiteside, Sybex's publishing intern, for his permissions expertise. Also, a tip of the hat to Harry Helms for turning up in an unexpected place yet again.

Special thanks go to Susanne Beeler, Amy Forrester, Wayne Hall, Larry Judy, Becky Lasater, and Debra Morner for proofreading, research, and various other helpful acts.

Contents at a Glance

Introduction. . . . . *xvii*

CHAPTER 1   Why Bother with Security? Threats to Your System, Your Data, and You. 1

CHAPTER 2   Basic PC Security Logistics & Tricks 11

CHAPTER 3   Simple & Direct—Protecting Your Information with Passwords and Settings . . . 25

CHAPTER 4   Protecting Your Files and Folders with Disguise and Misdirection 49

CHAPTER 5   Hiding Files, Folders, and Applications 67

CHAPTER 6   How to Keep Your Files from Giving You Away 79

CHAPTER 7   Data Encryption 97

CHAPTER 8   Virus Protection. 111

CHAPTER 9   Internet Safety and Privacy 135

CHAPTER 10   E-Mail Protection 161

CHAPTER 11   The Internet Revisited: Software Helpers. 177

CHAPTER 12   A View from the Other Side. 197

CHAPTER 13   Reviews, Recourses, and Resources. 209

APPENDIX A   Products and Web Sites in This Book. 223

APPENDIX B   Glossary of Terms 231

Index *245*

Table of Contents

Introduction . . . . *xvii*

CHAPTER 1 Why Bother with Security? Threats to Your System, Your Data, and You 1

Just Snooping Around? 2

The Value of Information 3

Information and Vulnerability 4

At What Cost Is Personal Information Revealed? 4

What about the Destruction or Alteration of Information? 5

Compromising Data: What's at Risk? 5

Data Destruction 6

Online Threats 7

Information and Privacy Protection Strategies 8

Tactics, Anyone? 9

CHAPTER 2 Basic PC Security Logistics & Tricks 11

Who's Looking over Your Shoulder? 12

Monitoring the Monitor 12

Don't Save It—Print It! 13

Mail Call 14

Empty the Trash 15

Preventing Disastrous Deletions: Backing Up Your System 16

Off-System Work Disks and Storage 17

When You Leave Your PC 18

Temporarily Disabling Your System 18

Looking for Tracks in Files 20

When You Do Turn It Off 23

Shutting Down Securely 23

Shutdown Precautions 24

CHAPTER 3 Simple & Direct—Protecting Your Information with Passwords and Settings . . . 25

What to Protect: An Overview. 26

Simple Settings and Adjustments for Security. 28

Clearing the Documents Menu 28

Emptying and Setting the Recycle Bin 30

Removing and Renaming Desktop Program Shortcuts 31

Removing and Renaming Start Menu Selections 31

Hiding the Taskbar. 34

Preventing File Alteration 35

Preventing Folder Alteration and Deletion 37

Windows Password Systems. 37

Screen Saver Passwords 38

Multiple User Profiles and Passwords 39

Dial-Up Passwords. 40

Network Password Protection for Files and Folders 41

Power-On Passwords 42

A Better Idea: Real Password Software 42

Shareware Programs. 43

Commercial Software. 47

CHAPTER 4 Protecting Your Files and Folders with Disguise and Misdirection 49

Disguising File Displays and Default Folders 50

Altering Recently Used File Lists 50

Misdirection with Deceptive Filenames and Extensions. 53

Misdirection with Alternate Folders 54

Creating Read-Only and Password-Protected Files with an Application . . 54

Saving Files as Read-Only. 55

Password-Protecting Files As You Save Them 56

Off-System Storage and Archiving 57

Floppy Disk Storage. 58

ZIP Drives 59

Tape Backup Drives 59

CD-ROM Storage 60

Storing Files Online 60

Archiving Files 61

CHAPTER 5 Hiding Files, Folders, and Applications 67

Purloined Files? 68

Now You See It, Now You Don't: Making Files and Folders Invisible 69

Background: File Attributes 69

Setting File Attributes 70

Setting Folder Attributes 71

The Final Touch 72

Hiding Applications (Programs) 73

What's in a Name: Hiding Programs by Changing Their Names 74

Using Archives to Hide and Protect Files 75

Hiding Out in the Archive 75

Password Protection for Archives 76

Some Important Cautions 76

CHAPTER 6 How to Keep Your Files from Giving You Away 79

Computer Data and Data Formats 80

Binary Data 81

Breaking the ASCII Code 83

How Information Is Stored on Disk 85

Why Deleted Files Aren't Really Gone 86

Getting Rid of Deleted Files 87

Word Processor File Peculiarities 88

What's Really in Those Files? 89

How Deleted Text Is Stored in a Document's Disk File 89

Getting Rid of Deleted and "Undo" Text 92

So, Where's the Risk in Sharing a File? 93

A Big Security Hole—Temporary Files 93

Finding and Cleaning Out Temporary Files Manually 94

Disk-Cleaning Utilities 95

CHAPTER 7 Data Encryption 97

What Is Encryption? 98

How Data Is Encrypted 99

How Data Is Decrypted 101

Encrypted Data Forms and Formats 102

Applications for Encryption 104

Encryption for File Storage 105

Encryption for E-Mail 105

Encryption for Data Transmission 105

Encryption Software 106

Encrypted Magic Folders (EMF) 106

Norton Secret Stuff 106

Pretty Good Privacy 108

Private File 2 109

SecurePC 2 110

CHAPTER 8 Virus Protection 111

What Are Computer Viruses? 112

Where Did Viruses Originate? 113

Why Do Viruses Exist? 115

What Kinds of Viruses Are Out There? 115

What Do They Do? 115

Applet Viruses: A Potential Plague? 118

How Can a Virus Get into My System? 123

Downloads 124

E-Mail Attachments 124

Shared Files on a Network 124

Shared Disks 125

Protecting Yourself against Viruses 125

Staying Informed 126

Anti-Virus Software 127

Dr Solomon's Anti-Virus 128

McAfee VirusScan Online 128

McAfee Virus Scan Deluxe for Windows 95/98 129
Norton AntiVirus 2000 130
Don't Panic: Virus Hoaxes 132

CHAPTER 9 Internet Safety and Privacy 135
Internet Risks: A 60-Second Primer. 136
How Did We Get Here?. 137
The Good Ol' Days 137
Modern Times 138
Getting to the Roots of the Problem 139
Basic Online Security Issues 139
Passwords 139
Your Identity. 143
Your Credit Card and Checking Account Numbers 145
Online Data Security 146
Browser and Internet Data Security Features 147
Download Security 148
Online Privacy Offline 149
Offline Download Security 149
Finding & Deleting Records of Online Activities. 150
A Private Entrance. 151
Checking Out the Stash. 154
Eliminating Cookies. 156
Bookmarks and Favorites Lists 157
Special Notes for AOL Users 157
When Your Personal Filing Cabinet Isn't 158
Don't Leave Tracks. 159

CHAPTER 10 E-Mail Protection 161
E-Mail and False Threats to Privacy 162
So, Can Others Intercept My E-Mail? 162
What About My Sysop? How Much Can System Operators See? . . 163

Real E-Mail Risks Online 164

    Indecent Exposure? 165

    The Proper Address 167

    Is Encryption the Answer? (And If Not, What's the Question?) 170

    Protecting Your Privacy from Spammers 173

E-Mail Risks Offline 175

CHAPTER 11   The Internet Revisited: Software Helpers 177

When Cookies Aren't So Tasty 178

    What Are Cookies, and Why Are They on My Hard Drive? 178

    Cookies and Your Personal Information 181

    Do-It-Yourself Cookie Cutting 182

Surf Anonymously with a Proxy Server 187

    How Does a Proxy Server Work? 188

    The Anonymizer: A Simple Proxy Server 189

    Other Public Proxy Servers 190

Wiping Out Your Online Trail with Software Helpers 190

    Stop Giving Yourself Away with Your Bookmarks 191

    Get Rid of Telltale Files 192

    Two Specialized Internet Safety Helpers 192

A Few Words on Internet Monitoring Programs 193

    How Do I Know If I'm Bugged? 193

CHAPTER 12   A View from the Other Side 197

Password Security and Insecurity 198

    Human Password Hacking 199

    Software Password Hacking 200

A Solution for E-Mail Insecurity 201

Stealth Logging Programs 202

    What If I Am Bugged? 204

    Prevention Is Still the Best Cure 205

High-Tech Spying with TEMPEST 205

Hacking and Other Things Out of Your Control 206

CHAPTER 13 Reviews, Recourses, and Resources 209

Someone Got Your Password(s)? 210

Password Recovery 210

At Work 212

At Home. 212

Prevention Is Still the Best Cure 212

Getting a New Computer? 213

Take What's Yours 213

Clean It Up. 213

Passwords, Anyone? 214

Fooling the Web 214

A Few Notes on Web E-Mail Directories 215

When Breaking Up Is Hard to Do. 216

More Privacy Tools 217

Anonymous Remailers 217

Check Your Surfing Privacy 218

The Enonymous Advisor 218

Fortify for Netscape 219

Freedom 219

PrivacyScan. 219

Proxy Servers 219

Search Engines 219

Privacy Resources 221

Anonymity on the Internet 221

Center for Democracy and Technology (CDT) 221

Cypherpunks 221

Electronic Frontier Foundation (EFF). 221

Electronic Privacy Information Center (EPIC). 221

The Privacy Page 221

Privacy Rights Clearinghouse (PRC). 222

PrivacyTimes 222

APPENDIX A Products and Web Sites in This Book 223

APPENDIX B Glossary of Terms 231

Index 245

Introduction:
Threats and Promises in the Little Box

Something over 20 years ago, the Information Revolution bloomed full upon us (or, as some view it, was sprung upon us). It came replete with promises of the paperless office, more efficient means of record keeping, improvements in how we carried out common tasks, telecommuting, instant news, and other things undreamed of even by science fiction writers.

Along with such promises came threats. *Beware*, some cried, *the modern Frankenstein will steal money from your pockets and take jobs away. Computers will shape your thoughts and feelings. You will unwillingly and unwittingly provide big business and government with everything they need to enslave you. More than ever, important things in your life will be at the mercy of maliciousness and accidental destruction. Privacy will cease to exist—everything you do, say, and even think will be filed away in your dossier.*

The end of privacy was the worst of the threats. Within the next decade or two, we were told, our entire lives would be stored in massive databases on mainframe computers. Compiled by faceless, inimical government and corporate entities, the databases would ensure that nothing could remain private.

Still, it seemed for a time that the promise of computers far outweighed any threats—threats which, in any case, seemed to be blown out of proportion. Indeed, until the latter half of the 1990s, fears such as those just cataloged were more the stuff of sensationalistic journalism and entertaining films and novels than reality.

The future (that particular future, at least) is nevertheless here, and it isn't what it used to be. Indeed, the reality is at times more frightening than the fears. Yes, our privacy is diminishing. Endless facts about us, from vital statistics and records of events in our lives to our tastes in food and fun, are indeed filed away in massive databases. We are under surveillance every time we use a credit card, order a product, receive treatment for an illness or injury, interact with courts and other legal entities, or change our residences. Insatiable data-gathering systems wait at every turn to record what we do.

Still, they don't know everything, do they? Our thoughts remain private, along with correspondence, conversations, and many of the things we do for entertainment, education, or implementation of new career goals or personal plans when we're alone and unobserved .

Unfortunately, that's not quite true. In fact, the threats are now more personal. In addition to the myriad means that government and corporate entities have to compile information about us, it is now possible even for smaller organizations and individuals to learn things about us without our knowledge.

Just who are these organizations and individuals? They could be anyone, from your supervisor at work to your neighbors, friends, or relatives. In some instances, complete strangers can get into your most personal business. Worse yet, no sophisticated, high-tech surveillance devices are required; information can be gathered through the computers you use at work and home.

Can information really be gleaned from your personal computer so easily? Should you be afraid of what might be found on your system? Yes, and *yes!*

This Is Your Life

How can this be? I'll show you, with a quick stroll through your home and work PCs.

Here's that letter you wrote to your brother six months ago telling him off. Remember? You thought better of sending the letter and just dropped it. But your PC didn't drop it— even though you neither saved nor printed out the letter, your computer showed it to me! Imagine if it had been your brother browsing your system instead of me.

Hey—what's this? You told everyone that you hadn't heard from *her* in nearly a year— but here is a rather intense bit of e-mail you received just last week. (Sure you deleted it, but here it is.) That's nothing—take a look at your reply! Oh, stop blushing. No one else can get their hands on this—or can they?

Wow! There's quite a bit more here about that relationship and other things, but I don't want to embarrass you unduly. So, let's take a look at what you've been doing at work. I'm sure your PC will prove you to be a diligent employee.

Here we are at your cubicle. Whoops! Look at these photos. You wouldn't want your department head to know about them. Yes, I believe you when you say you visited that Web site by accident and didn't download anything—but would your supervisor believe it? And how about that guy in MIS? The sad fact is that you don't even have to download anything from the Web for it to be found on your computer.

What else have you been doing? Here's something commendable: According to the Properties dialog box accompanying this document you have open, you spent exactly 18 minutes this week working on that past-due project report.

Moving on, let's look at the rest of the trail for the week. What's that? You were careful to delete all of *those* files? It doesn't matter; you left a trail. Take a look at this menu. According to this, you worked on writing a letter to the editor of *TV Guide*, planning your vacation, cropping some family photos, and sprucing up your resume both today *and* yesterday.

Here's your expense spreadsheet, in not one, but *two* versions! Looks like science fiction to me. And, oh—here's another fun group of Web pages you visited, according to Netscape and Internet Explorer records!

All right, all right, I'll stop. You get the idea: Anyone who can get their hands on your computer can learn far more about you than you would like. All it takes is a little time and the appropriate knowledge. Even if you have nothing to hide, do you want anyone to have this much access to your life?

What about your boss, your brother, friends, your children, or significant other? Can you keep them away from your PC?

No? Well then, read on....

Damaging Acts

Lest we forget, there is also the potential for your data to be deleted or corrupted by hands other than your own. Vandals or innocents playing with your computer can wreak havoc with data that you don't keep backed up or on hardcopy.

Keeping track of matters financial, historical, and personal with our PCs is so very easy that we often forget that we've placed all our eggs in one proverbial basket. We thus risk losing everything to one malicious act or accident.

Online Threats

The online world has counterparts of nearly every aspect of the real world. You can shop, communicate, bank, chat, research, and more. You can also be scammed online, as well as hoaxed, harassed, stalked, and worse.

Online threats usually involve information. The threats can be minimized—or even nullified—if you maintain control of your information, which means you need to control what information about you gets out. This includes, in some instances, your opinions, as well as your identity, credit card numbers, occupation, location, and other facts.

Why This Book?

Given that personal information is so valuable and vulnerable, and privacy is a vital concern, it's time for a guide to PC privacy on the job and at home. Hence this book, in which I show you how to keep your private information and your computing activities private.

You will learn what's at risk and how to eliminate those risks. For example, you'll find out how to keep others who have access to your PC from seeing what you've been writing in e-mail and MS Word documents, etc.; what you've been doing with Excel and other applications; and what sites you've been visiting on the Web.

Perhaps best of all, you'll be able to protect your privacy without special tools or techie knowledge. This is a book for the average PC user, not for PC geniuses. To that end, I'll show you various techniques and settings you can use to protect your data and to avoid leaving a trail from which someone can reconstruct your computing activities. I'll also show you where PC applications such as Word, Internet Explorer, and Netscape keep extra, hidden copies of your tracks and how to get rid of those copies. In addition, you'll learn about some useful software that can help with all of the above.

Another vital tool you will take away from this reading is the knowledge to encode and/or password-protect vital data and programs. Plus, you'll see some software and techniques that are useful to protect your system from invasion by viruses and Trojan horse programs and from accidental or willful data destruction. You'll also discover how to retain your privacy in e-mail and on the Internet.

Spies Like Us?

It may have occurred to you that, in telling you how to protect your data, this book also tells you how to find hidden and unprotected data on others' computers. What you do with the knowledge gleaned from this book (beyond protecting your own data and privacy) is up to you. If you feel a need to "check out" someone else's PC, you'll certainly know how to go about it. But think before you snoop; you may not like what you find, and you may find that you're meddling with someone who can fight back very effectively.

How to Use This Book

The best way to use this book is simply to read it. But you don't have to sit down and read the entire book cover-to-cover. If you're like most PC users, you already have specific questions about certain situations or software. If that's the case, feel free to jump to the chapters that deal with your concerns. You may want to skip around the chapters for useful and interesting tidbits, or read each chapter until you feel like moving on to the next.

Whatever your approach, I suggest that you read Chapters 1 and 2 first. After that, you're on your own—but I do suggest that you take the time to try out the tips and tricks in this book. Putting the tips into practice will enhance your knowledge of how your PC works and make you a better user.

Also, keep this book handy as your reference to PC privacy and security. You may not want to keep it near your PC, though, lest someone use it to find what you've protected! You will want to browse the accompanying CD, too, as it contains several programs that can help you protect your privacy.

Special Elements in This Book

At the beginning of each chapter, there's a bulleted list. This is an overview of the major topics covered in the chapter. Use this as a quick-reference guide to the chapter, bearing in mind that related topics are covered, as well.

Throughout the book, you will find text that is set off and identified as shown and described below. These are notes, tips, warnings and sidebars that call your attention to information of special value.

This is an example of a note. It elaborates on or illuminates an element or topic discussed in nearby text.

This is an example of a tip. Here, you will find quick facts and how-to information.

Be careful when you see this icon. It marks a warning about a situation in which you may get into trouble by deleting valuable data—or worse.

Sidebars, or Boxed Text

Text set off in a box such as this one is called a *sidebar*. You saw one implemented earlier in this introduction: It was titled "Spies Like Us." A sidebar provides an extended discussion of a topic in nearby text, and/or of related material.

In addition, a sidebar may present an illuminating anecdote or background of interest that isn't directly related to the topic at hand.

You will also find that for your ease of use we have set words that you need to type into your computer in **boldface**. *Italics* are used to show emphasis or to highlight a word or phrase that will be defined in the book.

Moving On

I hope you find this book useful, and perhaps a bit entertaining. If you find errors or omissions, or if you have suggestions, feel free to drop me a line at:

banks@sybex.com

Now it's time to get busy protecting your data and your privacy!

PC CONFIDENTIAL

CHAPTER 1

Why Bother with Security? Threats to Your System, Your Data, and You

- ✔ The value and vulnerability of information
- ✔ What's at risk
- ✔ Snooping and data destruction
- ✔ Online threats
- ✔ Information and privacy protection strategies

The Times
COMPUTER BREAK IN!
How to protect yourself and your computer

The purpose of this chapter is to introduce you to the importance of information and privacy in modern life, and to the threats to information and privacy that unfortunately exist right inside your own PC.

Just Snooping Around?

Before we get into defining information and its value, I should tell you up-front exactly what sort of potentially sensitive information is "at risk." So, give me two hours with your home or office PC and I might find, among other things:

- ✔ Files you deleted months ago (without using UNERASE or similar programs)

- ✔ E-mail messages you've read and deleted, online or offline

- ✔ E-mail you've composed and sent

- ✔ Entire Web sites (including graphics) you visited months ago

- ✔ Sentences and paragraphs that you deleted from letters or other documents in progress—still lingering even though you never printed or saved them (Where's the risk? Perhaps you made rash comments or put sensitive information in a document and then thought better of it.)

- ✔ Your online trail on a day-to-day basis, including files you downloaded (even if you deleted them)

- ✔ Precise dates and times that you used your computer, including information about when and how long (or how little) you worked on a project

- ✔ The source of much of your software—whether it was legally purchased by you, or copied/borrowed from someone else

All this information and more can be had without extensive technical knowledge or special software tools. Thus, the risk increases: co-workers, supervisors, employees, spouses/partners, children, friends, enemies—anyone can learn far more than you ever want known about your online and offline activities.

If you think you have nothing to hide, consider these examples of people who were betrayed by their PCs:

✔ A policewoman carefully deleted personal e-mail referring to job-hunting from her work PC—but she was written up for on-the-clock misuse of the computer system because two menus tipped off her supervisor that she was using the system to work on her resume.

✔ A man found himself in divorce proceedings because his wife chanced upon some letters to a "special" friend—letters that he never even saved to disk. These were of the sort that were innocent in intent but could be easily misinterpreted— and were.

✔ A woman learned that her entire financial history was open to a friend who had stopped by to use her computer for word processing.

✔ A college student made some perhaps injudicious remarks in a public messaging system—remarks that returned to haunt him two years later, when he applied for a job with a major corporation.

✔ Two ISPs provided extensive information to police about the time and place and name of a teenager who was using a stolen credit card number to access online pornography.

With the exception of the woman whose financial history was compromised, you will be interested to know that no claims can be made in these cases that anyone's privacy was violated. Logs of Internet traffic were all that were used in the stolen credit card number case, and in the other cases, people stumbled on the information during routine use of a shared PC. (There was no special effort made to view the damning information, as it were.)

The point is, information figured in each of the examples. In each instance (except for the financial history) the information's value became apparent only when it was compromised—all in all, some excellent exemplifications of the fact that value is often relative.

The Value of Information

Information drives nearly every element of contemporary Western civilization, and almost nothing happens without the appropriate information. For example, when you buy an airline ticket and pay with a credit card, information about you is collected and shared. The same is true when you apply for a car or home loan, have a prescription filled, or start telephone and utility services. For each of these transactions, information is shared, exchanged, and collected. In addition, new information is generated and stored.

That airplane for which you bought the ticket? It doesn't leave the gate until quite a bit of information has been exchanged—about the weather, the passengers, the crew, and the airplane itself. Similarly, nothing is shipped—by truck, rail, air, post, or courier—without an extensive information interchange.

There are few things you can do in the modern world that do not involve collecting, sharing, generating, or accessing information. Multiply the information that is involved in things you do on any given day (buying, renting, subscribing, ordering, borrowing, paying, loaning, traveling, applying) by several hundred million people, and it's easy to see that the total quantity of information involved is nothing short of staggering.

Information is *valuable*. So valuable, in fact, that a significant portion of every sector— including business, research, industrial, and government—is devoted to collecting, manipulating, sorting, and storing information. Providing access to information is itself a major business activity.

What, then, *is* the value of information? Sometimes the value represents a fixed amount (usually set arbitrarily), such as $500 for the names and addresses of ten thousand people who buy a certain kind of music. Often, however, the value of information is subjective. For example, the fact that someone you don't know in a town a thousand miles from you is planning a divorce or a major business move or a career change is worthless to you. However, to that person's spouse or business partner or employer, the information could be very valuable, indeed. It is even more valuable to the person involved, who wants to keep it private.

Information and Vulnerability

Our concern in this section is with both sorts of information—that with subjective value as well as that with objective value—and with keeping private information private and safe.

At What Cost Is Personal Information Revealed?

For some, the revelation of private information may have devastating personal consequences. For example, if a network administrator was perusing staff e-mail at random and discovered a hot romance between two employees (in an atmosphere where fraternization was prohibited), revealing the content of the e-mail could cause problems for the two involved—at work or at home. Similarly, if the network administrator discovered correspondence discussing a job offer between an employee and a competing company, the revelation of that information could cost the employee their job.

(Incidentally, a network administrator would not be violating privacy either way. By precedent, information created on a company computer, during company time, is the "property" of the company.)

Mostly, though, having something known that you'd rather keep to yourself is annoying, or perhaps infuriating. Either way, when a snoop gets hold of information you don't want anyone to have, it is at the very least an invasion of privacy.

What about the Destruction or Alteration of Information?

Data destruction is another matter. Unless you keep backups (disk or hardcopy), when data is gone, it's gone. Sometimes it can be reconstructed, but only at the cost of time and effort (and perhaps money) and of always wondering if the data is the same.

Compromising Data: What's at Risk?

Is it really that bad? Can someone get so much information from my PC that I should feel threatened? Yes, and yes.

What's more, no specialized software or hardware is required, so with a little effort, anyone can get information about you and what you do on your computer. A dedicated snoop can see what you've been doing with a computer at work or at home. This person can even find out when you have used a friend's PC or one in a library, classroom, or anywhere else.

Consider just what sorts of things you do with your computer that might leave or imply information you would be uncomfortable sharing, or that might give the wrong impression. Think about it now, and you won't have to worry about it later.

You need to take the necessary precautions now to guard your data.

"Deleted" Files: A Cautionary Tale

In a sense, I began this book in the early 1980s when, among other things, I was freelancing as an acquisitions editor for a New York book publisher. Certain experiences with computer data opened my eyes to how vulnerable PC privacy really is.

The owner of the company (who shall remain anonymous) was beginning to learn to use PCs and typically sent info I needed on disk rather than printing it out. It was his way of forcing himself to learn faster.

He eventually became a fairly adept PC user, to the point where he developed sophisticated spreadsheets and databases to handle much of his business record-keeping. At the same time, I was more adept, thanks to having been involved with personal computing since 1979. I was known as the guy to contact if you needed to recover or reconstruct documents from trashed disk files as well as those accidentally deleted.

In helping others recover data, I occasionally happened upon interesting files and fragments of files. These included personal letters, plot outlines, profit-and-loss statements, and whatnot. One day I decided to take a look at what the publisher might have deleted from the disks he sent to me.

What I discovered was a large window on this publisher's business activities. Among other tidbits, I found letters and spreadsheet material that would have alienated some of the publisher's best-selling authors and their agents—not to mention investors.

I pulled that data from a few recycled floppy disks, using some special software. Nowadays, it's far easier to get information from a computer. In addition, far more of it is available on the typical PC, all conveniently collected in one place—your hard drive.

Data Destruction

In addition to snooping, there's the potential for someone to destroy important files and settings on your PC. This could be the result of malicious intent, or it might be an accident. (Yes, those things happen; I've seen several instances of system files deleted by youngsters or adults who "got lost" while using a PC and started trying everything they could click on.)

The damage may not be confined to deleted files. More creative vandals might make subtle changes in files in an attempt to cause problems. For instance, the value of a name/address/phone number database can be destroyed by the alteration of one or two digits or letters in each entry.

As if that isn't enough, there are also viruses and Trojan horse programs. Some are subtle in how they change or delete things on your system, and some are blatant. Either way, their activities are troublesome at best and tragic at worst. (Chapter 8, "Virus Protection," goes into greater detail about viruses and Trojan horse programs.)

I'll repeat this advice in other chapters, but you should know that the best defense against viruses and Trojan horse programs is to know your source. If someone gives you a disk of unknown origin, you may not want to run any programs it may contain. If you don't feel confident about a Web site or online service from which you're downloading, don't download anything.

Mostly, the risk of damaged or deleted data can be dealt with by planning ahead and taking the appropriate precautions.

If you find that files on your hard drive have been deleted accidentally or intentionally and you have no backups (see Chapter 2, "Basic PC Security Logistics & Tricks"), don't panic. Try to recover the deleted files using your system's undelete or unerase utility. Such utilities are normally self-guiding and simple to use.

Online Threats

Speaking of viruses and Trojan horse programs, what about the most common source of these threats, the online world? Downloads can be dangerous, but they are not the only threats you may encounter online. Often, the biggest threat is people.

Under the cloak of perceived anonymity, individuals often do things they would not otherwise consider. The Internet is the venue of all sorts of scams and hoaxes, as well as harassment, stalking, outright theft, and more.

A little information goes a long way online. Given a bit of personal information about you, an online malefactor can cause all sorts of problems for you, online and off. With the right information, you can usually avoid problems online and eliminate almost any that come up.

The problems don't stop when you go offline, however. Your Web browser may keep surprisingly detailed records of what you do on the Web. What you download may also be recorded. The e-mail program you use and even your ISP may also create trails that the informed snoop can follow. Fortunately, these trails can be eliminated by altering settings and making some judicious deletions, as described in Chapters 6, "How to Keep Your Files from Giving You Away," 9, "Internet Safety and Privacy," and 10, "E-Mail Protection."

Information and Privacy Protection Strategies

Online or off, protecting your information and privacy comes down to one thing: controlling information. You must control where your information is stored, limit access to it, and preserve its integrity. The basic strategies include:

Securing your system   When and where possible, limit who has access to your computer, at work and at home. This may include considerations such as password protection and physical location. It also includes second-hand access via software that might turn out to be viruses or Trojan horse programs. (Chapter 2 and Chapter 3, "Simple & Direct—Protecting Your Information with Passwords and Settings.")

Hiding information   If no one but you knows where your information is stored, the risk of privacy violation or information destruction is greatly reduced. To this end, you may use tricks like bogus filenames or "invisible" filenames and directories. You also want to wipe out any tracks to your data that involves, among other things, clearing file and document menus in Windows. (Chapters 3, 4, "Protecting Your Files and Folders with Disguise and Misdirection," 5, "Hiding Files, Folders, and Applications," 7, "Data Encryption," and 10.)

Protecting information from destruction/maintaining integrity   Here, the concern is preventing your information from being deleted, altered, or corrupted. To this end, tactics such as backing up data, locking files, and password protection go a long way. (Chapters 2, 3, 4, 5, 8, and 11, "Odds and Ends.")

Removing information from accessible areas   Where extremely sensitive information is involved, hiding and locking files may not be enough. You may have to resort to such tactics as keeping working files on a floppy disk or keeping data only as hardcopy. You will also have to root out system-made data backups. (Chapters 3, 4, and 5.)

Eliminating your PC from the loop   You may want to give some thought to whether you really need to create or store certain kinds of information on your PC. (Chapters 2, 3, 5, and 7.)

Wiping out your trail   Windows and certain applications are simply too compulsive about keeping a trail of what you've been doing in recent sessions. You can eliminate most of the trail with settings; the rest you can clear out manually. (Chapters 2, 3, 6, 10, and 11.)

Tactics, Anyone?

Implementing the aforementioned strategies requires that you take certain precautions, both before and after creating, accessing, or storing information on your PC.

Some tactics are geared to specific applications; others involve Windows itself and/or how you handle information. The ensuing chapters describe the necessary tactics in detail. We'll begin at the beginning, of course, with the basics in Chapter 2. There, you will find useful information about locating your PC and certain peripherals, dumping useless files that can cause problems if a snoop finds them, making backups, and taking precautions when you leave your PC.

PC Confidential

CHAPTER 2

Basic PC Security Logistics & Tricks

✔ **Locating your system for security**

✔ **Printing or copying sensitive e-mail**

✔ **Deleting files for good**

✔ **Backing up files**

✔ **Securing your data and system when you leave your PC**

✔ **Checking your PC following an absence**

✔ **Clearing your own tracks from the Documents menu**

✔ **Taking precautions when shutting down your PC**

The Times
COMPUTER BREAK IN!
How to protect yourself and your computer

Much of what this chapter has to say is basic and may seem obvious to some readers. Still, it makes sense to start at the beginning, with the most common and simple means of protecting your privacy and your data. You'll probably find some tricks here that hadn't occurred to you.

For those of you who are fairly new to the world of PCs, this chapter is intended to give you a jump start. It provides advice and techniques you can use right away without any additional knowledge or software.

Who's Looking over Your Shoulder?

Among the most obvious and often neglected elements of PC security is location. Most of us locate our PCs for convenience. We think in terms of the nearest power source, the best spot on a desk or table, and so forth. However, if you are concerned about security with your PC activities, you must take into account the fact that anyone in your workplace or home can see exactly what you are doing by simply looking.

Monitoring the Monitor

Because anyone can happen by and see what you are doing by looking at your monitor, whether or not you are away, you ought to give some consideration to your monitor's location. The best place to set up—which may seem obvious—is with your chair set so that your back faces a wall and the monitor faces you. This way, no one can look over your shoulder or otherwise see what's on your monitor unless you want them to.

Moving things around may not be practical in a work environment, but you might also try obscuring your monitor from a sidewise view with a briefcase or other large object. Be sure the obscuring object is something that looks like it belongs on your desk; otherwise you'll only draw attention to the fact that you are trying to hide something.

Much Ado about Nothing?

In the early 1980s, I was doing some on-site work as a technical writer for a documentation company. One of the company's projects involved the then-secret IBM AT computer, just weeks away from public announcement. IBM naturally wanted to keep the machine a secret and went to great lengths specifying the precautions to be taken to guard against information leaks.

One morning I entered the office suite to find everyone in the midst of rearranging their desks and computers. An order had come down that all PC monitors had to face away from windows. This seemed rather extreme, but everyone complied.

As it turned out, IBM employees had been spending time in the parking lots and woods surrounding the building, using binoculars to read what was on PC screens. They figured that if they could read monitors from vantage points around the building, competitors' spies could do so as well.

Again, this seemed to be a bit extreme, but maybe the IBM employees knew something we didn't.

Don't Save It—Print It!

Printers also provide an opportunity for compromising your privacy. Consider placing your printer so that the output is not readily viewable. If you work in a networked environment and share a printer, your best bet is simply to avoid sending anything but legitimate work to the printer. A case in point: I knew a university professor who routinely printed out things on a shared printer in her department. The printer was several rooms away from her office, so she had no idea who might be seeing what she printed. She never gave it a thought—until someone questioned her printing invitations to a cookout. (The person who discovered that she was using the office equipment for personal business happened to be a die-hard "company person," who wanted everything run by the book. This individual also made a practice of citing others' errors in the workplace, as a means of gaining points with administration.) If you have something you want to print out and have access only to a networked printer at your job, copy the file in question to a floppy disk and use your home PC or one at a copy shop to print the data. (Remember to delete the file from your hard drive after you've copied it.)

Mail Call

E-mail, whether in a networked or non-networked environment, is the most vulnerable point for most PC users at work. Take these precautions:

- ✔ Do not store copies of messages you've sent on your computer's hard drive. Ditto incoming messages that you wouldn't want someone else to see.

- ✔ If you want to save incoming mail messages, put them on a floppy disk. (If you already have an accumulation of incoming and outgoing mail messages, you might want to put the messages in one file, if your e-mail program offers this option.) Alternatively, you can simply print out the messages. Don't forget to delete the originals—because there may come a time when you find your e-mail under scrutiny! (The safest course is to save your mail on floppy disks, or to print out messages. Even if your e-mail program offers password protection of folders, the system administrator can probably find a way around that.)

- ✔ Make sure that deleted messages are really gone. Deleting e-mail messages doesn't always delete them. Depending on the e-mail program you use, deleted messages may simply go into a Trash folder, which must be emptied before the messages are truly deleted. (See the next section for more details on the Trash folder and the Recycle Bin, which are responsible for handling deleted files.)

- ✔ Check into your work PC environment, if you are connected to a network. It may be that your e-mail is stored on the server and backed up, even though you delete it. This is very common in large networked environments.

Naturally, these same precautions apply to home PCs.

Empty the Trash

You may not be aware of this, but under its default setting, the Windows Recycle Bin actually *stores* "deleted" files, until you empty the Recycle Bin. These files can be instantly undeleted or viewed from the Recycle Bin.

Because of this, you should periodically empty the Recycle Bin. To do so, open the Recycle Bin and select File ➢ Empty Recycle Bin, as shown in Figure 2.1.

Figure 2.1

Emptying the Recycle Bin

The Recycle Bin is a good idea if you want to be able to recover accidentally deleted files. However, if you would rather skip emptying the Recycle Bin and instead have files permanently deleted, follow these steps:

1. Right-click the Recycle Bin icon on your desktop.

2. Select Properties from the menu displayed. This brings up the Recycle Bin Properties dialog box displayed in Figure 2.2.

3. Click the Global tab.

4. Click the check box labeled Do Not Move Files To The Recycle Bin. Remove Files Immediately On Delete.

5. Click OK.

Remember that if you set the Recycle Bin to remove files immediately, you will not be able to undelete files once they are deleted.

Figure 2.2

Setting the Recycle Bin to remove files immediately

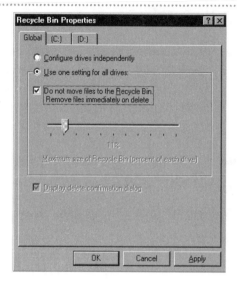

Preventing Disastrous Deletions: Backing Up Your System

Whether you fear someone is deleting your files intentionally or accidentally, or whether a virus has been introduced or you have a system crash, there is only one way to ensure that you can always access data files—that is to back up your system.

You may have created a *rescue* or *system disk* when you set up your PC. A rescue or system disk is a disk that contains enough of the operating system to start your PC from drive A and some information about your PC's configuration. You may want to store this safely away against the potential misfortune of a hard drive crash, but there will be no compromising information on such a disk.

This has nothing to do with data files you create, however. Data files are those files you create using an application—a word processor, spreadsheet, graphics editor, and so forth— or with information you receive from an outside source (such as an e-mail message or files copied from a floppy disk). All important data files should be backed up (copied) on an alternate media, such as floppy disks, a tape drive (some can be used to back up *everything* on your hard drive), or ZIP disks. CD-ROMs may be a good option for this, too, but only for data that you do not intend to edit or otherwise change, as data on CDs cannot be edited.

The media you use depends on your budget, your work habits, and the size and number of files you need to keep backed up.

If you use a floppy or ZIP disk to back up your data files, it's a good idea to create directories and subdirectories on the disk that mimic the directories under which the files are stored. This greatly simplifies the task of finding files later.

You should be cautious about where you store your backups, too. Store backups where no one else can easily get to them and store the disks in a dry environment that doesn't get too hot (say, over 85 degrees Fahrenheit).

Off-System Work Disks and Storage

If you have database, spreadsheet, word processor, or other files that you don't want others to see, don't keep them on your PC's hard drive. Instead, create or copy the files on a floppy or ZIP disk. (And don't forget to delete the originals if you created and/or worked on the files in question on your hard drive.)

Here's a special note to those of you working in a networked environment: You may or may not be aware that your work files are saved on the company's server—in which case they can be accessed. If you are going to work on personal files at work, use a floppy disk for your work disk. Create and save any files you need on that disk only.

If you use a standard $3^1/_2''$ floppy disk and your files are very large, you will probably reach a point where you can't open or save a file on the floppy. If this happens, copy the file to your hard drive to work with it, copy it back to the floppy, and delete the hard-drive copy when you're finished working with the file.

When labeling floppy or ZIP disks that contain sensitive data, consider using misleading labels. Rather than writing "Financial Databases" on a floppy, for example, use the more innocuous "Old Recipes." Just remember what you named the files, so you don't lose track of them!

Again, where you store the disks is important in terms of accessibility and safety.

After you copy files to a floppy, check to make sure they are actually *on* the floppy before you delete the versions on your hard drive. View the floppy's directory by clicking on it in Windows Explorer, or view the disk's directory from DOS. If you don't double-check, you can end up losing files altogether.

When You Leave Your PC

When your PC is unattended, others may have access to it. The following are some tips on how to render your system inaccessible to others, how to check to see whether someone has been using your PC while you were gone, and some precautions to take when you shut your PC down.

Temporarily Disabling Your System

Most of us do not like to turn off our PCs if we are going to be away from them for only a few minutes. Still, if there is a risk of someone getting into what you're doing, there is always the option of using a password-protection program for the entire system (see Chapter 3 and the accompanying CD, which contains some password-protection software). If you don't have a password-protection program installed yet, you will most likely have to turn off your system.

Or will you? Another and sometimes better option if you don't have a password-protection program installed is to disable your system temporarily. This will make it more difficult for those who aren't very knowledgeable about computer hardware to take a peek at what you're doing. It won't stop determined snoops who know about PCs, though. But never fear, there are more tricks and tips to thwart them in later chapters.

Temporarily disabling a system is also useful if you're using someone else's PC and, therefore, cannot add a password program.

Disabling options include:

- ✔ Turning off the monitor
- ✔ Unplugging the monitor cable (the power cable, or the cable between the monitor and the PC)
- ✔ Unplugging the keyboard and mouse cables

Such precautions are helpful in deterring the computer-illiterate from trying to get into your PC. Of course, if you are not very knowledgeable yourself about PC hardware, you probably shouldn't be messing around with these things. However, if you do disconnect a cable or two, either hide it or take it away with you.

Software solutions for the problem of people snooping around your computer while you're away from it include the aforementioned system password protection, as well as dropping out to DOS in full-screen mode. The PC novice, presented with the screen shown in Figure 2.3, isn't going to be able to do much—unless, that is, he or she knows enough to type **EXIT** and press Enter to return to Windows and whatever applications you have running.

Figure 2.3

Displaying a simple DOS screen is often enough to deter the idle curious from browsing your system.

Speaking of novices, if you are in or near that category as a PC user, here's how to get to the DOS screen shown in Figure 2.3. First, open the Programs menu from the Start menu. Click MS-DOS Prompt, and you will be "in" DOS.

If you go to DOS but it is displayed in a small window that overlays the rest of your windows, press Alt+Spacebar to view the DOS window's menu. Select Maximize on that menu, and DOS will expand to fill the screen.

To return to another application from the DOS screen, press Alt+Tab. To exit DOS entirely, type **EXIT** at the C:> prompt (C:\WINDOWS>**EXIT**).

Looking for Tracks in Files

Do you have to leave your computer on and open to others when you are away? Are you unable to prevent others from turning it on when you leave? If so, you may wonder whether someone has opened a specific file while you've been away from your PC. Here's a fast and easy way to check, using the Windows Explorer:

1. Start Windows Explorer by selecting it from the Programs menu off the Start menu.

2. Navigate to the directory where the file is stored.

3. Right-click the filename and select Properties from the menu displayed.

You will see the File Properties dialog box displayed in Figure 2.4, which uses a file called `Multiple Stock Quotes by PC Quote, Inc.` as its example. Midway down, you will see when the file was created, when it was last edited, and when it was last accessed (opened).

If the date/time the file was last accessed is after you last used your PC, an unauthorized person opened the file.

You can also view the Properties dialog box by right-clicking a file from the list that is generated when you select Open on an application's File menu.

Figure 2.4

Check a file's properties to see whether someone opened that file while you were away.

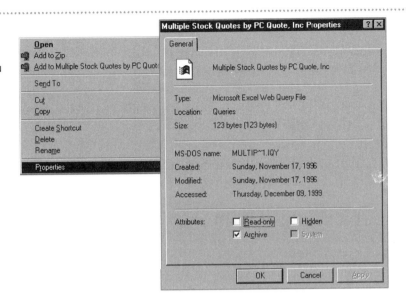

To see whether someone has been using a specific application to open your files, check the application's File menu. At the bottom of the menu you will find a numbered list of files; these are the files most recently opened with that application. If you see the name of a file you haven't opened recently, or that the order of the files is different from when you were working with that application, someone has opened the file(s) in question. If this is the case, check the Properties of the file(s) for more information. (Note that the file list will not be available if you disable it as described in Chapter 4.)

Make sure you check a suspect file's properties *before* you open it. If you don't, you will obliterate information about the most recent access of the file by opening the file yourself; Windows changes that information as soon as a file is opened.

Another way to check for unauthorized file access is to look at the Documents menu, off the Start menu. To view it, go to Start ➤ Documents; or click on Start and type **D**; or press Alt+Esc and type **D**. Select Documents and you will see the list shown to the right in Figure 2.5.

Figure 2.5

The Documents menu shows the files most recently opened by any and all applications on your system.

If you see a filename that is not among those with which you've been working recently, check the properties for that file. If the filename is totally unknown to you, it may have been created by someone using your PC; the Properties dialog box will show the date and time the file was created.

To view one of the files, simply click its name; Windows will open it using the application that created it.

Clearing *Your* Tracks from the Documents Menu

Want to eliminate *your* tracks from the Documents menu? It's easy!

1. Select Settings on the Start menu, and then select Taskbar (Start ➤ Settings ➤ Taskbar). You'll see the Taskbar Properties dialog box shown in Figure 2.6.

2. Press the Start Menu Programs tab on the Taskbar Properties dialog box, and then click the button labeled Clear Under Documents Menu.

Figure 2.6

With the Taskbar Properties dialog box, you can clear the Documents menu on the Windows Start menu.

When You Do Turn It Off

If you are surrounded by people who know more than a little about using PCs, your only option is to turn off your system. This can dissuade snoops, because no one wants to initiate the beep and other signals that occur when a PC is turned on to alert the owner that someone is starting their computer.

If you want to check whether someone has rebooted your computer and then turned it off in your absence, the accompanying CD has several programs that will help.

Shutting Down Securely

When you leave your computer unattended overnight or longer, you will most likely want to turn it off. This will often deter the aforementioned computer-illiterates.

You cannot, of course, rely completely on this deterrent in most instances. So, you need to take extra measures to protect your confidential data.

Shutdown Precautions

Before you shut down your computer, there are two things you will want to do to protect your data:

✔ Back up important data files.

✔ Copy sensitive data to a floppy disk or other media, and store the floppies in a safe place. As always, delete the original data files.

Beyond that, you might want to consider removing a cable so that no one can turn on the computer. The best choice is probably the power cable to the PC itself. (Note that this measure can be thwarted by someone who has a power cable—or knows enough to remove one from another PC.)

There are additional precautions that involve changing settings for applications and/or for Windows. Those are discussed in the next chapter.

PC
CONFIDENTIAL

CHAPTER 3

Simple & Direct— Protecting Your Information with Passwords and Settings

- ✔ **What to protect**
- ✔ **Simple settings and adjustments that will enhance security**
- ✔ **Password protection provided by Windows**
- ✔ **Real password protection**

In this chapter, we'll take a look at the password protection that Windows provides for your system, as well as password protection from add-on programs. I'll also show you some simple settings and adjustments you can make to Windows that will greatly increase your security.

What to Protect: An Overview

Your PC can be viewed in layers, with the overall system (your hardware) being the outer-most layer, as shown in Figure 3.1.

Figure 3.1

PC "layers"

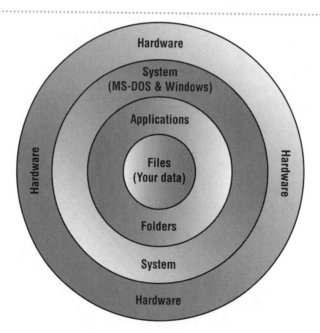

Hardware

System
(MS-DOS & Windows)

Applications

Files
(Your data)

Hardware

Hardware

Folders

System

Hardware

The next layer is Windows, followed by your applications and the directory (folder) system, and finally, your files and the data they contain. Obviously, you want to protect your data, but you do not have to focus all your efforts on data. Any of the layers can be a focus for protection, as you will see. Before going into further detail about password protection options, here's a quick rundown of what you will need to know:

Your Computer and Windows   As stated above, your computer hardware is the outermost layer. Security options begin here with turning off the system when you are away; however, this is not always an effective deterrent. Blocking physical access to the system by locating it where not just anyone can get to it, such as in a locked room, is the next step. You might also remove physical components, such as the power supply and connecting cables or the keyboard. Of course, these measures are not always practical—particularly in a work environment or when you are using someone else's PC.

Windows itself offers several password schemes, but only one is of any practical value and, as you will learn, is easily circumvented. However, as you will also learn, it is possible to add more effective password protection to your system.

Applications   Protecting your applications can be accomplished in several ways. You can rename applications to make them look like games or non-application files. You can also hide applications in a couple of different ways—putting them in the "wrong" folders, for instance, or using deceptive folder and file names, as I will show you in Chapter 4.

Directories (Folders)   The directories (also referred to as *folders*) on your hard drive or floppy disk can be renamed or simply hidden. With the appropriate software, you can add password protection to directories. (Windows also offers a means of password-protecting folders and their contents for networked computers *only*.) Or you can use a couple of other techniques to keep snoops who browse by directory out of your more important files.

Files   Password protection for files is afforded by some applications. Windows lets you password-protect specific files on networked systems so they cannot be shared. As with directories and application filenames, you can rename or render invisible important files. Some general password-protection programs can also be used to protect files, which I will show you a little later in this chapter.

Simple Settings and Adjustments for Security

There are a number of settings and adjustments you can make to afford some additional security to Windows. I showed you a couple of them in Chapter 2, and I will go into them in a bit more depth here. They're all free, fairly easy to implement, and include:

✔ Clearing the Documents menu periodically

✔ Emptying the Recycle Bin, or changing its settings (alternately, you can delete files from DOS)

✔ Removing or renaming the program shortcut icons on your desktop

✔ Removing or renaming program selections on the Start menu

✔ Hiding the Taskbar

✔ Preventing a file from being altered or deleted

✔ Preventing a folder from being altered or deleted

Clearing the Documents Menu

The first place to start covering your tracks is the Documents menu on Windows' Start menu. You saw how to do this in Chapter 2, but let's review it here. Pop up the Start menu and select Documents. You'll see a list of the last 15 or so files you've had open with any application, as shown in Figure 3.2.

Clicking one of those filenames starts the required application, with the selected file open. This means that anyone can look at your work or personal files without even having to search.

Fortunately, it's simple to clear this menu. Click on the Settings menu, and then select Taskbar (Settings ➤ Taskbar). Press the Start Menu Programs tab, and then press the Clear button at the bottom of the page that is displayed, as illustrated in Figure 3.3. (Note that you are *not* deleting files by doing this. Only the list of filenames goes away.)

Once the menu is cleared, it will take snoops a little more time to find your files. If you're lucky, they'll just become discouraged and give up.

Figure 3.2

Windows' Documents menu

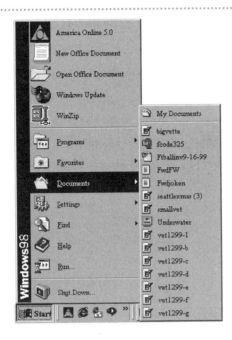

Figure 3.3

Clearing the contents of the Documents Menu

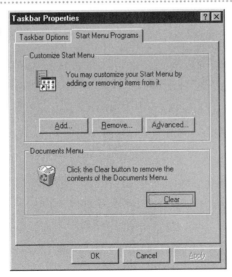

Emptying and Setting the Recycle Bin

The Recycle Bin is a great place for snoops to "go fishing" for choice information. As noted in Chapter 2, the Recycle Bin keeps on hand any files that you delete with Windows Explorer or with a Windows application such as Word. Thus, it is possible for anyone to examine files you've deleted.

There are actually three ways to handle this problem:

✔ Empty the Recycle Bin daily or more frequently. Do this by right-clicking the Recycle Bin and selecting Empty Recycle Bin, or double-clicking the Recycle Bin and selecting File ➤ Empty Recycle Bin.

✔ Set the Recycle Bin so that files are permanently deleted (you saw this method not long ago in Chapter 2, but here you get the details, as opposed to theory). To do so, open the Recycle Bin, select Properties from the File menu, click the Global tab, and click the check box labeled Do Not Move Files To The Recycle Bin. Remove Files Immediately On Delete. Then click OK. (You will not be able to undelete files after setting this.)

✔ Delete files from DOS. Select from the Start menu Programs ➤ MS-DOS Prompt; change to the directory that contains the file(s) you wish to delete; type **DEL**, followed by the name of a file to delete.

Files deleted in DOS are not easily recovered—if they can be recovered at all. In addition, it is very easy to accidentally delete the wrong files from DOS. Therefore, I recommend that you do not use the DOS DEL command unless you are accustomed to working in DOS. (Similarly, if you set the Recycle Bin so that it does not hold deleted files, you will not be able to retrieve them.)

A Byzantine Solution

If you are dealing with a more sophisticated snoop, and you want to let them think that you are not deleting files from the Recycle Bin and therefore have nothing to hide, try deleting only your sensitive files with the DOS DEL command. You can do this from DOS, or you can delete selected files from the Recycle Bin.

The reason for this is, if someone sees that you have deleted files in the Recycle Bin, they may well believe that those are the only recently deleted files there are. This may well discourage the snoop from looking further.

Removing and Renaming Desktop Program Shortcuts

Given access, many people will start clicking desktop shortcut icons just to see what's what and what they can get into. You can discourage this by either deleting the shortcut icons or renaming them. If you rename a shortcut with a misleading and uninteresting name (like *System Tools*), it may be ignored. Renaming is an alternative only if you feel that you must have that shortcut on the desktop. (Again, make sure *you* remember what you've called it.)

✔ To delete a desktop icon, right-click it, and select Delete on the menu, as shown in Figure 3.4.

✔ To rename a shortcut, right-click it, and select Rename on the menu. You will then be able to type in a new name for the shortcut.

Figure 3.4

Deleting a desktop icon

Removing and Renaming Start Menu Selections

Selections on the Start menu are easily deleted or altered, and either of these options will go far in preventing others from rooting around your hard drive.

Deleting Start Menu Items

To delete or change items on the Start menu, right-click on the Taskbar and select Properties, or select Settings ➤ Taskbar on the Start menu. Click the Start Menu Programs tab, and you should see the dialog box shown in Figure 3.5.

Figure 3.5

The Taskbar Properties dialog box with the Start Menu Programs page displayed

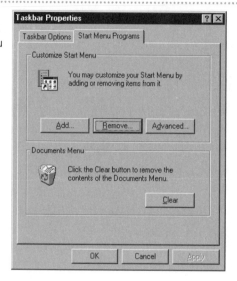

To remove a selection from the Start menu, first press the Remove button in the Taskbar Properties dialog box. This brings up a window containing a list of the folders on your hard drive, as shown in Figure 3.6. You can delete these folders, browse through them, or delete program files. To perform a deletion, which is what we're primarily concerned with here, click once on the desired item, and press the Remove button.

The items you remove from the Start menu remain on your hard drive, so you can still use them. You can still run a program that has been removed from the Start menu via the Start menu's Run command, or with a desktop shortcut. And you can still access removed folders and files through normal means.

✔ To run a program that isn't on the Start menu, open the Start menu and click Run. Enter the name of the program in the Run dialog box and click OK.

✔ To run a program with a desktop shortcut, double-click the icon for that program on the desktop. If there's no shortcut, you can create one. Right-click on the desktop, click New, and then click Shortcut. Follow the instructions in the Create Shortcut dialog box (basically, enter the name and location of the program you want to run, and a name for the shortcut).

Figure 3.6

The Remove Shortcuts/
Folders dialog box

Yet another approach to running a program is to start at the My Computer icon or use Windows Explorer to make your way down the succession of folders and sub-folders to the actual program. Once you've arrived at the program you want to launch, double-click its name to run it.

Remember, items deleted from the Start menu are not deleted from your hard drive.

Editing/Renaming Start Menu Items

To rename a Start menu item, click the Advanced button shown on the Start Menu Programs page of the Taskbar Properties dialog box you saw in Figure 3.5. This will open Windows Explorer with the Start menu folder displayed. To rename an item, right-click it and select Rename from the context menu that appears, as shown in Figure 3.7.

Type in the new name in the ensuing dialog box. (You can also delete items from this display by selecting Delete instead of Rename from the context menu.)

Figure 3.7

Windows Explorer showing the Start menu folder

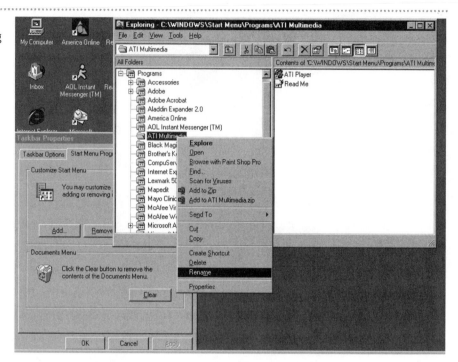

Hiding the Taskbar

A simple Taskbar setting that may dissuade the unsophisticated snoop and idle browsers is Auto Hide. Shown in Figure 3.8, this selection makes the Taskbar invisible for all practical purposes, hiding the Start menu and any programs you have running. (What it actually does is "push" the Taskbar outside the normal viewing area, although the Taskbar will show up if the mouse cursor is hovered over its location.)

To set this attribute, follow these steps:

1. Click Start.

2. Click Settings ➢ Taskbar to open the Taskbar Properties dialog box.

3. Click the Taskbar Options tab, if necessary.

4. Click the check box labeled Auto Hide, then click OK.

Figure 3.8

Taskbar Options settings

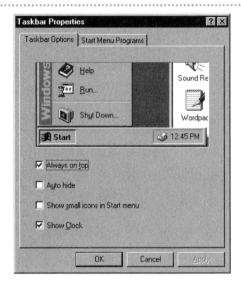

Preventing File Alteration

If you fear someone accidentally (or intentionally) altering your files, Windows provides a small hedge against this happening. You can use Windows Explorer to set appropriate attributes so that files cannot be altered, by setting the *Read-only* option.

The Read-only attribute is a system setting that prevents changes in a file. You can view or copy a file, but you cannot change its name or contents—hence the name *Read-only*.

Follow these steps to set up this option:

1. Start Windows Explorer.

2. Open the appropriate folder, and right-click the file you wish to protect. Then select Properties on the menu displayed. You will see the Properties dialog box, as shown in Figure 3.9.

3. Click the check box labeled Read-only and press the OK button. The file is now protected from editing changes.

Figure 3.9

The File Properties dialog box for a file called better

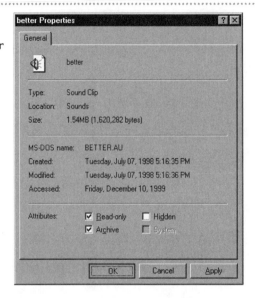

If you want to change multiple files in the same directory to Read-only status, select all the files in question at once by holding down the Ctrl key as you left-click each of their names. Then right-click any of the filenames to display the Properties dialog box and set the Read-only attribute for all the selected files at once.

Setting the Read-only attribute prevents someone from editing and saving a file with a Windows or a DOS application. It also prevents deletion from DOS. However, anyone can still delete your Read-only file from Windows Explorer, although Explorer will ask whether you're sure you want to delete the file first. Still, you may not be the person who gets to answer whether you're sure you want it deleted, so be aware that this is not a completely saboteur-proof method.

You can set files created with certain applications—such as Microsoft Word—to be Read-only when you save them. Some applications allow you to create that setting, or you can use the file's Properties dialog, which you can open with Windows Explorer. You can also password-protect files within many of the same applications. We will take a closer look at these topics in Chapters 4 and 5.

Preventing Folder Alteration and Deletion

You can protect entire folders from being renamed or altered in the same fashion as individual files by following these steps:

1. Start Windows Explorer.

2. Highlight the folder(s) you wish to protect.

3. Right-click, and select Properties on the context menu displayed.

4. Click the Read-only check box and press OK.

Yes, you *can* set the Hidden attribute (for which you can see a check box on the General page of the Properties dialog box), which will indeed hide files from Windows and DOS applications and DOS directory commands. A system setting, the Hidden attribute literally hides a file or folder from DOS directories and application file lists. More on that in Chapter 5.

Windows Password Systems

There is little that the Windows password system can do for you as far as security goes, because it is designed more for retaining the preferences of multiple users than as a protective system. Still, there are some worthwhile elements that provide some security, such as a screen saver password and networking protection for files and folders. As noted, the multiple–user-passwords system doesn't do a lot in terms of protecting files. The dial-up password protection system, on the other hand, does a good job.

There is also a power-on or startup password system that you can access through your system's *CMOS settings*. (CMOS stands for Complementary Metal Oxide Semiconductor. CMOS settings hold important elements of your PC's operating system. These include the date and time, information on what sort of disk drives you have, and more. The information is stored on a chip—of the CMOS type—that has a programmable memory that is kept "alive" by a tiny battery. Your computer reads this information every time you turn on its power.) We'll look at each in the following pages.

Screen Saver Passwords

The screen saver password system is a fair first line of defense for times when you need to be away from your PC for a short while, but you don't want to turn it off. When you set up a screen saver password, the system will ask for a password *after* the screen saver is activated. To set a screen saver password, follow this procedure:

1. Click Settings on the Start menu, and then select Control Panel (Start ➤ Settings ➤ Control Panel). Double-click Display. (Alternatively, you can right-click your desktop's wallpaper and select Properties.) The Display Properties dialog box will be displayed.

2. Press the Screen Saver tab and click the check box labeled Password Protected. Then press the button next to it, labeled Change, and enter a password in the ensuing dialog box, as shown in Figure 3.10. (You will have to enter the password twice to confirm it.)

The screen saver password system is fine if you plan to be away for a brief time. But you need to be aware of a major weakness in the system: If someone really wants to get into your PC, all they have to do is *restart the computer*. There is no password protection until the screen saver is activated by its timer.

Figure 3.10

The Display Properties dialog box with the Change Password dialog box displayed

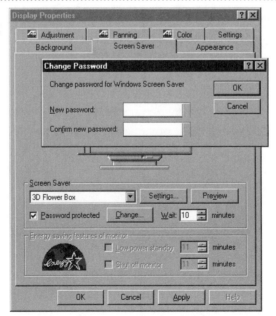

Windows NT users have an additional option when it comes to password protection: locking the workstation. This is done through the screen saver. When the workstation is locked, no one can get into the system without the current user's password; but there's more. Anyone who tries to reboot the system to get around the password protection will still find themselves faced with having to enter the password of the user in question. Of course, anyone with administrative privileges can still log on, overriding your password protection.

Stronger Screen Saver Password Protection

If you want to create a boot-up password with your screen saver, try this: with Windows Explorer, find the .SCR file that corresponds to the screen saver you have active. (The .SCR files are in your /windows/system folder and have names that match the selections listed on the Screen Saver page in the Display Properties dialog.)

Right-click the screen saver file and drag it to this folder:

```
/Windows/Start Menu/Programs/StartUp
```

A pop-up menu will appear. Select Create Shortcut(s) Here. Now the screen saver you set up will start whenever Windows starts and will request a password. (You must of course have set a password on the Screen Saver page of the Display Properties dialog for your desktop.)

Multiple User Profiles and Passwords

Windows offers a multiple-user profile option that saves personal preference parameters such as the desktop layout and appearance, Start menu items, and so forth.

The settings for each user are password protected, but this does not block access to any applications or programs. When a PC with multiple user setups is started, a dialog box asks for a username and password. However, you can bypass this by pressing Escape or canceling the dialog box.

If you wish to set up multiple-user profiles, select Settings on the Start menu, and then select Control Panel. Double-click the Passwords icon. You'll see the Password Properties dialog box, which is self-guiding. Again, however, settings you make here have nothing to do with security for your files, programs, or system.

Dial-Up Passwords

The Windows dial-up system requires a username and password, which are used to log on to the system you are dialing. Note, however, that this password setup is likewise meaningless in terms of system security. The password and username are used to log on to a dial-up system, such as an ISP.

As you can see in Figure 3.11, there is a check box in the Connect To dialog box labeled Save Password.

The password is retained, but only during the current session; when you turn off your PC, the password is gone. (The main reason it is there is to simplify repeated logons to a dial-up system during a given session.) *Not* clicking that Save Password check box will keep someone from logging on to a system with your user ID and password, but that's the limit of security here.

Figure 3.11

The Connect To dialog box with Save Password option

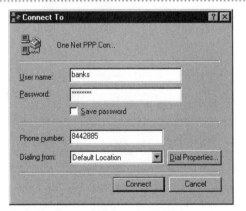

If your PC is set up for one or more users and you override the system password dialog, the Save Password check box is not available in the Connect To dialog. If you logged on with a user ID and password, you would use the same password with the Connect To dialog as with the system password dialog. (The system password is the initial logon request that Windows makes when there are multiple users on a system. You can get around this by simply clicking Cancel, or pressing Escape.)

Network Password Protection for Files and Folders

If you use a networked PC at work, you can grant access to and protect files and/or folders by setting file or folder properties.

The quickest way to get to a file or folder's properties is to start Windows Explorer, and then right-click the file or folder in question. Select Properties from the menu, which will give you the Properties dialog box, as shown in Figure 3.12.

Figure 3.12

A Properties folder's Sharing page

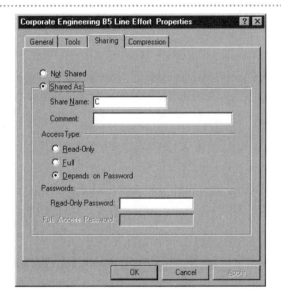

On a networked system, a Properties folder has two sheets: General and Sharing. If you want to require password access from others to access a file or folder, click the Sharing tab. This will give you the Sharing page to make these selections. If you want to set the type of access (Read-only, or read–write/change) to a file or folder, you need to access the General page, which I'll describe how to do later in the book.

Your network administrator can, of course, access any and all files, folders, and programs on your system, whether or not they are password-protected or hidden.

Power-On Passwords

A power-on password system requires that you enter a password as soon as a PC is turned on. Once in place, the PC will not load its operating system (neither DOS nor Windows) until the correct password is entered.

The exact process of setting up a power-on password varies from one PC to another—sometimes even those PCs made by the same manufacturer have variations in this process. However, the first step in setting a power-on password is to access your system's CMOS settings. This is usually done by pressing F1 or another designated key at startup. (You will see a message telling you which key to press when you first turn on your computer.) From there, follow the instructions and prompts displayed on your screen to set the password.

Your power-on password can be bypassed by someone starting your PC with a system disk in drive A. To prevent this, go into your system's CMOS settings, and look for a setting such as Boot Options. Select that, then follow the prompts until you find an enable/disable setting for Boot From Floppy, Check Drive A, or similar.

Be extremely careful when you go into your system's CMOS settings! It is easy to render your system inoperable by doing something like accidentally setting the wrong hard drive type. You should also know that clearing a power-on password if you've forgotten it can be a tedious and difficult project.

A Better Idea: Real Password Software

Although Windows' network password protection works fine for short periods of time, and the screen saver password system has its uses, real password software is the only way to go—that is, if you want a high level of security for files, folders, or the entire system.

You can replace Windows' token password protection with add-on shareware and commercial programs that provide real protection. We'll examine a few of those here.

Note that software discussed on the following pages is a sampling of the better products available. There are other products that offer the same features, but which cannot be included here due to space limitations. If you wish to see what else is out there, most computer magazines offer reviews of new products as well as periodic roundups of software by category.

Most of the programs mentioned here have additional functions beyond providing password protection. Thus, you will see some of them again in later chapters, and on the accompanying CD.

Shareware Programs

Shareware programs are a great way to try out software before you buy it, and sharing copies of a shareware program is usually encouraged. The basic premise behind a shareware program is simple: Try the program, and if you like it, pay the registration fee. If you don't like the program, you don't pay. All of this is done on the honor system. You get shareware free by downloading it, getting a copy from a friend, or obtaining a copy from a disk or CD such as the one accompanying this book.

Some shareware is fully functional. Other shareware programs may offer only limited functionality, and some work only for a predetermined amount of time. Many have frequent pop-up reminders to encourage users to pay a registration fee. No matter what the limitations of unregistered shareware, these are eliminated when you pay a registration fee and receive a code that unlocks the program.

You can download shareware on AOL, CompuServe, Delphi, and other online services, as well as many Web sites, including Download.com, Shareware.com, and Wugnet.com.

There are shareware programs and, it follows naturally, password-protection programs for virtually any application, from word processing to spreadsheets. The following shareware programs offer solid password protection, which is why I draw your attention to them here.

Black Magic   Black Magic is perhaps the simplest program that password-protects your desktop. The program can be set up to lock your desktop automatically, and it logs outsiders' attempts at getting through. Figure 3.13 will give you an idea of the options Black Magic Offers.

ScreenLock   ScreenLock secures access to your PC with password protection on more than one level. You can set up ScreenLock to keep Windows from starting without the proper password. One example is shown in Figure 3.14, which requires that the user respond to a question whose answer is the system's password. (And yes, for those

Monty Python fans out there, the correct answer, or password, in this instance was set to: "Is that laden or unladen?" Of course, you would not want to set your reply to something that someone else could figure out. No password should be guessable.)

Figure 3.13
Black Magic's setup options

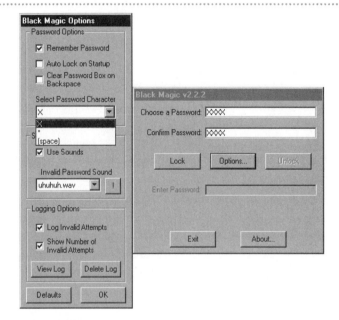

Figure 3.14
ScreenLock allows you to base a password on the answer to a question, which makes it easier for you to remember your password.

In addition, you can start ScreenLock with a *hot key* combination when you have to leave your PC unattended. As you can see in Figure 3.15, ScreenLock can also be used as a screen saver. ScreenLock can be set to keep a log of any attempts to bypass its security that were made while you were away from your desk.

Figure 3.15

ScreenLock functions as a screen saver at the same time it is logging attempts to bypass its security.

A *hot key* is a combination of two or more keys which, when pressed simultaneously, activate a program or function. Some examples of hot key combinations might be Ctrl+1, Alt+L, and Shift+F9.

Windows Task Lock   Windows Task Lock provides a simple but effective way to password-protect specified applications, no matter how they are executed. Options and features include sound events, password timeout stealth mode, multiple-language support, hot key activation, and encryption. Figure 3.16 shows how easy this utility is to configure.

WinGuardian   WinGuardian can be used to require a password to access Windows at startup or password protect any program window. It can also block MS-DOS programs and the MS-DOS mode itself. WinGuardian comes with 20 ready-to-use protected program windows for applications such as the Control Panel, File Manager, the Run selection on the Start menu, etc.

WinZip WinZip, the popular file compression and archiving program for Windows, offers a useful password-protection scheme. You can set up an archive so that any files added to it are password-protected and cannot be removed or copied from the archive without the password you have set. This feature has some very interesting applications, which we'll explore in more depth in Chapter 5.

Figure 3.16

Configuring Windows Task Lock is simple.

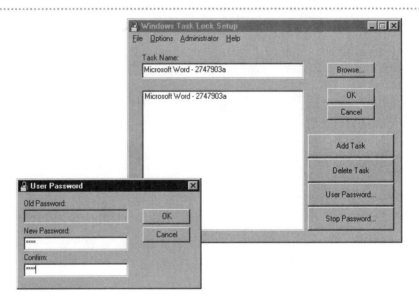

Archived Files and WinZip

An archived file can contain one or more other files, one of the cool features of archives. Another cool feature is compression, which often greatly reduces the size of the files in the archive, which in turn means the file takes less time to download (and less space in storage).

There are several forms of archived files, the most popular of which is the .ZIP archive, originated by PKWARE's PKZIP, a shareware program. .ZIP is the de facto standard for archiving in the PC world, online and off. (See http://www.pkware.com/ for more information.)

Continued on next page

Archived Files and WinZip (continued)

WinZip, another shareware program, is the most popular program for unpacking (unzipping) downloaded .ZIP files and for creating .ZIP files for transmission or storage. WinZip also creates self-executing archive files, which unpack themselves when run as a program under Windows. (See http://www.winzip.com for more information. You will also find WinZip on the accompanying CD.)

Commercial Software

Commercial software is software that you buy in computer stores and other shops, or via mail-order or Web sites. Besides not being free initially, one of the big differences between shareware and commercial software is that commercial software tends to be more professional in appearance and packaging. Commercial software is sometimes better in design, but not always. Finally, commercial software is usually produced by companies unlikely to drop out of the software business, so you can count on new versions and updates, as well as guarantees on media.

The following programs are among the best of their type:

AutoShutdown   Among the more interesting commercial software offerings that provide password protection is AutoShutdown, from Barefoot Productions. In addition to some interesting functions, AutoShutdown offers worthwhile password protection.

Cyber Patrol   Cyber Patrol is a filtering and tracking program that can be used to limit access to a PC and the Web. It also keeps track of what someone does with a PC (of value if you let others use your system) as well as limits access to PCs. Naturally, Cyber Patrol offers password protection for various elements of your PC. The system can be configured to accommodate as many as nine different users, each with their own username and password. Each user can be limited to specified directories and programs. Figure 3.17 will give you an idea of Cyber Patrol's capabilities.

Norton Utilities 2000 and Norton Utilities 8 (for Windows 3.*x*/DOS)   This venerable set of utilities is unbeatable in overall functionality, particularly when it comes to security issues. Permanent file erasure, damaged or deleted file recovery, and many more features make this indispensable for those who depend heavily on their PCs.

The package of course offers password protection functions, as well. (Note that versions are also available for Windows 95/98 and Windows 2000.)

Private File   This product, from Aladdin Systems, provides a graphic approach to file protection. Drag and drop a file into the desktop drop boxes provided by Private File, and the file is compressed and encrypted. You must have the proper password to either encrypt or decrypt files.

Security 98 for Win95/98   This program is touted as an armed guard for your computer. Security 98 is primarily designed to protect against viruses, handle cookies, and track a PC user's activity on the Web. However, it can also perfrom specialized encryption. For the purposes of the topic at hand, Security 98 also offers a feature that you can use to limit access to files and directories.

Figure 3.17

Cyber Patrol setup screen

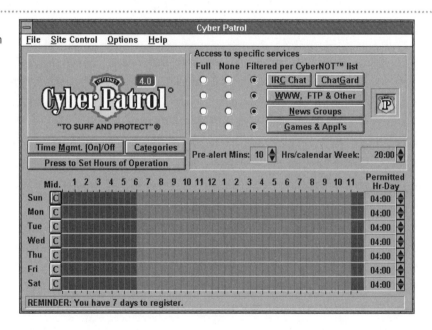

Now that you have the basic knowledge you need to protect your files and your privacy by setting passwords and making simple adjustments to Windows and your applications, let's take a closer look at what you can do with files. Chapter 4 focuses on some tricks you can use to hide your data—and how to overcome some tricks that your data may play on you.

PC CONFIDENTIAL

CHAPTER 4

Protecting Your Files and Folders with Disguise and Misdirection

- ✔ Disguising file displays and default folders
- ✔ Misdirection with deceptive filenames and extensions
- ✔ Misdirection with alternate folders
- ✔ Off-system storage media
- ✔ Using archives to hide files
- ✔ Additional archive applications

This chapter examines a variety of ways to disguise your sensitive files, cover tracks that lead to them, and set password protection and more with applications.

From there, we segue into off-system storage and archiving—with quite a few tips and tricks in between.

Disguising File Displays and Default Folders

The old maxim, "Out of sight, out of mind," can be applied to files and folders on your PC. After all, if certain files and folders can't be seen, no one will know they exist, right?

Perhaps. A diligent snoop will often find more than you want him or her to find, with a little knowledge, time, and motivation. However, the idle browser, given access to your PC, generally has no idea what you have stashed away if it isn't easily visible.

Speaking of visibility, there are techniques whereby you can render files and folders invisible to most applications, DOS, and, sometimes, Windows Explorer. These are detailed in Chapter 5.

Thus, to protect your files and privacy from idle curiosity (and from those who aren't quite up to expert level in their knowledge of PC applications and options), this chapter will teach you tips, tricks, and techniques for rendering any file you wish almost impossible to find.

Altering Recently Used File Lists

Your favorite applications leave definite pointers to important files and to what you've been doing with those applications of late. The most obvious pointers are in the Recently Used File List on the application's File menu, as shown in Figure 4.1.

Figure 4.1

Microsoft Word's Recently
Used File List

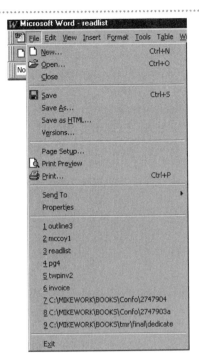

This list shows the files you've opened in order, beginning with those most recently opened. This is a convenient tool if you open certain files regularly, because it provides shortcuts to those files.

The Recently Used File List also makes it easy for anyone to open any file on which you've been working, without having to search for it, because the information about the file's location is stored by the application and keyed to the item selection on the list.

Although this may be obvious, someone may learn quite a bit about what you've been doing—even if you've deleted the files on the list. For instance, a Recently Used File List on your PC at the office consisting of `resume.doc`, `shopping.doc`, `project8.doc`, and `gifts.doc` would strongly imply that you have been working more on personal business rather than company business. Therefore, it may be a good idea to forgo the convenience of fast access to your recent files from this list in favor of privacy—which you can do. Many applications that provide such a file list (Microsoft Word, Excel, and PowerPoint, among others) allow you to specify from zero to nine files on the list.

To specify the number of files shown on the list, you must change the program option that controls this. That can usually be edited via an Options dialog box, as shown in Figure 4.2. To get to this box, select Options on the Tools menu, then click the General tab.

Figure 4.2

A program's Options dialog box

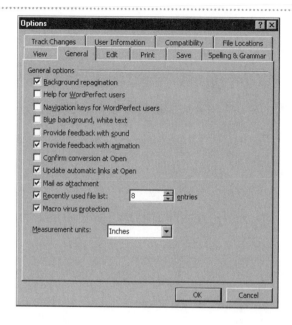

This dialog is from Microsoft Word (Excel, PowerPoint, and other programs have similar Options dialog boxes). As you can see, the General sheet is displayed and shows a selection for setting the number of entries in the Recently Used File List. If you uncheck the check box labeled Recently Used File List, no list will be displayed.

The number of filenames on the Recently Used File List is normally from zero to nine. A few applications may restrict the number to fewer, but each of the Microsoft applications here lets you have a list of as many as nine. This is independent of Windows itself, which has no control over the number of filenames an application can display.

To muddy your file tracks a little more, set the number of entries in the Recently Used File List to 1. Then, whenever you leave your PC, make sure the last file you open has an appropriate- or innocent-seeming name (such as schedule.doc or bizlet.doc). This will imply, to some, that you have been working only with that file.

Misdirection with Deceptive Filenames and Extensions

If you want to further confuse the issue of where your data is stored, consider using filenames that have no relationship to the file content. For example, if you have a file named resume.doc, rename it as oldinfo.doc; or use calendar.xls instead of budget.xls.

This has two advantages. First, the name itself will be misleading, as in oldinfo. Second, if you select a filename extension that an application cannot "see," anyone snooping with your word processor, spreadsheet, or other program won't see it either. I often use .DLL, which no application recognizes as one of its "native" files, and which most people will disregard.

Here's the step-by-step procedure:

1. Open Windows Explorer and navigate to the directory where the file you want to rename resides.

2. Right-click the filename.

3. Select Rename on the menu displayed.

4. Type in the file's new name (filename *and* extension).

5. Press Enter.

6. You will get a message that says, "If you change a filename extension, the file may become unusable. Are you sure you want to change it?" Click Yes.

Using this dodge requires that you remember the names and extensions you use, and that you rename any such files to their original names before you open them. If you do not rename the file before you click on it, chances are you will get an Open With dialog box asking with which application you want to associate the file. Since *you* will know in which application you created the file, scroll down the list until you find the correct one. Anyone else who clicks on this file will have to guess at the program or application, and will find themselves out of luck if they get it wrong.

Do *not* keep a list of your covert filenames on or near your computer system. Someone might find it, rendering this security feature moot.

You can change the default extension under which some applications save files in the applications' Options (go to File ➤ Save As, click the Options button, and go to the Save [*Application*] File As drop-down list) or Settings dialog boxes. (What the dialog box is named depends on the application.) Be sure that you don't set the file type in the application's Open dialog box to that of your covert files, or *only* your covert files will be displayed. Neither do you want to set the type to All Files.

Misdirection with Alternate Folders

Most applications have specific work (or *default*) folders, to which they default when you go to open a file. This makes it very easy for someone to find your files, because most people tend to look for things where they expect to find them. (For example, most snoops would look for a folder named LETTERS if they wanted to find letters. They would probably not look for letters in a folder named DOSUTIL.)

That being the case, you probably want to keep your files in a folder other than the default. You should also avoid the obvious folders, such as My Documents.

Instead, keep your files in a folder with a name that has no relation to what the files are. You might, for example, create a folder called UTIL or SYSTEMA on your C drive as your work folder. At the same time, let the default folder (file location folder, or work folder or directory, for some applications) remain a place where you do not keep important files.

You can change the folder in which some applications look for their files initially (the default folder) via the program's Options or Settings dialog box. Using Word as an example, the sequence would be Tools ➤ Options ➤ File Locations. For Excel, Tools ➤ Options ➤ General, and for PowerPoint Tools ➤ Options ➤ Advanced.

Creating Read-Only and Password-Protected Files with an Application

Among the more interesting of many applications' features is the ability to save a file as *Read-only*. You can also password-protect files with many of the same applications when you save them.

Saving Files as Read-Only

As discussed in Chapter 3, a file with the Read-only attribute set cannot be altered and saved (some applications will not let you make any changes in a read-only file, while others will let you make changes but will not allow you to save the file's changes). This protects the file from malicious or accidental alteration, should someone open it without your knowledge. In that chapter, I showed you how to set the Read-only attribute from Windows Explorer. Now I will show you how to save the file as Read-only using the application that created the file.

To save a file with the Read-only attribute set from within an application, follow these steps:

1. With the file open, select Save As on the application's File menu. The Save As dialog box will appear.

2. Enter the name for the file in the Filename text box and press the Options button. The Save dialog box will appear, as shown in Figure 4.3. (If this is a file that has already been saved and perhaps reopened, simply use the filename in the filename field or click on the existing filename.)

3. Click the check box labeled Read-Only Recommended at the lower-right of the Save dialog. Click OK, and then click the Save button on the Save As dialog box.

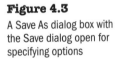

Figure 4.3

A Save As dialog box with the Save dialog open for specifying options

Setting a file as Read-only does *not* set a password. Anyone who opens the file can change the Read-only attribute, unless you password-protect the file as described in the next section.

Password-Protecting Files As You Save Them

If you want to password-protect a file, follow this procedure:

1. Select Save As on the File menu and press the Options button in the Save As dialog box.

2. In the Save dialog box (Figure 4.3), enter a password in the Password To Open field. Optionally, you can enter a password in the Password To Modify field next to it. This permits you to set up differing levels of access for a file—to view or to edit.

If you move or copy a file with the Read-only attribute set, and/or with password protection set by the application used to create it, the attribute or password set remains with the file. (This is true even if you copy the file with a new name.)

3. After you enter the password, you will be prompted to enter it again for verification, as shown in Figure 4.4.

Passwords can consist of letters or numerals. Letters in passwords are *case-sensitive*, which means that if you use a capital letter or letters in creating a password, you must capitalize the same letters when you give the password to open a document.

Saving a file as Read-only or password-protected with the application that created it does not protect it completely. In most instances, you can still read (view) the file with other applications—including the simple DOS file-editing program, EDIT. More on this in Chapter 6.

Figure 4.4

Verifying a newly created
file password

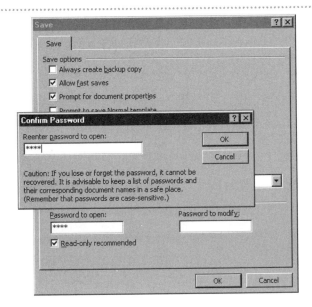

Again, these techniques are to protect your files from those with little
or moderate PC experience. If you feel the techniques described here
are not enough to protect extremely sensitive files and/or folders, consider using additional password protection—such as what I described
in Chapter 3.

Off-System Storage and Archiving

For really sensitive files and files you want to use elsewhere, off-system storage (i.e., not
on your PC's hard drive) is the way to go. Off-system storage may take the form of floppy
disks, high-capacity disks (ZIP or others), or even tape or CD-ROM drives. You might
also consider storing files online—at any of several Web sites that offer free file storage
(including altavista.com) or, if you use an online service as an ISP, in your online
storage space. (I don't recommend this, but many people do it.)

If you store more than one or two files off-system, you need to consider archiving the files. As this section explains, archiving is an excellent means of file management and storing files in "compressed" form.

Floppy Disk Storage

Floppy disks are the de facto standard when it comes to off-system storage. Every PC has one or more floppy disk drives, and $3^1/_2''$ floppy disks are inexpensive, reliable, and don't take up much space.

With these features, floppies are ideal for storing sensitive information. When you need to view, edit, print, or otherwise access the files, you can do so from the floppy or copy the needed files temporarily to your hard drive. (Don't forget to copy any edited files back to your floppy and to delete the copies on the hard drive.)

You should already have backups of your important data files stored on floppies. (If not, back up that data now!) Copying files is pretty much a no-brainer, whether you do it from DOS, with Windows Explorer, or with a copying/backup utility.

You may be tempted to disregard labeling floppy disks used for off-system storage because you are certain that you will remember what's on the disks. Don't do it! Before you know it, you will have 10 or 20 disks without labels, and every time you want something that's on one of the disks, you'll waste time looking at the directories of one disk after another. Label your disks!

The only real negative here is the 1.4-megabyte (MB) capacity of the standard $3^1/_2''$ floppy, which may be limiting if you have several large files (or a lot of small files). Archiving, to be discussed shortly, can help.

If you back up or frequently store data off-system, consider making *two* copies of everything, on separate disks. This is good "insurance" against disk failure (it does happen), data corruption, or floppies getting lost or damaged.

ZIP Drives

ZIP drives are fast becoming standard equipment for many PC users, as well as *on* many new PCs. ZIP disks are not cheap, but they are relatively small in size and offer a big bonus over standard floppies: They can store 100MB.

ZIP drives and .ZIP files are not related in any way, save by name. The companies that produce archiving software are entirely separate from Iomega, the company that manufactures ZIP drives and disks.

With this much space, you need not be concerned about having to go to a second disk immediately. Still, you may be surprised at how quickly files can add up to 100MB. Today's applications create large files as a matter of course. Some types of files—graphics in particular—are large by their very nature. So, you could be into two or even three ZIP disks for storage—not counting backups—before you know it.

At present, the main disadvantage of ZIP disks for off-system storage is cost. ZIP disks cost 40 to 50 times as much as floppy disks. In addition, if your PC did not come with a ZIP drive, you will have to buy one. But with those disadvantages aside, ZIP disks are as reliable as conventional floppies, and one ZIP replaces as many as 70 floppies.

When you want to copy a large number of files for off-system storage, consider keeping those files in one folder, created for that purpose. Name the folder COPY (or whatever else you wish), and when you want to duplicate its contents, simply copy the entire folder (that is, assuming the floppy or ZIP disk to which you are copying has enough room for the contents of the folder).

Tape Backup Drives

Tape backup drives, once the standard for backing up important data you couldn't afford to risk losing, are still used but are declining in popularity. Still, they have their place, for chores such as backing up an entire system. However, tape backup drives are not the best option because they are too cumbersome and expensive for the average computer user.

CD-ROM Storage

With fast CD-ROM drives and burners as affordable as they are, it might seem that CDs are an ideal off-system storage medium. This isn't quite true. CDs are ideal for files you won't be editing or changing in any other way, but they are impractical for data that you use and edit frequently. Once information is burned to a CD it cannot be changed without altering it in its original program and then completing the entire burning process again.

Don't neglect safe physical storage for your off-system storage media. Heat and humidity can damage disks and tapes and render them useless. Disks and other media are susceptible to physical damage, too. Along with this, keep in mind that you will want to keep your off-system files in a place that is secure from snoops.

Storing Files Online

For those of you who are fairly new to the online world, the idea of storing files online may seem odd, or even impossible, but it is neither. There are Web sites that specialize in storing your files. (Personally, I do not trust these, since files thus stored are out of the owner's control, in more ways than one. Someone may hack into the Web site and its host computer, and obtain access to and damage or delete files. A malicious employee at the site may do the same. Or, the site may disappear one day, along with your files.)

If you use an online service, such as Delphi or CompuServe, for your ISP, you will find that the service has set aside a certain amount of personal file storage space—with no special software required.

If you use a conventional dial-up ISP, and the ISP offers space for personal Web pages, you can set up your own page and use that space to store files. A simple *FTP* (file-transfer protocol) program is all you need to upload and download files to and from your online space.

Need a good ftp program for your PC? Try WS_FTP. It is available for download at many sites and included on this book's CD.

AOL and CompuServe users can use a similar ploy, uploading files to their Web-page space. The necessary file-transfer programs are built into AOL and CompuServe access software.

If all that seems a bit too complicated or otherwise impractical, you have one other option: E-mail files to yourself. Better yet, e-mail the files to a second e-mail address.

Don't have two ISP or online service accounts or screen names? Free e-mail sites, such as Excite and AltaVista, allow you to attach files to e-mail you send and to receive files attached to e-mail. However you set them up, having two e-mail accounts means that you can send files to account B from account A, then allow the files to reside in storage at account B. Having more than one account is also handy because almost all ISPs, online services, and Web-based e-mail services have a file-size limit that you cannot exceed. Of course, transmitting files as .ZIP archives can solve that problem. See the next section, "Archiving Files," for details.

However you store files online, there are two potential problems. First, your access may be limited by connectivity problems with your system or phone lines or with the host system. Second, you could lose your files if the host experiences a hardware or software problem.

Archiving Files

If you are going to store your files on portable media or online, it is a good idea to archive them, for several reasons. Archiving files (storing them in archives created with PKZIP or WinZip) results in the files being compressed and taking up less space. This can be important when you want to put a large number of files (or a number of large files, as the case may be) on floppy disks. Storing them in an archive means they take up less space—as much as 90 percent less space.

Archiving also simplifies file management. You can store multiple files—two files, 10, 50, or more—in one archive if necessary, which means you don't have to worry about copying all the files you saved on disk. In one operation, you can simply unpack the archive into the hard drive folder where you need the files.

Certain kinds of files do not compress much—or anything at all—when they are archived. These include graphics files. Still, archiving provides a means of organizing related graphics files.

There are several formats for archiving. The most popular of these include .ARC, .ARJ, and .ZIP. The .ZIP archive format is by far the most popular, and the one on which we'll focus here.

Four popular archiving programs use the .ZIP format: PKZIP (the original), WinZip (a program that began life as a simplified front end for PKZIP but quickly became its own entity), Aladdin Expander (a program that unpacks archives), and Quarterdeck Zip-It. Figures 4.5, 4.6, 4.7, and 4.8 show these programs' main screens.

Figure 4.5

PKZIP's main screen

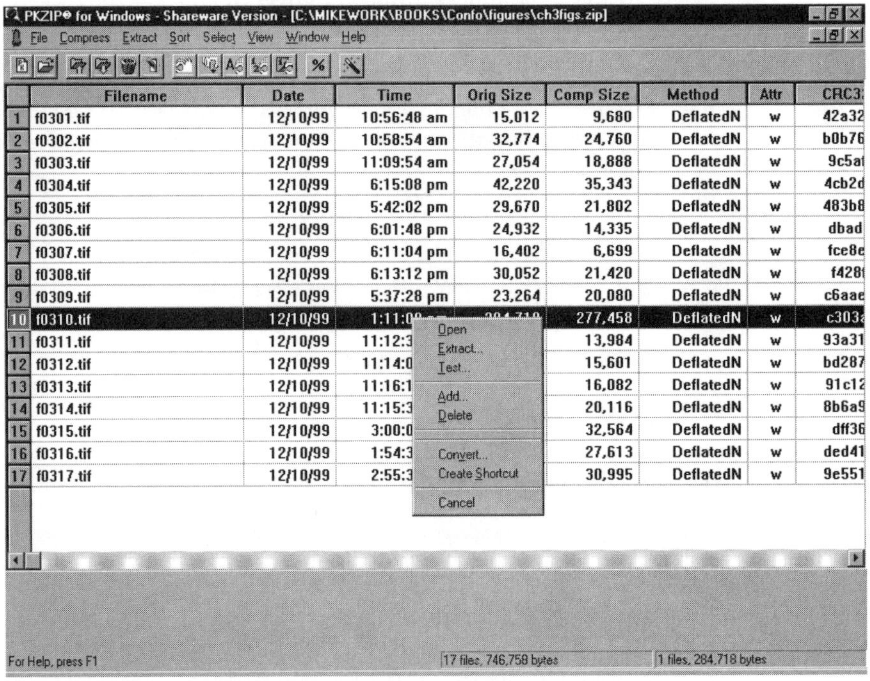

Both PKZIP and WinZip are shareware that can be downloaded. You will find PKZIP at http://www.pkzip.com. WinZip's site is http://www.winzip.com. (You can also check the CD that is included with this book.) Of these two shareware programs, WinZip seems to have the most utility and to be easier to use. However, that is my opinion; you may find otherwise. Both programs offer similar features (drag-and-drop capability, extensive user help, the ability to create self-extracting archives, virus scanning, viewing or extracting specific files from an archive, and more) and differing approaches to various tasks. Try one, and if you find it difficult or user-belligerent, try the other. As mentioned, these are shareware programs, and it costs nothing to try them.

Figure 4.6

WinZip

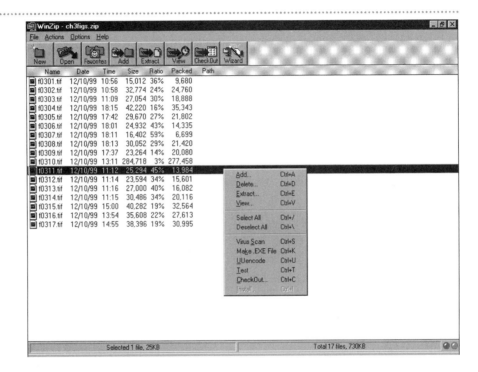

Aladdin Expander, on the other hand, is *freeware* (which means you do not have to pay to use it). You can download Aladdin Expander at http://www.aladdinsys.com. The advantage of Aladdin Expander is that it also handles MIME-encoded files that are often used on the Internet, as well as Macintosh archives.

It is probably a good idea to have Aladdin Expander on your desktop, even though you will need another program to create archives. In addition to the advantages just noted, it also has a user-friendly drag-and-drop interface, as shown in Figure 4.7.

Quarterdeck's Zip-It (Figure 4.8) is a relatively easy-to-use program that offers most of the features PKZIP offers. It comes with a *plug-in* (an add-on program) that works with Netscape or Microsoft's Internet Explorer to handle archived files as you download them. Quarterdeck is not free, but can be purchased at a price of around $30–$40, with a rebate offer included in the package.

Figure 4.7

Aladdin Expander

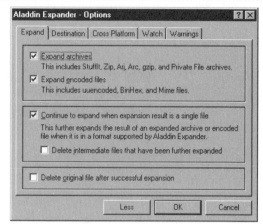

Figure 4.8

Quarterdeck's Zip-It archive program

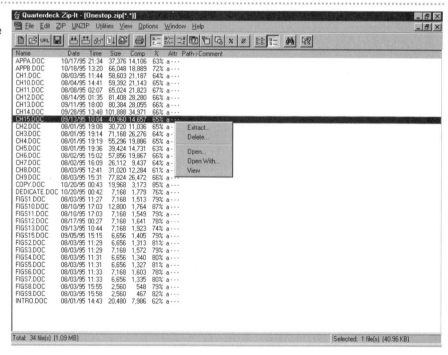

With rare exception, one program isn't necessarily "better" than another that has the same function. There is usually no absolute "best." What is best is more often than not a very subjective decision. A given program may function better for you and suit your style of work and your needs more than others that acquaintances or co-workers may strenuously recommend. If a program works for you, it's the best. Use it. But don't be averse to trying new things.

Putting Archives to Work for You

Whichever program you use, your primary applications will be creating .ZIP files containing files that you don't want others to have. There are several ways to approach this.

Storing Archives on Your Hard Drive   If the only others who have access to your PC are those who are not PC mavens, you might consider simply putting all the files you want to protect into one or more archives. Locate the archives in some buried subfolder you create—such as \windows\system\temp\files. The files will be effectively invisible to novice PC users *only*. Take it a step further if you like, and give the archive a different extension, such as .DLL or .RFX—whatever you like—as discussed earlier.

If you want to keep the tools to retrieve your archived files out of the hands of unauthorized viewers, don't leave a desktop shortcut/icon or Start menu selection for a program like WinZip or PKZIP. Instead, delete any shortcuts and remove the selection in question from the Start menu. When you want to run the program, use the Start menu's Run selection. (Review Chapter 3 for details on how to remove shortcuts and Start menu selections.)

Off-System Storage of Archives   If your PC is accessible to others at home or in your workplace who know how to open .ZIP files, you will want to move everything to off-system storage. Archiving will be helpful here as well, reducing the space required by the files you store off-system.

Archiving files seems to help guard against data corruption. In some 10 years of experience, I have found that files that are not archived on floppy disks are more likely to be corrupted than files that are archived. Of course, ideally, you should keep *two* copies of everything you archive, on two separate disks.

Packing and Unpacking/Zipping and Unzipping Archives

As with anything to do with computing, archives and archiving software come with some esoteric language and redundant terminology. Here's the short version: When you put files into an archive, it is referred to as "packing" the archive; removing files is referred to as "unpacking" or *extracting* the files. With .ZIP archives, packing and unpacking are often referred to as *zipping* and *unzipping*.

As noted previously, you will probably be using PKZIP or WinZip to create archives and to extract files from archives. Fortunately, these processes are pretty much intuitive with either program. One bit of advice regarding creating, adding files to, and extracting files from archives: It is not a good idea to create or unpack large .ZIP files on a floppy disk. The programs sometimes require more room than a floppy affords to do their job. If you have an archive that is larger than 300 megabytes on a floppy, it is probably best to copy it from the floppy to your hard drive before you do anything with the archive.

If you plan on downloading files from Web sites or online services, you will find that you cannot do without PKZIP or WinZip. The majority of program and data files online for PCs are in .ZIP format, since this reduces download time and provides the convenience of transmitting the multiple files required by most applications in one download.

As you can see, disguise and misdirection, along with off-system storage, are very effective privacy protection aids. But now it's time to move into more subtle realms of file protection—including invisibility—in Chapter 5.

PC CONFIDENTIAL

The Times
COMPUTER BREAK IN!
How to protect yourself and your computer

CHAPTER 5

Hiding Files, Folders, and Applications

- ✔ Hiding files in the open
- ✔ Making files and folders invisible
- ✔ File attributes—what they mean and how to set them
- ✔ Windows Explorer and invisible files
- ✔ Hiding and renaming program files
- ✔ Using archives to hide and password-protect files
- ✔ Important cautions when changing file locations, names, and passwords

I n this chapter, we delve into some of the more esoteric methods of hiding and disguising information on your hard drive.

We begin with hiding a file "in the open," and then take a close look at how to make data, program files, and folders invisible, as well as give you a good foundation on these topics. From there, we'll cover some outlandish techniques for hiding programs. Then it's on to using archives to hide and to protect your important data and program files.

Purloined Files?

Perhaps the simplest way to hide a file is to place it where no one would expect to find it. You might, for instance, store a Word or Excel file in your /windows/system folder rather than in the application's work folder. Thus, as with the letter in Poe's tale "The Purloined Letter," the file can be "out in the open"—complete with a correct filename and extension—and never be spotted (and thus truly purloined), simply because the snoop would *expect* the file to be somewhere else.

Most people—particularly when pressed for time—will not do a folder-by-folder search for files with the desired extension and contents, which means they would never spot the file or files you've hidden. Still, you can't count on everyone being short on time and motivation, so hiding the file out in the open, under its own name, isn't always a solution.

Fortunately, there are several other solutions to the problem of hiding a file on your hard drive. As covered in earlier chapters, you can rename the file (just the beginning of the filename or the filename and extension) or password-protect it. You might even make the file—and perhaps the folder it is in—*invisible*.

If you have a large hard drive, it may be, unbeknownst to you, divided into two virtual "drives." For example, a 3.2-gigabyte (GB) drive might be divided into drive C and drive D, with most of the space allocated to drive C. (Take a look at your system now—you may be surprised.) The unused drive can be a good place to hide files—particularly encrypted files, about which you can read more in Chapter 7.

Now You See It, Now You Don't: Making Files and Folders Invisible

It may have occurred to you that the ability to make files invisible would give you a great way to hide them. If so, you'll be interested to know that you can indeed make both data and program files invisible. The same is true of folders.

What Do You Mean by "Invisible"?

The Invisible attribute prevents applications and DOS from "seeing" (or displaying the filename of) a file. Under the proper conditions, it also prevents Windows Explorer from seeing the filename. The file is still there, however, and can be acted on by DOS or application commands as long as you know the filename to use.

Doing this doesn't require you to obtain special software; nor does it require any technical knowledge (although the following section gives you some useful background). If you can point and click, you can make any data file, program file, or folder invisible.

Background: File Attributes

As you may know, PC files have certain *attributes* (an attribute is a property or characteristic). In Chapter 4, we explored the Read-only attribute, which prevents editing a file. There are, however, four file attributes in all. These are:

Read-only This prevents changes from being made to a file. It also prevents deleting the file from DOS with the DEL command. (You can still delete the file via Windows Explorer and some applications.)

Archive   An archive is typically any binary data or program file. This attribute is used by the system to identify files that need to be included in a system backup.

Hidden   A hidden file is one that does not show up in a directory display. This includes file directories and lists displayed by DOS and applications. As you will learn, it sometimes—but not always—includes Windows Explorer file lists.

System   System files are operating system (MS-DOS and Windows) files. They are normally protected from deletion and alteration.

For our purposes, only the Read-only and Hidden attributes are of interest.

Setting File Attributes

A file's attributes may be set using the application that created it, although this is not true for all applications. (As you may recall, you learned how to set a file's attribute to Read-only in Chapter 4.)

Any attribute can be set for any file with Windows Explorer. To set an attribute with Windows Explorer, follow these steps:

1.   Right-click the name of the file whose attributes you want to set.

2.   Select Properties on the context menu displayed. The File Properties dialog box will appear, as shown in Figure 5.1.

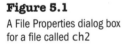

Figure 5.1

A File Properties dialog box for a file called ch2

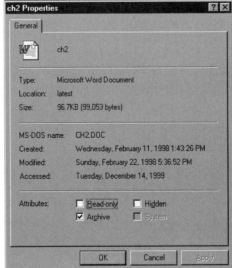

As you can see, the attributes are listed at the bottom of the dialog. To set a file's attribute, click its check box. To remove an attribute, uncheck its check box.

It doesn't matter whether a file is a data file or a program file; attributes are set in the same way for both.

Setting Folder Attributes

Folders have the same attributes as files, as illustrated in Figure 5.2, which shows the properties of a folder that contains multimedia files.

Figure 5.2

A Folder Properties dialog box for a folder named Multimedia Files

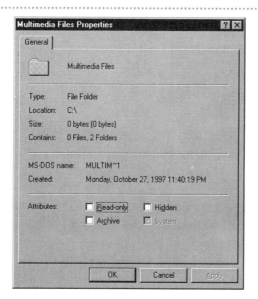

You can view the attributes of any folder with Windows Explorer. To do so, follow these steps:

1. Open Windows Explorer and right-click on any folder.

2. Select Properties on the menu displayed, and a Properties dialog box appears.

3. To set a folder's attribute, click its check box. To remove an attribute, uncheck its check box.

The Final Touch

Whether it's a data file, program file, or folder you're working with, to make an object invisible on your hard drive you must set the Hidden attribute in the object's Properties dialog box. After you have done this, the file or folder should no longer show up on a DOS directory, an application directory, or a list.

You're not in the clear yet, however. There remains one additional step to complete invisibility: You must make an adjustment to Windows Explorer's options.

Even after you make a folder invisible, its contents are still visible when you include the folder name in a directory search. Still, unless someone knows the folder exists, they won't be able to view the files therein, because they won't know enough to perform a search for it by name.

The Windows Explorer Exception to Invisibility

Having set the Hidden attribute for a file or folder, you will not be able to see the file or folder with Windows Explorer—unless Windows Explorer is set so that it displays files for which the Hidden attribute is set.

To check this, open Windows Explorer's View menu and select Options. The Options dialog box will appear, as shown in Figure 5.3. Click the radio button labeled Hide Files Of These Types to clear it and enable Windows Explorer to display Hidden files and folders; or click the button so that it's selected to prevent Windows Explorer from displaying Hidden files and folders.

Although setting Windows Explorer not to display Hidden files will prevent others from viewing them, this attribute is easy enough to change, as you've just seen. So, if you expect a snoop who has more than a modicum of PC knowledge to get their hands on your system, be aware that this trick won't necessarily keep anything from them for long.

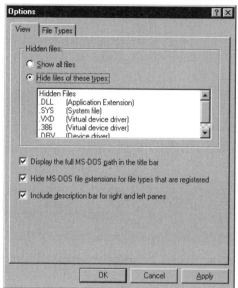

Hiding Applications (Programs)

Hiding an application can be a useful dodge; if someone can't run the application that created a given file, they can't see that file. If you combine several techniques you've learned from this book, you can all but insure that no one will be able to find the application.

The steps to hide an application are simple enough:

1. Remove the program from the Start menu, per Chapter 3. If there is a shortcut/icon for the program on the desktop, delete that (and empty the Recycle Bin).

2. Move the program and its files to a new folder. If you have a partitioned drive, create the new folder on the virtual drive that is least-used or unused (normally, drive D).

3. Make *all* of the program and support files—*plus* the folder they are in—invisible by setting the Hidden attribute.

(If you do this, be sure that the Documents List on the Start menu is cleared, and that you've set the application file as Hidden with Windows Explorer. If you don't, someone can simply click on an item in the Documents List, or on the application's name in Windows Explorer, and the program will start right up.)

Want more? Okay, here's an additional step: Rename the program file something that isn't even a program name, so that even if a snoop comes across it, they won't recognize it as a program. Perhaps grazu.exe. If this sounds preposterous, read on.

What's in a Name: Hiding Programs by Changing Their Names

Does the name grazu.exe seem improbable for a program? Is it so bizarre that it couldn't possibly work? Try it for yourself using these steps:

1. Open Windows Explorer, and then open the directory /Windows.

2. Right-click on the filename sol.exe, and select Rename on the menu that appears.

3. Type in **grazu.exe**, or **sybex.exe** if you like, and press Enter.

If you recall from the section in Chapter 4 titled "Misdirection with Deceptive Filenames and Extensions," you can use just about anything for the filename extension, so long as you remember that you will have to change the extension back to the original before you yourself can open the program. This is because Windows will not know with what application it should associate the program until you tell it, either by returning the extension to the application's default, or by selecting the correct program from the Open With dialog box. Please review Chapter 4 for a more thorough explanation of this tactic.

Avoid renaming the program with the same name as another program. Using the name of another program will at the very least create a lot of confusion, and at the very worst, if the program is in the same folder, it will overwrite the original program, rendering it completely unusable.

4. Double-click on the name you entered; the game Solitaire will start. (Don't forget to name it back, unless you want to hide that program file, too.)

Note that if you haven't altered the extension, you can still start the program from the Start menu. This is because the program file's internal name hasn't been changed, which means that the system can find and run it.

You should not rename other support files that are included in a folder with a program file. This is because some programs seek support files by their directory names, and changing the name (filename and/or extension) would render them invisible to the program.

Using Archives to Hide and Protect Files

You should be familiar with WinZip from the preceding chapter. If not, take a few minutes to read about WinZip and install it on your system. (The latest version of WinZip is included on the CD accompanying this book.)

Hiding Out in the Archive

In Chapter 4, I showed you how you can use WinZip archives to store files off-system on floppy disks efficiently and safely. WinZip archives can likewise be used to store files on your hard drive and are guaranteed to be unfindable by anyone who doesn't know about archives and WinZip or PKZIP.

For an extra modicum of security, rename the .ZIP file something besides .ZIP. You can always change the filename extension back to .ZIP, in any event.

At the same time, you might consider hiding WinZip, as well, using the techniques described in the section titled "Hiding Applications" a few pages back.

WinZip allows you to run programs from an archive. This may be useful for protecting a small program that you don't use often. Add password protection as described in the next section, and no one else will be able to run the program, even if they know how to use WinZip.

Password Protection for Archives

As I mentioned many pages ago, WinZip offers password protection for archives. You can add a password when you create an archive or any time thereafter. Simply open the archive you want to password protect and select Password on WinZip's Options menu. You will see a dialog prompting for a password, as shown in Figure 5.4

Redundancies and Recursions: Multiple Passwords and Archives?

In case you have been wondering, yes, you can place a password-protected file (say, a Word file that you password-protected with Word) in a password-protected archive and retain the benefit of protection from both passwords.

Similarly, you can add .ZIP archive files to another .ZIP archive file. (This step makes for good housekeeping if you have a number of related .ZIP files around.) If you have a password on an archived file that you put into another archive that has its own password, the password protection still applies. (The .ZIP files you add won't be compressed again, though.)

You can also place encrypted files in an archive under password protection.

Some Important Cautions

By now, you may be ready to start moving, renaming, and rendering invisible all sorts of files—and hiding the applications you use with them. Before you get too far into planning (or doing) that, remember that the more you change things, the more you have to remember. Think about how much you need to remember in order to get through the password barriers you've set up and find the bogus names of programs you want to run, or to find programs and files that you've hidden and/or removed from the Start menu.

How much protecting of files you do is entirely up to you. If you write such information down to give your memory a crutch, I can only caution you keep the paper on which it is written on your person—in your purse or wallet or checkbook, perhaps. You might also keep a second copy hidden away, in case you lose the first. After using your new setups enough, you will have in your memory everything you've written down; but until

Figure 5.4

Adding a password to a
WinZip archive

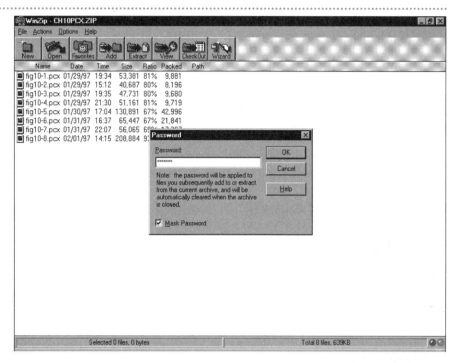

that time, you don't want to lose the passwords and names and locations that are the keys
to all of your important data. (There are programs designed to "crack" passwords, but
there is no guarantee any of these will work.)

Once the password is set, no one can open, run, view, or extract a file in that archive
without giving the password. The protection is also added to any files subsequently added
to the archive.

Don't choose simple passwords. Anything that is connected with you
personally (birthday, hometown, child's name, significant other's name,
pet's name, and so on), someone who works or lives with you—or who
simply knows you fairly well—can guess. More passwords are guessable than you might think. (It's also not a good idea to use the brand
name of your PC or the box of disks on your desk.) Try to create a
random string of characters and work to memorize that string, rather
than writing it down where someone might find it.

You may have heard of or seen password "vaults" or other protection programs that you can use to store passwords for other programs. I recommend that most folks avoid using these. You have all your eggs in one basket, and any such program's data files can be broken into.

Now that you know how to hide your files—on your system or off—it's time to introduce you to some files you probably didn't know existed. Created by Windows and your applications, these are files that are intended to help you, but which can give away everything. Get the lowdown on this and much more, in Chapter 6!

PC Confidential

CHAPTER 6

How to Keep Your Files from Giving You Away

- ✔ Computer data and data formats
- ✔ How information is stored on disk
- ✔ Why deleted files are not gone, and how to view them
- ✔ How to get rid of deleted files permanently
- ✔ What's hidden in your files
- ✔ What's hidden on your disk

N ow that you know how to hide your files—on your system or off—it's time to take a closer look at the files themselves and the potential for treachery they hold.

Before we get into that, I will explain a bit about how your PC handles and stores information. Then we'll look at how files are stored on disk, why deleted files aren't necessarily gone—and how to make sure they are. After that, you'll learn some interesting things about what's contained in many of your files in addition to the information you put there.

I will also introduce to you some files you probably didn't know existed. Created by Windows and various applications, these are files intended to help you, but they may do the opposite. Hidden away in subdirectories on your hard drive, they can give away a lot of information about you and what you have been doing with your PC. I'll show you how you can get rid of them.

Computer Data and Data Formats

Before we get into the ins and outs of files, let's take a brief look at how PCs handle data. I'll make this as painless and non-technical as possible. If you do not wish to read this entire section, that's okay, but read some of it. Even a little knowledge is useful in the realms we are exploring. (And—who knows?—you may find this information fascinating!)

All modern computers have one thing in common: they handle data in *digital format* (which is why they're called digital computers). This means that they perceive and handle data characters as *strings* (groups) of *binary digits*, which are explained in the next section.

The terms *digital* and *binary* are often used interchangeably. To clear up any confusion caused by that fact: *Digital* refers to discrete signals of any type—binary or otherwise—that do not vary in a continuous manner. Rather, such signals are identified by two specific values or states, such as *on and off*, *positive and negative*, or *1 and 0*. Digital signals change immediately from one state to another and are the antithesis of *analog signals*, which vary through the entire range between the two states. An analogy for digital would be a radio with only two volume settings: *high* or *low*. In contrast, a radio with a normal volume control that lets you set the volume anywhere between high and low would be analog. Binary is described in the section below.

Further, almost all computers (some mainframe computers excepted) use the same numeric code to represent each character—numbers from the *American Standard Code for Information Interchange* (or *ASCII*, which will be explained in coming pages).

Binary Data

Even if you're not technically oriented, I'm sure you've at least heard rumors about data being stored and manipulated by digital computers in something called *digital* or *binary data format*. If a computer uses binary data format, this means that each *character* (letter, number, symbol, or control character) a computer handles is manipulated and stored as a specific *binary number*. (There are several excellent reasons for this, one of which you'll discover presently.)

Binary Numbers

A binary number is a string of binary digits, such as "1010" or "10011." Only 0s and 1s are used in binary notation, as opposed to the numerals 0 through 9, which are used by the decimal system.

Unlike the decimal system that we use on a daily basis, the values of the numerals themselves (0 and 1) are not used to determine the total value of a binary number; instead, the values of the places marked by a 1 are summed. Each place has a set value. The first place on the right in a binary number has a value of 1, the second place a value of 2, the third place a value of 4, and so on, with the value doubling with each place.

Again, the value of a binary number is determined by adding up the values of the places that contain a 1. If there is a 0 in a place, that place's value is not counted. Table 6.1 shows some examples of digital numbers.

Table 6.1: Examples of Binary (Digital) Numbers

Binary Numeral	Decimal Value
00001	1
00010	2
00100	4
01000	8
10000	16
100000	32
1000000	64
10000000	128
...	...
00110	6
10001	17
11111	31
100001	33

Consulting Table 6.1, it's easy to see that the binary number *00011* (or *11*) is the same as the decimal number *3* (add the values of the places: 2 + 1 = 3). Similarly, the binary number *1010* is the same as the decimal number *10* (add the value of the places that contain a 1: 8 + 2 = 10). Nothing to it, right? Right! Keep this up and you'll be a binary math wizard in no time.

A complete binary number is often referred to as a *byte*. The 1s and 0s that make up binary numbers are called *binary digits*, a term which is usually shortened to *bits*. As you will learn, there are either seven or eight bits to a byte.

Why Do PCs Use Binary Numbering?

As you can see, only two states—*on and off*, or *high and low*—are required to represent any binary number. This means that such numbers can be processed very rapidly within a computer, which handles data as varying electrical values.

Breaking the ASCII Code

Still, there has to be a way to represent letters, numerals, and other characters, and to send control signals and the like. This is done by using an agreed-upon set of decimal-numeric values to represent all such characters. The computer uses a code of binary numbers that are the counterparts of that decimal numeric code. This results in the computer using a binary number to represent each and every character.

In Table 6.2, you will see the decimal value of a number, the binary numeral that represents that number, and how that number in binary is interpreted by a digital computer. (The ellipses mark where I have jumped to a new set of numbers.)

Table 6.2: ASCII Character Set

Decimal Value	Binary Value	Character Represented
65	1000001	A
66	1000010	B
67	1000011	C
68	1000100	D
69	1000101	E
70	1000110	F
71	1000111	G
72	1001000	H
...		
103	1101011	g

For example, an ASCII 71 (binary *1000111*) represents the uppercase letter *G*. An ASCII 103 (binary *1101011*) represents the lowercase letter *g*. Other values represent the rest of the alphabet (in upper- and lowercase), numerals, punctuation marks, spaces, special controls, and graphics characters. This system goes all the way up to 255 (*11111111*), which is the largest binary number a PC handles.

> The characters—letters, numerals, punctuation, and so forth—that the binary numbers in the ASCII code represent are usually referred to as *bytes*; hence the unit of measure of file size, RAM, and other PC elements, known as *kilobytes* (or *K*). Each K is 1024 bytes (characters) in size.

Those are the basics of data handling and storage in your PC. Now, we'll take a quick look at disk storage.

Important Note: ASCII and Binary Data

It is important that you take note of the fact that computer data is classified in two general types: *ASCII* and *binary*. The distinction is based on what sort of characters make up the data. ASCII data is composed of ASCII characters 0 through 127. These are certain control characters, all the letters of the alphabet (upper- and lowercase), spaces, punctuation, and numerals.

Binary data is composed of any of the characters in the ASCII code from number 128 through 256. These are additional control characters and DOS graphic characters, as well as special characters such as ®, ß, and ±. Except for those special characters, ASCII characters from 128 through 256 are not normally displayed by word processors and most other programs, although they do have token representations that may be displayed by certain programs. (See Figure 6.3, in a later section, for an example.)

Also of note is the fact that ASCII data is often referred to as *7-bit* data, and binary data is referred to as *8-bit* data. This is because, as you may have noticed in looking at Table 6.1, there are at most seven elements (bits) in the binary numbers representing the first 128 ASCII characters, while ASCII 128 through 255 require 8 elements.

How Information Is Stored on Disk

Computer disks include in their makeup a magnetic material. Data is stored on the computer, either on hard disk or floppy, in patterns of magnetized areas. Each area is called a *sector*. Each sector can store a set number of bytes (512, for instance, or 256). Sectors are sometimes arranged in groups called *clusters*. Sectors (and clusters) are laid out in *tracks*. Figure 6.1 is a graphical representation of this arrangement.

Figure 6.1

How data is stored on a computer disk

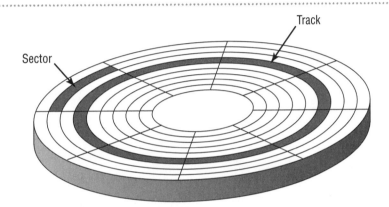

Actually, the important thing to take away from these discussions is not so much *how* data is stored, but how your PC keeps track of *where* data is stored. This is done using something called a *directory track*. A disk's directory track contains information about each file—its size, where it is stored, and so forth.

The bytes of a file are not usually stored in adjacent sectors. Files may be stored in sectors anywhere on the disk. Information as to where each sector's successor is located (adjacent or non-adjacent) is stored on that sector.

As you may surmise, scattering the data contained in a file randomly across non-adjacent sectors is inefficient. Have enough non-contiguous data on a hard drive, and it slows down file retrieval. This is why it is a good idea to *defragment* your hard drive from time to time, using the defrag utility that came with your hard drive, or with a commercial utility program such as Norton 2000. (Defragmenting a hard drive involves moving the data for each file from scattered sectors to contiguous sectors.)

Why Deleted Files Aren't Really Gone

And now we come to a really interesting aspect of disk file storage: *When a file is deleted from a hard drive, the data on the disk that makes up the file is not really deleted*. Instead, all information about the file is removed from the directory track. After that, the sectors that were occupied by that file are available for use, as your system sees things. Eventually, the sectors are written over by data for new files, but the data in the sectors is not erased or removed.

So, there are sectors with all the data for a "deleted" file on them, but no information on the directory track as to where they are. That's as good as gone, right? Wrong!

Certain utilities, such as Norton Unerase, can find deleted files' sectors and display them—and even bring them back as a file that a PC and its applications can read. This goes for hard drives or floppy disks. Figure 6.2 shows a portion of a deleted file as viewed with an undelete utility. Note that Norton Unerase shows as near a view of the reconstructed file as is possible.

Figure 6.2

A portion of a deleted file, as seen by Norton Unerase

Even if some of the disk sectors where a deleted file was stored are already overwritten by data from a new file, it is still possible to see the rest of the file's data with an unerase utility. Unerase utilities find all deleted files still on your hard drive, then locate all existing sectors containing data from a specified file. The utilities allow you to view the file, then save it as a new file.

If you don't use your computer a lot and don't create and save a large number of new files, the odds are that deleted files (or big chunks of them) are going to be around for a long time. Even if you do a lot with your PC on a daily basis, some files and pieces of files will survive.

There you have it—even files you've deleted can be found, viewed, and brought back. Can you stop others from trying to see deleted files? If they have the knowledge and the tools, no, you can't! Can you plug up this hole in your privacy? Yes, with the right kind of utility, several examples of which are described in the following section.

Getting Rid of Deleted Files

The answer to the problem of data from deleted files remaining on a hard drive or floppy disk is to write over the sectors where the file was stored. This is sometimes called *zeroing-out* the sectors, as many of the utilities fill in the sector data with binary 0s. Some utilities also overwrite with random data, and most can be directed to overwrite sectors several times. There are in fact U.S. Department of Defense standards regarding clearing deleted data from disks that the better utilities meet.

You cannot overwrite or otherwise clear out data from sectors without one of these utilities. I'll show two of the best to you here. (These utilities have additional functions that we'll examine in Chapters 7, 9, and 10.)

McAfee Office 2000

This software utility suite includes programs that handle disk repair, removing programs, and cleaning up hard drives. As a part of these functions, the programs can do a thorough overwrite of deleted file space to clear out data for good.

Norton Utilities 2000

Norton Utilities 2000 is *the* standard in the field of disk utilities. Perhaps best known for Unerase and its disk repair tools, Norton Utilities 2000 offers a sheaf of disk repair and management tools. Among these are WipeInfo, a utility that can clear all traces of selected files or entire folders.

The Norton WipeInfo utility can also wipe the free space on a hard disk, ensuring that previously deleted information is not left on the disk. The technique used by Norton Wipe-info conforms to the method specified by the U.S. Department of Defense.

Quarterdeck Remove-It

This disk cleanup program (which also removes backed-up Internet files) is a good choice if you want to be sure you can restore what you wipe out—just in case you find that you've made a mistake. (Once you're sure about what you've deleted, you can dump it for good by emptying your Recycle Bin.) As a part of its hard-drive cleaning, Remove-It can over-write deleted data, as well.

Word Processor File Peculiarities

Harkening back to one of the examples in Chapter 1, have you ever been typing an important letter and included some comments of which you thought better and deleted? Everyone has, and you probably thought no more of the matter after you deleted the offending sentence or paragraph and saved the letter.

Perhaps you've also used an open document to make temporary notes—a telephone number, a meeting time and date, contact name, directions, whatever. You deleted the notes, then completed the document and saved it.

What if I told you that there is a good chance that the offensive remarks you deleted from that letter are in the letter still? And that the notes are still in the document you saved and sent on to someone else. Depending on what sorts of things you've done in your documents before putting them into their final form, those ideas may be chilling, or embarrassing, or shocking. In any of these cases, you certainly want to find out what may be in your documents that you thought wasn't, how to get the material out for good, and how to prevent it from lingering in the future.

Or, you may simply be curious as to how this can happen. In either case you'll find this section to be a real eye-opener.

What's Really in Those Files?

As far as most PC users are concerned, what is in their files is what they put there—letters, numerals, punctuation, and perhaps graphics. However, as with most things, there is more than meets the eye in files created with most PC applications.

Consider a document created with a word processor. In addition to the content typed in, the word processing program must store information about a number of elements having to do with the document's layout and format. Among these elements might be:

✔ Non-printing characters, which include tabs, carriage return/linefeed characters (which move down one line), and page breaks

✔ Line-spacing and margin information

✔ Information about which font to use

✔ Special text formats, such as bulleted lists and tables

✔ Graphics—both the graphic itself, and positioning and formatting information

✔ Links to other files

✔ Any special display or printing instructions—extra lines between paragraphs, justification, centering, and much more

As is probably obvious, there is quite a bit more data in a word processor file than you put in. (For those of you who may have been wondering, this explains why word processor files for even small documents can be rather large.)

How Deleted Text Is Stored in a Document's Disk File

Many word processors also store in a document file deleted text (in case you want to undo a delete) and sometimes material that you copied and moved elsewhere. This is particularly true of word processors that save your file for recovery against the possibility of a power outage or disk crash. You cannot see this material when you print out the document, nor when you view or edit the document with the word processing program. It is there, however—and it stays with the file even if you e-mail or copy it for someone else.

You can save a document to a file without all the formatting info, and without the deleted text. When you save the file, select a file type of ASCII, Text-only, or MS-DOS text—whichever of these your word processor offers.

Look at Figure 6.3 to see what a Microsoft Word file really contains. The odd shapes are 8-bit or binary characters that comprise information about document formatting. The regular letters and words are the regular 7-bit ASCII characters. They are often referred to as *literal characters*, or *literals*, and of course comprise most of a document's human-created content.

Figure 6.3

A typical word processor file may be composed of format information and deleted text, in addition to its intended content.

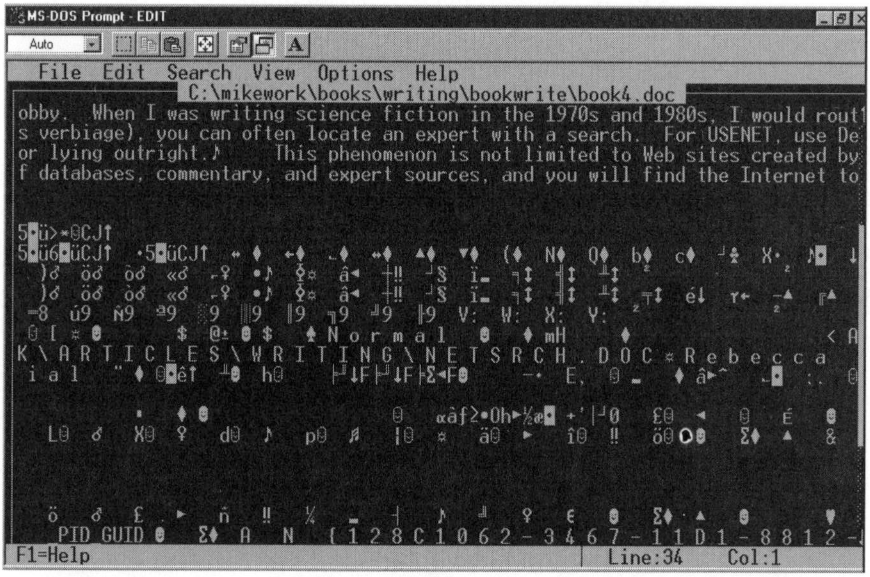

Deleted or "undo" text is usually stored near the end of the file. Again, thanks to special 8-bit codes, it is never displayed by your word processor, nor when the document is printed.

Large files and files that are open for a long time are usually saved for backup—along with deleted text—more frequently than small files.

However, you can view such undisplayed text by opening the document's file with another word processor. Sometimes Windows WordPad or Notepad will work for this—although you may find that a file is too large for one or both of those programs. You can also view a document file using the DOS program EDIT (which is what I used to display the text in Figure 6.3).

Looking at a File's Contents Using the EDIT Program in MS-DOS

(For the hypothetical example below, we'll use a file titled document.doc and located in the folder \letters on drive C.)

To open a file with the DOS program EDIT, first select MS-DOS Prompt on the Programs menu off the Start menu (Start ≻ Programs ≻ MS-DOS Prompt). Once you have a DOS window, move to the directory/folder where the file is located. (To do this, type **CD\LETTERS** at the C:\Windows> prompt and press Enter. *CD* stands for **C**hange **D**irectory. You will want to switch from the Windows directory to the directory you are looking for; in my example this would be Letters. This method works with single-word filenames only, which means you must use the DOS names of long directories/folders. For example, typing **CD\My Documents** will not work; you have to use the DOS filename, which is **Mydocu~1**. To see the DOS names of folders, type **DIR** at the DOS prompt.)

Next, type **EDIT** followed by the name of the file, and press Enter. (For our example, you would type **EDIT DOCUMENT.DOC**, and press Enter.) From here, you can move through the document with the Arrow keys, the PgUp and PgDn keys, and Home and End. You can also search the document, using the program's Search menu. (The commands are similar to those of Windows Notepad.)

Some word processors' files can be viewed from the MS-DOS prompt. When you are at the MS-DOS prompt and in the same directory as the file you want to view, type **TYPE** followed by the name of the document and press Enter. If the file is stored in standard ASCII format— or mostly so—it will scroll by on your screen. (If it is a Word file—or files for any of a number of other applications—you will see some odd-looking characters, but no text.) You can pause scrolling text with Ctrl+S and resume display with Ctrl+Q. If the text scrolls by too rapidly, type this command at the MS-DOS prompt (where the name of the file is document.txt): **more document.txt** and press Enter. One screen page of text will be displayed, with a More prompt at the bottom of the screen, and will not resume until you press a key.

Getting Rid of Deleted and "Undo" Text

If you want to be sure no deleted text is saved with your document, there's an easy way to be sure without even having to view the document with another program. Follow these steps:

1. Save the document.

2. Create a new document (click New on your word processor's File menu).

3. Reopen the original document.

4. Select the entire document (normally by clicking Select All on your word processor's Edit menu).

5. Copy the document (click Copy on the Edit menu).

6. Close the document.

7. Paste the copied content into the new document you created.

8. Save the new document.

Because you copied only the displayed content from the original document, that is all that is put into the new document.

So, Where's the Risk in Sharing a File?

You have most likely figured out this one by now. The risk in keeping edited document files on your PC's hard drive—or sharing them with others via e-mail or copying to a floppy disk—is that someone who is curious and has the knowledge can see what you deleted while creating that document.

So, if you are going to share a document with someone else as a file, create a new document and copy the original document to it. Save the new document and give *that* file to the person, because that new document won't contain any traces of your deleted material.

 Other kinds of applications, such as spreadsheets and database programs, may also save your character, word, and block deletes. So, it is recommended that you similarly copy documents created by those programs if you intend to share them.

A Big Security Hole—Temporary Files

Along with Windows, Microsoft Word and other applications have a habit of saving documents in progress, against the possibility of a system crash. Some applications also save text you have deleted, moved, or copied within a document. The text is saved in disk files—even if you have not saved the file on which you're working. The idea is fine, but sometimes this safety feature does not work. Whether or not it works, you end up with a bunch of useless temporary files.

Figure 6.4 will give you an idea of what you have to seek out.

To be fair, some of the files are there because of a disk crash or a power outage, but the majority are simply left over from editing sessions.

You can get rid of those saved snippets by going to the appropriate subdirectories and deleting the temporary files that various applications leave behind. Or, you can use any of several commercial programs designed to get rid of useless files.

The manual method (described in the next section) is worth performing at least once. Then, if you use a disk cleanup program, you can go behind it to make sure it didn't miss anything.

Figure 6.4

A typical collection of temporary files waiting to be deleted, identifiable by the tilde (~) symbol preceding the filename

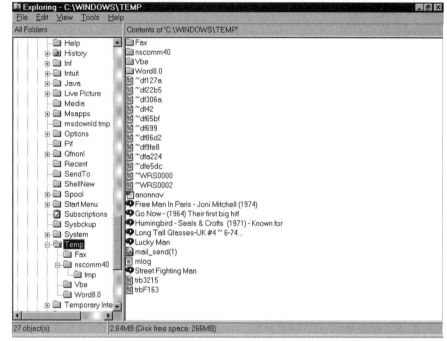

Finding and Cleaning Out Temporary Files Manually

The folders you'll want to check for useless temporary files are \windows\temp and all subdirectories below it. These may include directories with names such as \fax and \wordxx. The files will have extensions such as .TMP, but some will be complete .DOC, .HTML, or even image files, or some will have no extension at all. Many will have a zero (0) file size. The filenames will typically begin with a *tilde* (the ~ character), like this: ~wrdtemp.doc. The list in Figure 6.4 will give you some idea of the range of filenames.

Delete all of these by selecting them, then pressing the Delete key; you'll free up hard drive space in addition to getting rid of material that might attract snoops.

If you want to check out any of the temporary files, you can open most of them with the DOS EDIT program. Go to MS-DOS, move to the appropriate directory, and type **EDIT [*yourfilenamehere*].ext** to view a file.

You can also check out files with Word or Excel, or other applications that created them. Or, you might use a graphics program, such as Viewprint or Paint Shop Pro.

In addition, look for the temporary backup files that applications create when you have a file open. These usually have names such as ~document.doc, and you'll find them in your application work directories. They are sometimes left behind for no reason.

Use Windows Explorer to delete the files. Start Windows Explorer; then move to the folder where you want to delete files. To delete a file, click on it, then press the Delete key and confirm deletion. If there are multiple files to delete, you can highlight all of them, then press the Delete key. (Highlight multiple files by holding down the Ctrl key and clicking each file. Or, click on one file, then hold down a Shift key while moving down the list of files with an Arrow key.)

Close all applications before you try to delete temporary or suspect files. You may be surprised to find out that the application in question is using a file you're trying to delete. At best, you'll have to close the application(s) and start over. At worst, your system could lock up or crash.

Disk-Cleaning Utilities

A relatively new variety of utility is the disk-cleaning program. This type of program is designed to remove temporary and other useless files that many applications leave behind, and to help uninstall programs.

Such programs can help with getting rid of temporary files of the type discussed over the past few pages. They also perform some useful duties in getting rid of many other useless files. Two of the better disk cleaners are described below.

Norton CleanSweep

Norton CleanSweep is probably the most effective program of its kind, offering some features that similar programs do not.

A major focus of Norton CleanSweep is freeing up disk space, as implied by the program's main screen, shown in Figure 6.5. CleanSweep also seeks out temporary files of many kinds. Plus, you can customize CleanSweep to look for or exclude certain kinds of files, work in specified folders, and more.

Figure 6.5

Norton CleanSweep removes useless files.

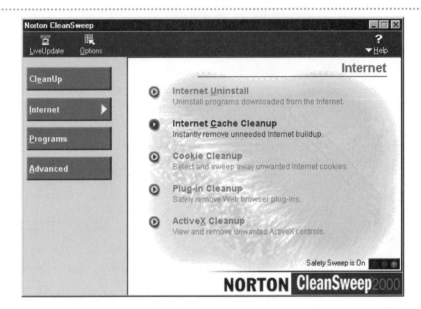

Norton CleanSweep also handles cleaning up leftover Internet files—a topic covered in more detail in Chapter 9—and adjusting and cleaning up the Windows Registry. If you buy Norton SystemWorks 2000, CleanSweep is included.

Quarterdeck Remove-It

Described in brief earlier, Remove-It also specializes in uninstalling programs and removing useless Internet files, but may also remove many of the temporary files you need to get rid of. Among the files Remove-It dumps are unneeded programs and .INI files, duplicate files, unused fonts and drivers, old faxes (some of which can take up tens of megabytes), icons and program groups that have no links or content, unused image and multimedia files, and more.

Okay! You know how to get potentially damaging material out of otherwise-innocent files, as well as what you need to get off your hard drive in terms of deleted files and useless temporary files. Now I'll show you how to add some strong protection to the files you keep, with data encryption.

PC Confidential

CHAPTER 7

Data Encryption

- ✔ What is encryption?
- ✔ How data is encrypted
- ✔ How data is decrypted
- ✔ Encrypted data forms and formats
- ✔ Applications for encryption
- ✔ Encryption software

This chapter introduces the concept of encryption for your computer files, a means of preventing others from reading or viewing files. I'll introduce the subject by explaining exactly what encryption is, with some background, history, and examples. You will also get some idea of the types of data encryption in use, and how encrypted data is unencrypted.

Then we'll get into applications for encryption, and a roundup of the better encryption software out there.

What Is Encryption?

Encryption is a means of altering a message or other document so as to render its content unrecognizable, by *encoding* it. (Encoding is the process of converting a plain-text or *clear* document into *code*. A code in this context is a system of representing data with a predetermined set of characters, numerals, symbols, words, and/or signals.) The concept of encryption also extends to computer files of any sort, from databases and spreadsheets to images or word processor files.

The idea, of course, is to prevent the data from being understood and used by those who don't have the means of *decoding* it. (Decoding is described in a later section called "Data Decryption.") Only those to whom you provide the means of decoding a file can read it.

Encryption has been around at least four thousand years. Among the earliest known uses of encryption was circa 1900 B.C., when an Egyptian scribe substituted unusual symbols for standard hieroglyphs in an inscription. Less than 500 years later, encryption was being used for religious documents and formulas, as well as government communications.

From the Middle Ages through contemporary times, the need for strong encryption schemes by military, diplomatic, and other government communications spurred the development of cryptography. With so much information exchanged among computers (on disk and via modem), businesses and individuals find data encryption of interest, as well.

A Simple Example of Encryption

A line in an encrypted text message produced by simple substitution of characters might look something like this:

```
lzdvrqwkhjuduubnroo.
```

On the face of it, lzdvrqwkhjuduubnroo looks like gibberish. However, if you knew that each letter was shifted three ahead in the alphabet (a to d, m to p, y to b—since you have to go back to the beginning to go past z—and so forth), you could easily work out that lzdvrqwkhjuduubnroo is iwason-thegrassyknoll. Add spaces between obvious word breaks and you have the sentence *in clear*, so to speak: I was on the grassy knoll.

This is a very basic example of encryption. Encryption by computer is based on far more complex patterns—and patterns within patterns.

How Data Is Encrypted

In practice, encryption is usually a process of *substitution*. An alternative value (also called a *token* or, where an individual character is involved, a *token character*) is substituted for designated elements of a message or other data. This is often done on the character level. For example, the letter *r* might be replaced by *m*, or the numeral *9* replaced by *3* or *0*. Letters and numerals are not, of course, the only characters used; a *?*, *&*, *#* or even a space can be replaced or used as a token character. Or, *bb* might be replaced by *2b* (for b times two). Combining these ideas, the word *three* might be encoded as *pkm2f* (assuming *p* replaces *t*, *k* replaces *h*, *m* replaces *r*, and *f* replaces *e*).

The above examples apply to text files. However, 8-bit or binary data can be similarly encoded by making substitutions. Other 8-bit characters might be substituted for the original characters in the document, or a mixture of 7- and 8-bit characters may be substituted. Or, nothing but 7-bit characters might be used for substitution. (This, in fact, is how many files are transmitted via e-mail; through encoding, the file is converted from 8-bit to 7-bit characters, which can easily be transmitted via conventional modem channels.)

Not incidentally, since a substitution like *4r3w* can be made for the character group *rrrrwww*, encrypted data is sometimes condensed or compressed, as well.

Special Data Encoding for 8-Bit File Transmission

Conventional data transmission with modems and telephone lines does not involve 8-bit characters as data. Data transmitted via modem must be in 7-bit format, because many of the 8-bit characters that appear in a binary file (a graphic image, for example) are used as control and signal characters by serial ports, modems, and the software involved in data transmission.

Therefore, when a binary file is converted so it can be handled as a 7-bit or ASCII file, 7-bit characters are substituted for 8-bit characters. The patterns of substitutions are preset based on the format (UUENCODE, MIME, or other). Thus, there is no problem with decoding on the receiving end of a data transmission.

An example of this type of encoding basically looks like random characters to a human viewing it, as in the line below:

    foXwAAAQMjpgsAAAEDAMsiJK9Ah6VAXVfobv34chAeLeWx

Of course, the program on the receiving system has the *key* (translating code) to translating the file back to its original format of binary data.

While this is not specifically encryption, you may want to know about MIME and similar data formats and how to unencode them. A shareware program that can handle this for you is Wincode. To download Wincode, visit http://www.winsite.com/info/pc/win3/util/wincode.zip.

Depending on who sends you what via e-mail, and depending on the e-mail programs you both use, you may receive images or other files attached to e-mail messages in MIME or UUENCODE format. Thus, you will probably want one or both of the unencoding programs just mentioned. (I recommend Wincode.)

For more information about 7- and 8-bit data files, bytes, and related computer data topics, please see Chapter 6.

Often during the process of encoding, each and every character is replaced—but not always. Too, substitution isn't always on a character-by-character basis. One character may represent an entire word or a group of bytes. Or, just to confuse things further, a word (or group of bytes) may represent one letter or numeral.

Most encryption schemes vary the pattern of substitution enough so there is no recognizable pattern that can be used to decode the message. The type of substitution made (one character for many, many for one, repeating or non-repeating patterns) and/or the patterns of substitutions, is referred to as the code, or the *cipher*.

How Data Is Decrypted

Decryption (also known as *unencryption* and *deciphering*) is a process of reproducing data from an encoded message based on a known code, or cipher. The code is decrypted using a list, table, or key.

In theory, encrypted data cannot be read without the key to serve as a guide or reference to all the substitutions that were made when it was encrypted. However, a simple, non-varying pattern of character substitution is fairly easy to decode. (For example, if *m* was always substituted for *r* and so on. Or, the shifted substitution demonstrated in the accompanying sidebar.)

A key may take any of a number of forms—perhaps a table showing a character-for-character or word-for-word substitution, or a more sophisticated set of substitutions. (The most popular of contemporary encryption techniques involve sophisticated mathematical algorithms.)

Assuming an encryption scheme or pattern(s) is too complex to be worked out, or "cracked," the only way you can read a hard copy of an encrypted message is with a table that lists the substitutions made. Or, in the case of a computer-encrypted data file, you must have a *decryption program* and the key to the encrypted data. (The original encryption program can normally function as a decryption program, too.)

Decrypting computer-encrypted files usually involves a password, either to run a decryption program, or to run a self-extracting archive that contains the encrypted file. The person who encrypts the data sets the password.

Encrypted Data Forms and Formats

An encrypted data file may take the form of characters substituted for characters (or single characters for groups of characters), as previously discussed. A text file in this form would consist of meaningless strings of characters. A binary data file would consist of strings of 7- and 8-bit characters with which no application program could work.

Furthermore, an encrypted data file might take the form of a *self-extracting archive*—a stand-alone program that creates a *decrypted* version of the encrypted data it contains. (See Chapter 4 for more information on archives.) Either way, a password is normally required to get at the encrypted data.

There are several possible approaches to e-mail encryption. In general, the stronger the protection, the more complex the scheme required to implement it.

Manually Encrypted Messages

The simplest approach is to translate a message manually into a code that the recipient understands. This might be a set of code words, or a cipher of character substitution. It may depend on a table of substitutions arbitrarily created by the people using the cipher.

The cipher may be based on a formula—perhaps the numeric value of each letter of the alphabet (1 through 26) multiplied by 2, with 9 added. (In this instance, "cab" would become "15 11 13.") Often, the types of encryption discussed in the three sections following depend on a mathematical formula, or *algorithm*, which is far more complex than this example.

Automating the Cipher

Another approach to encrypting e-mail is to use a special program that scrambles data by assigning each character a numeric value. (This is referred to as *hashing* the data.) A similar program on the other end can unscramble the code, provided the recipient uses a password specified by the person who created the coded message. This is the basis for a number of encryption programs and is usually easier than creating your own cipher through manual encryption.

Self-Extracting Archives

Taken a step further, a file might be encoded, then packed into a program that, when run, unscrambles it. The newly created program is, of course, a self-extracting archive.

The program is created by a special piece of software that first encrypts the data, then stores it in the self-extracting archive. All the recipient has to do is run the self-extracting archive. This requires that the recipient give the proper password. At this point the file is decoded. The self-extracting archive creates a file into which it reads the encrypted data into a clear text format. Norton Secret Stuff, discussed in a few pages, is particularly well-suited to this purpose.

Public and Private Key Encryption

The newest method of computer encryption is the *public key* and *private key* approach, in which the key to decrypting a message is contained within the message itself.

A major problem with encryption has always been to get the code key or cipher to the person who will receive an encrypted message. A system known as *public keys* and *private keys* was developed in the 1970s to allow encrypted messages to carry a guide to the code used to encrypt them. This is quite unlike older computer and non-computer encryption schemes, which required the sender and the recipient to have the same key.

A computer-based public key system uses a program that encrypts data based on the *recipient's* public key. The public key is a code that the recipient makes public, and which serves as a guide to encrypting a message (also known as the cipher, or the type of encryption used). The public key is created by the encryption program and is different for every user.

Once a message is encrypted, only the recipient can unencrypt it, using their private key. The private key is created the first time a user sets up the program and directs it to create the private key. The public key is created at the same time.

Both parties must have the encryption program. If person A wants to send an encrypted message to person B, they first obtain person B's public key. Public keys are shared via *public key servers*, as described in a few paragraphs. Person B puts his or her public key on a public key server. Person A obtains it, then in effect "plugs in" the public key to the program to encrypt a message that they then send to person B. Person B then "plugs in" his or her *private* key to unencrypt the program. The program reads the public key, which tells the program how to encrypt the message so it can be unencrypted by the private key. But not enough of the cipher is included to enable anyone to unencipher the message without the private key. So, at this point person B is the only person who is able to read the message sent by person A.

Thus, the private key combined with the encryption program is used to unencrypt a message that has been encrypted with the user's public key and the same encryption program. Without the private key to decode the encrypted file, the file is meaningless.

This method works particularly well for someone who needs to receive encrypted e-mail messages from many people. All the recipients can use the public key program to encrypt messages, but only the recipient can decrypt the messages.

Figure 7.1 illustrates the entire procedure.

Figure 7.1

Public key encryption and decryption

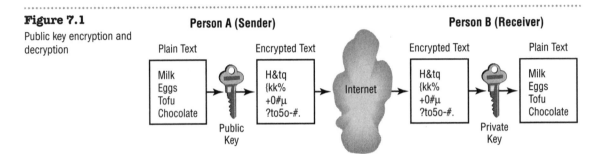

In addition to enabling the encryption of messages, the public key system can also be used as a means of authenticating a message or other data file as having come from the sender.

As noted, public keys can be made available on any of a number of public key servers on the Web. These are sites that store individuals' public keys at no cost, normally in a searchable database. You can find public key servers by entering the keyword/phrase **public key servers** into any search engine. The following URLs are those of two public key servers:

```
http://www-math.uni-paderborn.de/pgp/pks-toplev.html
http://www-swiss.ai.mit.edu/~bal/pks-commands.html
```

Applications for Encryption

Encryption is an excellent means of protecting information of any type. Text files, binary data and program files, and even graphics files can be encrypted for storage or transmission.

The primary application for data encryption is to protect information in files that others may be able to access. Depending on the level of computer knowledge possessed by someone who can access your PC, you may need to encrypt files stored on your computer's hard drive. This can be true even if the files are password-protected and/or invisible.

If you fear interception of your e-mail or of files you wish to send someone over the Internet, data encryption is also a good idea.

Encryption for File Storage

If you do not wish to go to the bother of copying files back and forth, or making files and folders invisible, you may find encrypting files a practical way to protect your information and still keep it on your PC's hard drive. Or, even if you do store sensitive files on a floppy disk hidden somewhere, you might want to consider encrypting those files against the chance that someone will find the disk.

Encryption is also an attractive means of protecting files on laptop hard drives. Because laptops are often in the position of being accessible to all sorts of people, their data is particularly vulnerable. If you keep sensitive files on a laptop—yours and/or those of clients or your employer—it makes sense to protect those files.

Too, you can use encryption to add an additional layer of protection to files and folders that are also password-protected and/or invisible.

Encryption for E-Mail

Many PC users are concerned that their e-mail might be read by others, perhaps by staff at their ISPs, or by someone intercepting it as it is transmitted. The 1986 Electronic Communications Privacy Act made it illegal to intercept and read private e-mail. That being the case, do you really need to consider encrypting your e-mail? The answer is "yes," because a law in itself doesn't prevent the act it prohibits. Too, system administrators or others within a company or organization are exempted from this law when dealing with employee e-mail. Further, e-mail can be mis-addressed or otherwise go astray.

Encryption protects e-mail messages against such threats. Since only you and the person(s) to whom you send an encrypted e-mail message can read it, there is no danger of information being compromised. Encrypted e-mail can be considered as analogous to sending a message in an envelope, as opposed to on a postcard.

Encryption for Data Transmission

If you plan to send sensitive data files to others, or to yourself for online storage (as discussed in Chapter 4), you will probably want to encrypt those files. This is also true of files you might store online.

If you encrypt e-mail or files you send to someone else, you must give the other person the password(s) required to view the data involved. It's not a good idea to send passwords via e-mail. Instead, give your recipients the password(s) in person or during a telephone call.

Encryption Software

Encryption is not exactly the most popular software category. Still, there are some good shareware and commercial programs that can handle pretty much any encryption need. Some of those we'll examine here are included with other software packages and are not available alone.

Encrypted Magic Folders (EMF)

Encrypted Magic Folders (EMF) lets you encrypt files in designated folders. At the same time, EMF can optionally make the folders and the files within them invisible to others. As shown in Figure 7.2, EMF uses a very simplified user interface. Click the folders you want encrypted, enter a password, and you're on.

Figure 7.2

EMF encrypts files and makes files and folders invisible.

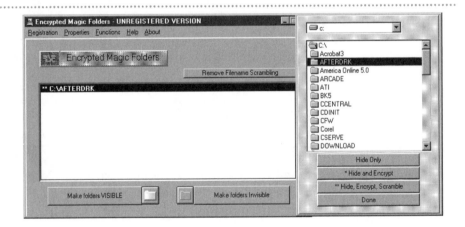

When you want to use encrypted files, reverse the process. You have to enter your password only once for full access to all of your files.

Encrypted Magic Folders is a shareware program.

Norton Secret Stuff

Norton Secret Stuff (NSS) is a program that is included with the Norton SystemWorks software suite from Symantec. It is a commercial program.

NSS creates self-extracting archives. The NSS user interface—shown in Figure 7.3—is simple and direct.

Figure 7.3

The Norton Secret Stuff user interface

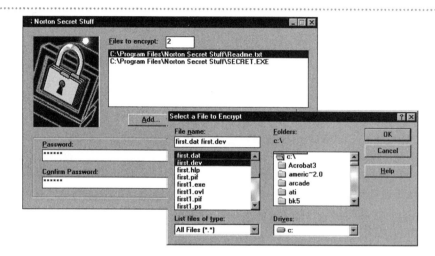

Simply select the files you wish to encrypt (you can include up to 2000 files in one self-extracting archive), enter a password, then click the Encrypt button. You are asked for a filename, and then NSS encrypts and compresses the selected file(s) in a self-extracting DOS program (which you can run from Windows).

To unencrypt files, double-click the self-extracting archive file from Windows Explorer (or select it from the Run option on the Start menu). NSS prompts you for the password. When the correct password is supplied, NSS restores the files to their original form. As the recipient of a message encrypted by NSS, you do not need the Norton Secret Stuff program to unencrypt files; all you need are the self-extracting archive (the encrypted file) that is sent to you and the proper password. No other program is required. This is because the self-extracting archive *is* a program.

The same is true of files you encrypt on your hard drive. You could, if you wished, remove NSS from your system and you would still be able to unencrypt files, provided you had the proper password.

On the whole, this is the simplest encryption program out there. Straightforward as it is, it is very effective in protecting files you want to transmit to someone else, as well as sensitive files you need to keep on your hard drive. I recommend it highly.

For more information about NSS and other Norton utility software, see http://www.symantec.com.

Pretty Good Privacy

The header above may seem facetious, but it is the name of what is probably the best public/private key encryption program going. Pretty Good Privacy (or PGP for short) is also the most widely used program of its type.

In addition to creating public and private keys, PGP of course encrypts messages using public keys, and unencrypts messages using an individual's private key. Plus, PGP provides message authentication with *digital signatures*, which are also created by the PGP program.

A digital signature is a unique identifying character string used as a means of verifying the authenticity of an e-mail message. The message is first *hashed*, which means each character is assigned a numeric value. Then a complex mathematical algorithm generates a string of numeric values that is almost impossible to duplicate or crack. The values are appended to the message as the digital signature and are stored by the system that generated them for later comparison as necessary.

Public keys and signature files created with PGP are text files and resemble the block of characters shown in Figure 7.4.

Figure 7.4
A public key created
by PGP

```
-----BEGIN PGP PUBLIC KEY BLOCK-----
Version: 2.6.2

foXwAAAQMjpgsAAAEDAMsiJK9Ah6VAXVfobv34chAeLeWxl
230LhBEskOAc01nwbWugMgSs39dfda996eWd5IFNhbGVzIDxzYcrn0hBEskBzeh
f3QJfoXou39Y29VfobvtPg==
=wPgw
-----END PGP PUBLIC KEY BLOCK-----
```

With PGP, you can create your own public key and distribute it to friends, associates, and others. One way to distribute your public key is to include it after your "signature" at the end of each message. (You can do this most efficiently by adding it to your *sig file*—also called a *signature file*—which is a user-definable block of text that many e-mail programs automatically place at the ends of outgoing messages.)

There also are public distribution servers for PGP public keys. Here, you can leave your public key for others, and obtain others' public keys. You will find a public key server located at this URL: `http://bs.mit.edu:8001/pks-toplev.html`.

PGP is the work of Phillip Zimmerman and is distributed as freeware.

PGP for PCs (MS-DOS Version)

PGP for PCs is a DOS application that works on files externally from the DOS command line. You type commands while running the program in DOS, directing it to act on a file you want to encrypt or decrypt. You will find the program on the accompanying CD, or at http://web.mit.edu/network/pgp.html.

If you prefer an easier interface than PGP for PCs, several DOS and Windows front ends are available for PGP. A list of these programs, with links and other useful information, can be found at this URL: http://home.earthlink.net/~rjswan/pgp/.

If most or all of your correspondents use PGP, you can use it to protect against unwanted junk e-mail and manage your e-mail more efficiently. If everyone who sends e-mail to you uses PGP to encrypt messages, you can simply use your e-mail settings to reject any e-mail that comes through unscrambled.

Private File 2

Private File is a commercial program that offers strong encryption and alternative-user interfaces. As shown in Figure 7.5, you can use a drag-and-drop interface to drop files to be encrypted or decrypted into a desktop dropbox. Alternately, you can use menu selections to encrypt and decrypt selected files.

Figure 7.5

Private File's drag-and-drop interface

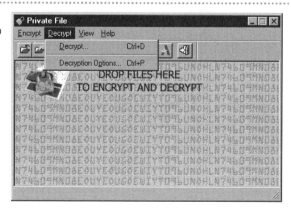

Files are encrypted and decrypted by the same program. A password is required for either action (you can enter a password of your devising, or Private File will generate a password at random), and files are compressed as they are encrypted. You can optionally delete the original file when you encrypt a file. (The deletion process matches a three-pass overwrite technique specified by the U.S. government. For details on how this works, see this URL: http://www.aladdinsys.com/privatefile/protect.html.)

Private File can also be integrated with an e-mail program to automatically attach files it has encrypted to messages.

Interestingly, Private File works between the Mac and Windows—which is to say you can share encrypted files between a Mac and a PC, provided each is running Private File.

Private File is a commercial program. For more information, visit Aladdin Systems, Inc., publisher of Private File, at http://www.aladdinsys.com.

SecurePC 2

SecurePC is a commercial product published by RSA Data Security, Inc. SecurePC is designed to be used as a stand-alone program to protect data either on one PC's hard drive or across a network. Once installed, the program works in conjunction with Windows Explorer, which speeds up file and folder encryption.

Files can be encrypted for later decryption by the SecurePC program, or you can use the program to create self-extracting archives.

In addition to encryption protection, SecurePC also offers optional start-up password protection—meaning that you must have a password to start Windows when this feature is implemented.

For more information about SecurePC, data security and standards, and what various companies are doing about security on the Internet, visit RSA Data Security's Web site, at http://www.rsasecurity.com/. This organization is responsible for designing and implementing most of the security standards in use on the Internet.

We will revisit the subject of encryption in Chapter 10. Now, however, it's time to address slightly less-cryptic topics in Chapter 8: computer viruses and how to protect your system from them.

PC CONFIDENTIAL

CHAPTER 8

Virus Protection

- ✔ What are computer viruses?
- ✔ Where did viruses originate, and why?
- ✔ What kinds of viruses are there?
- ✔ What do virus programs do
- ✔ Web browser applet viruses
- ✔ Anti-virus software
- ✔ Virus hoaxes

Welcome to the virus chapter! Here, we will examine exactly what computer viruses are, what they can do, and why they exist. Along with that, you'll learn about how viruses and Trojan horse programs can get into your system.

Once you understand computer viruses, I'll show you how to protect yourself against these virulent programs both online and offline. We'll look at precautions you can take, and what's available in anti-virus software. Finally, you'll find a few words on the subject of virus hoaxes.

What Are Computer Viruses?

In the most basic sense, computer viruses are programs or macros that take action—often destructive action—that you neither expect nor want them to take. They may display political or insulting messages on your screen, delete files on your hard drive, or wipe out your computer's operating system. Some virus programs operate on a time-delay basis, so that you'll use them and pass them on before you notice what they are. Many are insidious, slowly altering selected files until one day—*boom!*—your system doesn't work. The variations are endless, but the end result is the same: disruption or destruction of your computer operations.

Actually, the name *virus* is very appropriate. Computer viruses mimic the behavior of biological viruses in many ways. Just as a flu virus attaches itself to a human host, computer viruses attach themselves to programs or other files. Also like a flu virus, computer viruses are contagious, and some use the resources of a host system to reproduce themselves.

Most viruses are disguised as public domain or shareware software, but a few have been passed around disguised as or embedded in legal and illegal copies of commercial software. Those that slip into your system disguised as a legitimate program are often called *Trojan horse* programs.

Origin of the Name *Trojan Horse*

The name *Trojan horse* alludes to the gag that Odysseus and the Greeks pulled on the inhabitants of the walled city of Troy early in the 12th century B.C. The Greeks succeeded in sneaking soldiers into the city inside what appeared to be a giant wooden horse. As the legend goes, the Trojans believed that the horse was a gift from their gods and took it inside the gates of their walled city. Late that night, the soldiers inside the horse crept out and opened the gates for the Greek army—and Troy was history.

Obviously this is an appropriate name because Trojan horse programs appear to be something alluring—perhaps a great game, a hacking program, or even an illegal copy of an expensive commercial program. You learn otherwise, though, once you run the program and it steals information, damages your files, or otherwise vandalizes your system.

Where Did Viruses Originate?

The earliest computer viruses were most likely practical jokes between programmers on mainframe and mini-computer systems back in the 1960s. When the first personal computers came along, it was natural that the bright, technically oriented people who tended to buy them would think of clever and unexpected programs, and still more practical jokes.

This sort of activity was fairly harmless at first; but as more and more people got into personal computing, and the software tools for programmers and laypersons became more powerful and sophisticated, things started to go beyond jokes and pranks.

PC viruses were rather rare until the mid-1980s. (I suspect that most of the people who might have been writing virus programs before then were instead hacking into copy-protected software.) Until then, the means of distributing virus programs were next to none. As the sharing of software proliferated—by disk or modem—so did the incidences of malicious personal computer virus attacks increase.

Several sorts of *living*, or self-replicating, computer viruses made appearances during this time as well, invading mainframe and mini-computers, as well as specialized public and corporate computer networks, and disrupting e-mail and other operations. (Among these was the famous IBM network virus, which was capable of duplicating itself and moving through networks, almost as if it were a living, self-directed thing.)

As computer viruses started making the evening news in the late 1980s, even more of them popped up, in the manner of copy-cat crimes. Several were rather creative in concept and bold in implementation. At least one virus was publicly announced in advance by its perpetrator, who promised it would do nothing more than display a message about world peace on a certain date. There were even a couple of particularly insidious viruses disguised as virus-protection programs.

Today, it is estimated that at least two to three new computer viruses pop up daily.

A Little Caution Goes a Long Way

My own encounters with computer viruses have been relatively few and far between, considering the number of potential exposures I've had through downloads and disk-sharing. In more than 20 years of downloading thousands of files and getting freely distributed software on disk, I have experienced two virus attacks, both in the late 1980s. One piggybacked in a supposedly legitimate shareware database program and simply delivered the message, "Gotcha!" at periodic intervals. I got rid of that one by deleting the database program. Another virus program was much worse; it concentrated on altering file sizes—including the invisible system files on my hard drive—with the aim of filling up the drive. I had to reformat the drive to get rid of that one.

Some of my friends have not been so lucky—nor as careful. One seems to end up with a virus on her PC at least once a month, and another finds two or three on his PC every time he runs a virus scan (which is rarely).

The point is, I have always taken care with what I download and how I handle downloaded programs—I had to, because my computing history predates anti-virus programs. I've done the same with disk files. With a little caution and prudence in your computing activities, you can greatly reduce your virus risk level and perhaps never have to deal with a virus attack. That's what this chapter is about.

Why Do Viruses Exist?

People create computer viruses for any number of reasons. Motivations include, in no particular order:

✔ Revenge against a particular system or group of computer users

✔ The desire for a noteworthy accomplishment (albeit in anonymous fashion)

✔ Practical jokes

✔ Political statements

✔ Experimentation ("to see if it can be done")

The popular press has painted some virus creators as rogue geniuses. At the same time, media sources have claimed that others are maladjusted hackers who are ineffectual in their own lives and are acting out some deep-seated need to have control over things.

Whatever the reasons programmers create viruses and Trojan horse programs, those reasons hardly matter if *you* get one. So, you want to take every possible precaution against them.

What Kinds of Viruses Are Out There?

Viruses come in many different varieties. Some are activated only on certain dates (such as the infamous Columbus Day Virus). Others run only when you run a particular program, or when any program invokes certain system functions. Still other viruses go into effect as soon as you boot your system.

What Do They Do?

The actions a virus may take vary widely. As described in the following paragraphs, they destroy data, steal information, obstruct or prevent PC operation, or do odd things like reboot your computer or flicker your monitor. A few "merely" annoy you by interrupting your PC's operation.

One thing that computer viruses do not do is damage hardware. Neither do they physically damage disks. Data on disks may be damaged or destroyed, and devices such as your monitor or printer may do things you don't expect; but no physical damage is done.

The Destroyers

The best-known type of virus is the one that works happily away at data destruction, deleting all the files in a directory or on a hard drive, or corrupting or deleting system files as soon as you run a program to which they are attached. Others create progressively larger junk files on your hard drive in an attempt to fill it up. Some subtly change a number of program or system files on your hard drive, perhaps replicating or copying themselves within each of those programs, until a certain goal has been achieved—at which point none of your programs work.

Self-Replicating Viruses

Self-replicating viruses are particularly nasty, as they can be lurking in any of dozens or hundreds of files on your system. Even if you get rid of one or two instances of a self-replicating virus, there are probably more. Some may remain dormant until enough files on your hard drive are infected so as to insure that your system is trashed, and also to give you a chance to share one or more of the files they've infected. The bottom line is that their entire purpose would seem to be reproducing and spreading.

Data Theft

Some Trojan horse programs have been written for the express purpose of stealing user IDs and passwords to online services or ISPs. AOL users are a popular target for such programs, which run in the background when you are online, and e-mail or otherwise send your ID and password to the person behind the program. (Ironically, one of the most successful and threatening of such programs was one that promised free access to AOL. Thousands of people downloaded it and ran it.)

Some interesting macro viruses and Trojan horse programs have also been used to steal data—primarily to be used in self-replication. One of these viruses attacked a specific e-mail program, Outlook Express, and used address book entries to address copies of itself to others, where it infected each computer and repeated the process. Eventually, it reached tens of thousands of PCs.

Control Freaks

The sneakiest viruses can take over your PC and run or shut down programs seemingly at random. Some viruses are programmed to do these things for the sake of doing them. Others run programs at a certain time to steal data.

There are also Trojan horse programs that work behind the scenes to e-mail stolen data, as previously described, and to loot financial data from specific software packages.

A True Tale of Trojan Horse Treachery

In late 1996 and early 1997, a number of people in search of cheap thrills in the form of "free" online pornography learned that it was anything but free. Web sites offering "free" explicit pornographic images were liberally hyped in Usenet Newsgroups and in e-mail by spammers. Thousands of excited Internet users headed for the "free" Web sites in question and downloaded the "free" special software required to view the images.

A few weeks after downloading their free software, many were shocked to find charges for hundreds of dollars for long-distance telephone calls to the eastern European Republic of Moldova near Romania.

As it turned out, the special software required to view the images had a few tricks up its sleeve. After it was installed and activated, a Trojan horse element turned off users' modem speakers and surreptitiously dialed an international long-distance call routed to Moldavia. A server there apparently provided users with all the pornographic images they wanted—at $2 to $3 per minute.

Worse, some users continued paying the exorbitant rates after they left the porno site and surfed to other pages. In each case, the scammers—three people running two "companies" in the New York City vicinity—received approximately half the proceeds of the calls. In the end, they had taken Internet users for more than a quarter-million dollars.

The Federal Trade Commission shut down the operation in February 1997, apparently tipped off by AT&T, which noticed that an unusually large number of its subscribers were racking up large phone bills calling the same number in Moldova. Unfortunately for the porn-seeking victims, they will still have to pay their telephone bills to AT&T, despite the FTC's revelation that it was all a scam. They may eventually get all or part of their money back, as the U.S. Justice Department has frozen the assets of the companies involved.

The lessons taught by this classic Trojan horse program are both direct and subtle. First, don't use a program if you don't understand completely what it does and where it came from. Second, and perhaps more important, most things touted as "free" are anything but.

Macro Viruses

As you may know, a macro is a series of commands, menu selections, and/or other actions that have been pre-recorded. Most macros are specific to a given program (such as Word or Excel) and are used to simplify often-used command sequences. For example, a macro may be used to create a mailing list from a simple name and address list in a word processor's file. With a macro, instead of marking, copying, and pasting each individual name and address, you need perform these steps only once. Record the steps required, and you have a macro that you can run on designated names and addresses using far fewer keystrokes and saving you time to move on to other tasks.

Macros are obviously very useful, and many macros can be found for download on the Web. Of course it follows that macro viruses are hidden in macros for many popular programs. The macro viruses may perform some useful function, but at the same time they are damaging or stealing data. Some very well known macro viruses have been used to infect Word and Excel on thousands of corporate users' machines in the late 1990s.

The macros may be received in e-mail as macros, or they may be added to the target program by a Trojan horse program. Either way, they cause major headaches in corporate MIS departments.

Running Interference

Some virus programs never get around to doing what they were intended to do. Instead, they interfere with your PC's operation, making it beep or give error messages, or switching windows around. There are some viruses, however, that run this kind of interference on purpose.

Even such relatively "harmless" viruses—those that don't destroy data—are disruptive. Imagine being greeted by a derisive or political message every time you start your computer. Worse, imagine seeing the same message continually after x number of keystrokes while you're using your word processor. Or, what if your system stopped every few minutes and required you to correctly guess a number between one and ten before you could continue working?

Applet Viruses: A Potential Plague?

Applets are small programs that are sent to your system by Web pages and run on your browser. They are written in specialized scripting languages called Java, JavaScript, and ActiveX. (Note that ActiveX applets are officially named *controls*.) Applets are used for everything from generating forms to providing small display windows for special information. You can also use them to animate, and even navigate, a Web site.

The wildly growing popularity of Java applets, JavaScript, and ActiveX controls has created a number of security issues. Perhaps the most publicized case was in early 1997, when the members of a German hacker group announced a means of exploiting a weakness in Microsoft's ActiveX that would enable them to devise a way to hack into certain types of money transfers. That security hole has since been filled, but there are and will be others.

Even ActiveX's one real security feature is rather useless, as most Microsoft Internet Explorer (MSIE) users don't know how to use it. The security feature uses digital signatures (coded verification of an ID provided by a Web site, discussed in detail in Chapter 7) to verify that the person who created a given script or control is the same person sending it to you. Even if these signatures are implemented, however, an experienced hacker can work around them.

Plus, digital signatures do not prevent someone from creating a destructive ActiveX control that might delete or corrupt important files. Java has a similar destructive potential, although it boasts a stronger approach to security.

All of this points to the fact that security holes are not the only potential dangers offered by ActiveX and Java. Both ActiveX and Java can transfer programs to your system, and what they do there is wide open. Which is to say that, basically, these programs can do just about anything. This creates an inherent ability to host viruses. Symantec and other companies are developing or have recently introduced virus scanners that offer real-time detection and protection capability for such viruses.

JavaScript, the newcomer to this lineup, offers its own potential hazards. Among other things, a Web page with the proper JavaScript code can take over your browser and open it at any page the Web page owner desires—even a page without menus or controls, leaving you stranded without a way to navigate past it. If you close the browser, the JavaScript commands will simply reopen it. Similar things can be done with JavaScript in e-mail messages sent to Netscape's e-mail program.

Using Settings and Programs to Protect Yourself against Harmful Applets

Because of the potential dangers I've outlined, Web sites that download ActiveX Control, or Java or JavaScript applets to your browser should be approached with caution—as should the entire field of Internet applications. If you feel the least bit uncomfortable with a site or its applets, don't use the Web site.

Better still, surf the Web with Java, JavaScript, and ActiveX turned *off*, as described in the paragraphs following.

Some Web sites require that you have Java or one of the other scripting languages enabled. If you're surfing the Web with ActiveX, Java, and JavaScript turned off and you come to a scripting-language–enhanced page that you would like to access, turn on the desired scripting language; then reload the page. This will enable all of the features the site offers.

Disabling Java, JavaScript, and ActiveX with Netscape   To turn off Java and Java-Script with Netscape, select Preferences on the Edit menu. You will see the Preferences dialog box, as shown in Figure 8.1.

Figure 8.1

Disabling Java and JavaScript with Netscape

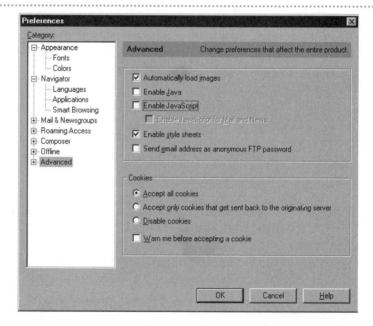

Press the Advanced label and uncheck the Enable Java and Enable JavaScript check boxes.

The most you can do to disable ActiveX controls with Netscape is to select Stop Animations on the View menu.

Disabling Java and ActiveX with Microsoft Internet Explorer   With MSIE 5, open the Tools menu and click Internet Options. Click the Security tab on the Internet Options window, and then press the Custom Level button at the bottom of the Internet Options dialog box. For MSIE 4, open the Edit menu and click Internet Options. Click the Security tab; then press the Custom Level radio button and press Settings. Scroll down to Java and open it; then check the Disable Java box. The Security Settings dialog will be displayed, as shown in Figure 8.2. Here, click the Disable radio button corresponding to each of the Java options.

To disable ActiveX, open the Tools menu and select Internet Options ➤ Advanced ➤ Multimedia and uncheck the box labeled Play Animations, as illustrated in Figure 8.3.

Figure 8.2

Using MSIE's Security Settings to disable Java

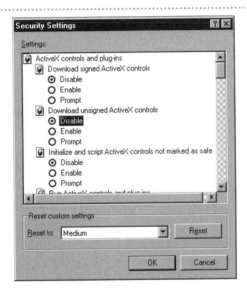

Figure 8.3

Disabling ActiveX animations is a good idea.

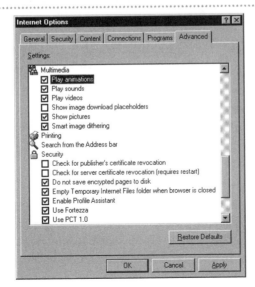

You can also set these options by selecting Start ≻ Settings ≻ Control Panel ≻ Internet Options. (Note that the dialog box thus displayed will be labeled Internet Properties, rather than Internet Options.)

Note that Microsoft apparently chooses not to recognize JavaScript officially—even though JavaScript commands work with MSIE. Thus, there is unfortunately no way to disable JavaScript with MSIE.

Many "harmful" Java programs are the result of inept programming, and/or failure to test a Java applet in more than one environment. The desire to have all varieties of color, movement, and action on Web pages results in many *soi-disant* "programmers" focusing more on how a page *looks* on their own PC's screen than on how their code is written. This in turn results in your browser, or even your entire system, locking up or crashing because of the number of items it needs to load to display the pages. Because there is no one certifying or otherwise validating the quality of Web sites, you have all the more reason to Web-surf with Java turned off. (There really isn't any central Web site content or quality monitoring organization. What rating services there are tend to rely heavily on subjective judgement.)

McAfee Guard Dog   If you don't want to bother with changing your browser settings, you might consider using McAfee's Guard Dog program. It is designed to protect your system from viruses and Trojan horse programs that can come in via Java applets and ActiveX controls.

Guard Dog also scans and removes viruses from downloaded programs and e-mail attachments. Further, it can block cookies, clean up trails you leave behind on your PC when you're surfing the Web, and protect sensitive information. The product is fully updateable at the publisher's Web site: http://www.mcafee.com.

Norton Internet Security 2000   Norton Internet Security 2000 is designed to stop viruses and other attacks via Java applets, ActiveX controls, and even IRC chats. As implied by the main menu in Figure 8.4, NIS 2000 also allows you to set parental controls so as to limit children's access to certain Web sites.

Figure 8.4

Norton Internet Security
2000's main menu

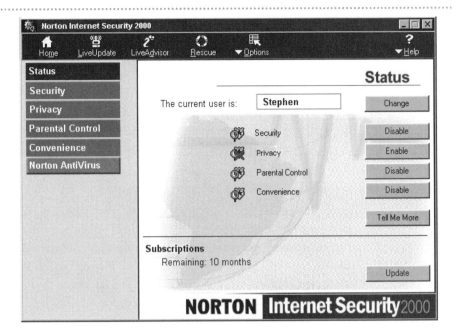

Other NIS 2000 features include protecting your e-mail address, credit card information, and other private information. You can also set up multiple user profiles and block
ads. Plus, NIS 2000 comes with Norton AntiVirus 2000.

For more information, see: `http://www.symantec.com/sabu/nis/index.html`.

How Can a Virus Get into My System?

A virus usually enters a system disguised as a program or a macro. For example, you might
download a file billed as a game and named `FUNGAME.EXE`. You might run it and, while
you were trying to figure out how to play the game, the program might be working in the
background deleting all files in the current directory—or all directories—or attaching a
virus to your boot file. (As noted earlier, Trojan horse is another, older, and very appropriate name for this sort of virus.)

The majority of virus and Trojan horse programs are disguised as public domain or
shareware programs to encourage their distribution. As noted earlier, however, a few are
disguised as or embedded in legal and illegal copies of commercial software. Also, a few

virus programs have been designed to take advantage of human greed, posing as a program that helps hack into Web sites or get free time with an ISP or online service, or offering some other unlikely benefit.

Downloads

For most viruses, downloads are the major means of getting into a computer, partly because so many files on individual PCs nowadays come in as downloads. The main reason, though, is that a virus-carrying file proliferates faster online than it does anywhere else on any other medium. Since those who create computer viruses seek wide exposure, most target the online world as the distribution point for their creations.

Viruses that spread online also have the best chance for longevity. It takes a long time from the initial discovery of a virus in a download before every last copy of it is stamped out. A good many people downloading it aren't plugged in or don't pay attention to online information sources, and some of them upload it elsewhere, putting it on online services or Web sites where still other unsuspecting victims can download it. And every new upload multiplies the potential number of computers exposed to the virus. Some will even e-mail the virus to their friends.

E-Mail Attachments

Viruses can come in programs or files that are attached to e-mail messages. Simply reading a message will not activate a virus; however, opening the attached infected file and/or running the attached program (or macro) will.

You'll find that programs attached to e-mail messages increase in frequency around major holidays. Even though such attachments may seem innocuous and appropriate, it's best that you just delete them. Even if you know who sent the file to you, be aware that they are probably forwarding something that came to them the same way and may not have checked to see if the file is a virus.

Shared Files on a Network

Shared files on a network often spread viruses rapidly. Be aware of your system administrator's policies on shared files, virus threats, and related matters. Take care to avoid running e-mail attachments on the network, and let the system administrator know immediately if you find a suspicious file.

Shared Disks

In contrast, viruses that spread on disk proliferate rather slowly. Computer owners don't share programs on disk the way they once did now that everything you could want is online, free for the taking. But shared-disk virus-spreading is not extinct.

A friend or co-worker may unknowingly download a virus-laden program and pass it on to you on disk before anyone realizes what it is. Or, someone may be spreading copies of a popular shareware program that is infected.

In the rare instances when a virus sneaks onto a commercially produced disk or CD-ROM, nearly every copy of it can be quickly destroyed, because software publishers keep close track of where their products go. (This does happen, by the way. More than once an irate employee or a prankster has modified a software publisher's product before it was reproduced.)

Now that CD burners are affordable, you need to be careful about what programs you run from a homemade CD.

Protecting Yourself against Viruses

Prevention is always the best cure. You can do a lot to prevent a computer virus program from getting at your data or system.

Before proceeding, I should note that your computer cannot get a virus or be invaded just from the act of calling an online service or an ISP. Virus and Trojan horse programs that have been downloaded aren't dangerous unless you actually *run* them. (There is the possibility of a remote system sending commands to your system through certain kinds of communications software, but online services and ISPs aren't set up to damage your data.)

That said, here are some important virus-prevention tips:

✔ If there is no virus-protection program on your system, install one, and update it frequently.

✔ If your anti-virus program offers automatic, full-time protection, consider enabling it. This will scan downloads, and watch files and programs in your system.

✔ Be careful about what you download. If you have questions about a program in a download database, ask a sysop (the truncated version of systems operator, the person running the Web site or online service area where you found the program) if he or she has used the program and found it safe. Ask other users about the program. (In general, if a program has a lot of downloads—download counts for programs in databases are visible on some systems—and you've seen no complaints about it on bulletin boards, you are probably safe in downloading the program.)

✔ If you receive an e-mail with an attached file from someone you do not know, delete the file immediately. If the file is from someone you know, ask them where they got it and whether they have scanned it for viruses. (You may want to scan it yourself.)

✔ If a friend or associate gives you a disk with a program on it, ask them whether they know if the program is safe. Have they run the program themselves? Have they scanned it for viruses? Do they know where they got the program?

✔ Before running a new program, carefully examine the files in the program archive and read any READ.ME or similar text files—the authors of public domain and shareware programs often include a description, with file sizes, of the files in a program archive. If you see any files that aren't included in the description, don't use the program.

✔ Even if a program is not immediately suspect, scan it using one of the virus-prevention programs. (Some can be set to scan archives and programs as you download them.)

✔ If possible, run the program from a floppy disk the first time.

✔ If you suspect a program of carrying a virus, *don't use it*. Scan it with one or more virus-protection programs.

✔ When you buy a commercial program, make sure the factory seal hasn't been broken—neither the external packaging nor the internal packaging containing the disk or CD-ROM.

Staying Informed

As with any threat, staying informed about computer viruses is a good defense. Your best source of information about computer viruses is the Internet.

So-called "virus alerts" are frequently circulated via e-mail, but many of these are hoaxes. (See the section headed "Don't Panic: Virus Hoaxes" at the end of this chapter.) To stay abreast of real virus problems, you will do well to visit Web sites run by McAfee (`http://www.mcafee.com`) and Symantec (`http://www.symantec.com`) frequently. Each offers archives of information about computer viruses, as well as updates on the latest viruses threatening PC users. Each also provides information about the latest virus hoaxes.

Other important online resources for virus and anti-virus information can be found in these Usenet newsgroups: `comp.virus` and `comp.lang.java.security`.

Anti-Virus Software

Before we get into specifics about anti-virus software, you may want to get some idea of what such programs can do for you. Here's a rundown of the functions anti-virus programs may offer:

- ✔ Searching suspected virus programs for embedded messages of the type frequently displayed by virus programs

- ✔ Searching suspected virus programs for functions and operations that might damage your data (such as delete or disk-format commands)

- ✔ Checking system files for alterations

- ✔ Blocking a suspected virus program from issuing potentially damaging commands

- ✔ Placing virus programs in "quarantine," where they cannot be run

- ✔ Removing viruses from your system

- ✔ Repairing files damaged by a virus (these include legitimate programs, which sometimes act as "hosts" for viruses, as well as data files)

- ✔ Scanning downloaded files and e-mail attachments for viruses

- ✔ Scanning designated drives, folders, and/or files on demand, or on a preset schedule

- ✔ Updating themselves when told to, or on a predetermined schedule

- ✔ Automatically protecting your system as you use it, monitoring programs, files, and system resources

I've already mentioned two anti-virus programs that focus on protecting your system from Internet threats. Now, we'll examine the more worthwhile general anti-virus programs.

Dr Solomon's Anti-Virus

Designed specifically for Windows 3.*x* and Windows 95, with a version available for Windows 95/98 and Windows NT, Dr Solomon's Anti-Virus specializes in checking archives for viruses. Archive types covered include .ARC, .ARJ, Cryptcom, DIET, ICE, LZH, MS Compress, PKLite, .ZIP, and self-extracting archives made with LZExe and ZIP2EXE. It also detects macro viruses.

The program comes with free updates for the lifetime of the product. For more information, see http://www.mcafee.com.

McAfee VirusScan Online

McAfee.com operates a subscription service that features online virus scanning, as well as PC performance analysis, and a Windows advice and information source. The service's main Web page, shown in Figure 8.5, will give you an idea of what's offered.

These services are available by subscription at: http://www.mcafee.com/centers/anti-virus/virus_help_me.asp.

Figure 8.5

McAfee.com's online virus scanning service

McAfee Virus Scan Deluxe for Windows 95/98

VirusScan Deluxe, from McAfee.com, is designed to detect viruses on the Internet, across networks, and in software. Also among its options is the ability to scan some mail attachments for viruses before you open them. It can also scan downloads, including .ZIP, .ARC, and .ARJ files, as well as self-extracting archives. VirusScan Deluxe detects all virus types, including boot sector, file, multi-part, polymorphic, stealth, encrypted, and macro viruses. As an added bonus, it also detects MS Office 97/2000 viruses. Lifetime free updates via the McAfee Web site are included.

Included with the program are two utilities: First Aid and Oil Change. These you may wish to leave off initially. First Aid changes browser and related settings on your PC, and Oil Change automatically finds plug-in updates online and installs them.

The user interface, shown in Figure 8.6, is simple to use.

In addition to the preceding, McAfee VirusScan Deluxe comes with free updates for the life of the product. In addition to stand-alone versions, it is available bundled with McAfee Utilities Deluxe and McAfee Office 2000.

McAfee VirusScan is also available in versions for DOS, Windows 3.*x*, and Windows NT. For more information go to `http://www.mcafee.com`.

Figure 8.6

McAfee Virus Scan Deluxe's user interface

Norton AntiVirus 2000

Norton AntiVirus 2000 (NAV 2000) is perhaps the best-known anti-virus software in existence. Available alone or as a part of Norton SystemWorks 2000, Norton AntiVirus 2000 offers several levels of protection and a variety of operating options, including:

✔ Manual virus scan of designated files, folders, drives (including floppy disks and CDs)

✔ Manual scan of your entire system

✔ Full reports

✔ Automatic protection while you use your PC

✔ Automatic scanning of e-mail and attachments

✔ Virus scan of downloads (archives and stand-alone programs)

✔ Updateable virus definitions

As you can see in Figure 8.7, NAV 2000 offers a wide range of settings in every aspect of its operation.

Figure 8.7

Norton AntiVirus 2000 is very flexible in operation.

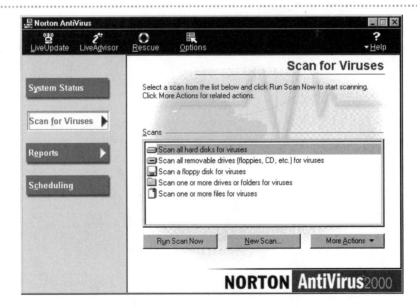

You can schedule complete or partial scans of your system on specific days/times or have the program remind you to do a scan. It will also remind you to update your virus definitions, if you wish. Updates are done online (Figure 8.8) at the Symantec Web site, and NAV 2000 comes with a free six-month subscription to the service. (Subscription costs thereafter are nominal.)

Figure 8.8

Updating Norton AntiVirus 2000 online

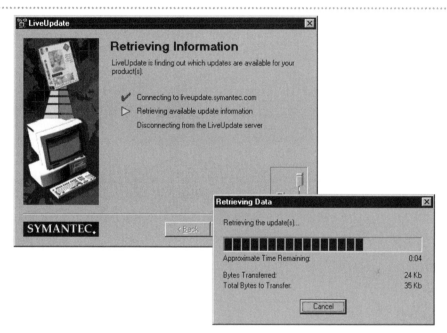

In addition, you can customize reports and alerts, automatic scanning at startup, scanning of e-mail attachments, and more. You can also customize whether the program runs automatically while you use your computer. If you set it for automatic operation, NAV 2000 watches for viruses while you work—even checking .ZIP files as you open them. The program also adds virus-scanning options to the right-click menu (used when you want to check a file's or folder's properties).

NAV 2000 also provides a comprehensive list of nearly 50,000 specific viruses, with details about each. As shown in Figure 8.9, this is a handy tool to help one understand viruses, or simply to satisfy curiosity.

Figure 8.9

Norton AntiVirus 2000's built-in virus database

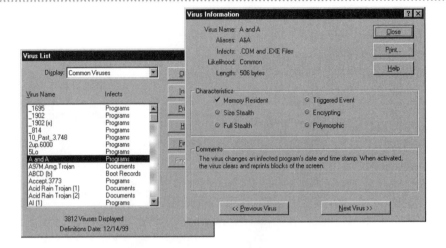

If the program spots a virus, NAV 2000 alerts you and lets you decide whether it should delete, repair, quarantine, or ignore the file containing the virus. If you allow the program to repair the file in question (the recommended option), it deletes the virus.

For more detailed information about Norton AntiVirus 2000, check this URL:

```
http://www.symantec.com/nav/index.html
```

Don't Panic: Virus Hoaxes

Every year seems to bring at least one major virus hoax. Recent examples have included the Good Times virus (it originated late in 1994); several viruses that were supposed to go into effect on certain holidays and destroy all data files on PCs; some that were supposed to spread as attachments to e-mail messages and destroy files if the messages were read; and, in 1996 and 1997, viruses that were "hidden" in word-processor macros.

While none of those viruses proved to be real, they ate up a lot of time and bandwidth on the Internet. They had individuals wasting time looking for protection from or cures for problems that didn't exist. In the end, the rumors and hoaxes were often as effective as real viruses would have been in wasting time and tying up resources.

Whether each of the viruses was an intentional hoax or just a kind of urban myth is impossible to say. Certainly, people perpetrate virus hoaxes for various reasons, and misinformed folks sometimes unintentionally start rumors.

While I don't advise taking the subject of viruses lightly, you might check around as to the authenticity of a virus scare before you take any action or waste a lot of time trying to find out what action to take. The sources mentioned earlier—McAfee, Symantec, and the Usenet newsgroups associated with virus issues—usually have the latest information on any virus or virus rumor or hoax.

Of specific interest in this topic area are these URLs:

- ✔ The Computer Virus Myths Home Page: `http://kumite.com/myths/`

- ✔ McAfee Virus Information Library/Hoaxes: `http://vil.mcafee.com/hoax.asp`

- ✔ Symantec's AntiVirus Research Center: `http://www.symantec.com/avcenter/`

Now that you are more familiar with the types of viruses you might encounter and how to prevent them, and you know the value of staying alert to potential plagues, real and staged, let's move on to something that is not a hoax—safety and privacy on the Internet.

PC CONFIDENTIAL

CHAPTER 9

Internet Safety and Privacy

- ✔ Internet risks
- ✔ How did we get here?
- ✔ Basic online security issues
- ✔ Online data security
- ✔ Download security
- ✔ Online privacy *offline*
- ✔ Special notes for AOL users

N ow it's time to take on the big one—the Internet! Thanks to media scares, more people are terrified of the Internet than of killer tornadoes, earthquakes, and hurricanes combined. But it's obvious that caution does not always accompany fear, because more people than ever before are being harassed, ripped off, hoaxed, and conned.

Despite their fears and concerns, the reason many people get trashed online in one way or another is simple enough: they are uneducated as to what they need to do to stay safe online. This chapter addresses that subject.

First, however, we'll survey some of the risks of being online, and I'll give you a bit of background on the Internet and the people who use it. Nothing technical—I'll give you just enough info to give you a feel for what's out there, and some history on how all this evolved.

Then we'll look at basic security issues online and how to keep a low profile yet still enjoy the Internet. Finally, I'll show you how to avoid leaving a trail of where you've been online for someone to find in your computer offline.

Internet Risks: A 60-Second Primer

You've seen it in the news, time and again: Someone is ripped off by Internet con artists. Someone else is taken advantage of in an online romance. The guy up the street is in hot water because of his monthly bill for online pornography sites—or was it a neighbor kid who stole his credit card number and used it to hit all the online dives? These are old stories, but unfortunately they are repeated time and time again.

Then there's the guy who was up to his neck in an online romance with a woman he'd never met. One day, his spouse happened to look in his e-mail inbox. Again, a repeating story, but the difficulty occurred offline rather than online.

Obviously, it's possible to get into online trouble both online and offline. (Rather Zen-like, isn't it?) Whether you cross paths with the wrong people online, or are uncomfortable with the evidence of where you've been and what you've been doing online tucked away on your computer for anyone to find, you are at risk. Fortunately, you can minimize those risks. To help you better understand what you face, let's take a look at where we are, and how we got here.

How Did We Get Here?

Perhaps you are unaware that the Internet and the *World Wide Web* (WWW, or simply the Web) as we know it, have only been around for a little more than a decade. Odd as that may seem, it's true. Before the Internet, the online world was little more than private *bulletin board services* (*BBSs*), and a few commercial *online services* like CompuServe and AOL. (The first commercial online services—CompuServe and The Source—made their debut late in 1979. AOL didn't come along until 1984, and Prodigy even later.)

A decade of growth has seen the online population multiply rapidly. Such growth has had its positive effects—the cost of getting online has dropped dramatically, for one thing. But it has also resulted in a host of problems of the kind unheard of in the early days of the online world.

The Good Ol' Days

In the early 1980s, the online world was a fairly quiet place. You lived your virtual life on BBSs and online services, with almost no interconnection to similarly isolated pockets of modem users. BBSs were generally free, but to get the best downloads and interact with the most people (in realtime chat and bulletin board postings), you had to use an online service with a national membership base. You used CompuServe or The Source, or perhaps The Well, BIX, or DELPHI—whichever you could afford. The number of users on those services could be counted in the thousands—or, in rare instances, tens of thousands. In aggregate, the online population may have approached 1,000,000.

Two things kept the population down: expense and the technical knowledge required. The cost of personal computers and modems was astronomical. Anyone who owned a personal computer was a dedicated hobbyist. 16K of RAM was a big deal, and it took a lot of tinkering and adjusting and trial-and-error to get online and stay connected. Some days, it seemed to many of us, we spent all of our online time either getting knocked offline, or griping about getting knocked off while we waited to get knocked off again.

Hackers and Crackers and Spoofs—Oh, My!

It was difficult to get into much trouble back then, because everyone pretty much followed the rules. This was true for every user, whether or not they wanted to follow rules, as system operators held absolute power over users' access. Unwritten rules about online conduct in messaging areas, e-mail, and chat rooms held equal power—thanks largely to the small sizes of the online communities. As in small towns where everyone knows almost everyone else, public censure served as an effective deterrent.

In those ancient times, when the online world's population was smaller than that of Wyoming, long before an Al Gore speechwriter coined the term "Information Superhighway," and before we were inundated with over-reaching analogies like "on-ramp" and "surfing the Net," there were few threats connected with being online. The most you had to worry about was being humiliated in a *flame war*. (A flame war—then as now—is an extended public argument that involves as much inflammatory and insulting rhetoric as possible without going beyond the boundaries of acceptable public behavior. They are quite entertaining if you aren't involved, and extremely emotional if you are.) That, and the possibility that someone might get your password and embarrass you by posting goofy messages in your name, or by running up charges on your account if you used an online service or pay-BBS, were the only threats to your peace of mind. Otherwise, those of us online busied ourselves uploading and downloading public domain and shareware programs, getting and giving answers to computing problems, playing online games, sharing chat and BBS postings about special interests, and occasionally socializing. Since it cost well over $1000 the get the equipment to get online, and anywhere from $6.00 to $18.00 per hour to stay there, we tried to make our online time count.

Modern Times

Everything has changed since those halcyon days of overpriced and under-populated online services. Today, computers do more and cost less. Getting online is a simple plug-and-go proposition. Low-cost, flat-rate access to the online world is the norm. The demographics have changed from computer geeks to anyone and everyone. However, there is less respect for the online world—and those who populate it—simply because it is so easy to access.

And no one, it seems, wants to follow the rules very much. Get your Internet access discontinued, and you can probably get online with another provider—or stay with the one who killed your access by claiming some sort of freedom-of-speech right, or making noises about your attorney.

Individuals treat the online world as something totally different and cut off from the real world—and this is what causes problems. People who would never dream of handing out their home addresses to, or starting an argument with, strangers in a mall do the equivalent online. They make it easy for others to find and harass them, and provoke anger with unseemly comments. Many interact with persons they would avoid like the plague in the real world. Why? Perhaps because it all seems so unreal and it is all under your control—or, is it?

Getting to the Roots of the Problem

There are two aspects of being online that contribute to most problems online. The first is a perception of anonymity. People don't know who you are and can't see you, so you can do or say just about anything you wish, right?

The second aspect is the unreal or surreal ambiance of the Internet. To many, other people they encounter online are just about as real as the characters in a computer game. This results in some people pretty much ignoring the possibility that someone they meet online can do them any harm. It also makes it easy for others to harass and steal from others—after all, the crimes aren't real to them.

You can, however, avoid trouble by watching whom you hang around with and what you do online. You can avoid those who are disposed to annoying others for fun and profit, not to mention those who are more goal-oriented in their online malfeasance: stalkers, con artists, and other sorts of criminals. The rest of this chapter shows you how.

Basic Online Security Issues

The most basic security issues online are those that involve things you do or use every time you are online. The gateway to these things is your password combined with your identity. In addition, you need to keep your credit card numbers secure.

Passwords

Online, your passwords are the keys to your life. If someone has your password(s), they can just about *be* you. By using your ISP or online service account and accessing various Web sites, here's what it is possible for someone to do:

✔ Read your e-mail

✔ Send out e-mail in your name

✔ Post bulletin board messages in your name

✔ Buy items online (if you have set up a charge with shopping Web sites, and/or if you have an account with an online service)

Although many people fail at it, protecting your password is relatively easy. All you need to do is remember these cautions, and act accordingly:

1. Do not give your password to anyone in your household or workplace.

2. *Never* tell anyone your password via e-mail or in chat rooms, no matter what the excuse given by the person asking for it. (Many troublemakers trick users out of their passwords by pretending to be an employee of an ISP or an online service.)

3. Make your password something lengthy and unique, like K9R3781. Avoid using anything like your child's birth date, your significant other's name, your dog's name, and the like; such passwords are too easy to guess.

4. Don't write down your password—*memorize it.*

5. Avoid downloading and running programs attached to mail, and programs offered at Web sites or online services that seem too good to be free. There is a good chance that such programs are designed to hack into your online software and e-mail your user ID and password to an online thief. (See Chapters 1, 8, and 10 for more information on such Trojan horse programs, and related items.)

Does Someone Have Your Password?

Until and unless a thief changes your password or does something particularly notice-able online, you probably won't know if your password has been compromised. If you use an online service where you can add charges to your card, you may not know you have a problem until the bills come in. Here's how you can check whether your pass-word has been stolen:

✔ If your ISP or online service provides a means of checking your most recent logon and -off times, use it occasionally. You may find that "you" were online when you really weren't.

✔ Strange e-mail referring to subjects about which you have no knowledge, espe-cially from people you don't know, can be an indication that someone else is using your account (and perhaps e-mailing or posting messages).

✔ Trying to log on to some systems (such as AOL) and getting a message that you are already logged on could be a warning flag. (This doesn't always mean someone else is online in your name, however. If you get this sort of message when you try to log on after being knocked offline, it probably means the system hasn't yet realized that you are offline.)

✔ You may be alerted to a problem when your ISP complains that you are logging on with multiple sessions. (Of course, if you really are doing that, you're going to get complaints; ISPs don't like any one user hogging more system resources than necessary.)

✔ In Newsgroups or bulletin board areas, if you find messages you didn't post—or replies to messages you didn't post—someone may be using your password.

✔ If you get a message from your ISP about excessive failures at logon, this may well be an indication that someone is trying to hack their way into your account by guessing your password.

✔ If you use an online service, you can watch for a banner at logon that tells you the date and time of your last logon. Not all online services offer this, but if yours does, make a habit of watching for the notification. Compare it with your last online session. (This is how I discovered that someone was logging on as me with one of my accounts on an online service. I changed my password, and that was that. Apparently, someone had guessed my password, and rather quickly. I was using a password that was only four characters long, so I was partly responsible.)

What to Do If Your Password Is Compromised

Ideally, no one will ever get your password, because you will be following the advice in the previous section. But if, by some unfortunate circumstance, someone does get your password, here's what you should do:

✔ If you can, immediately change your password. If you can't log on, telephone your ISP or online service's customer service number. (Be prepared to identify yourself, usually by providing your mother's maiden name or other information that was requested for that purpose when you signed up.)

✔ If you are not able to change your password, call your ISP or online service's customer service number and let them know what's happened. If extra charges have accrued to your account, you may be able to get an adjustment.

✔ If you frequent bulletin boards or other message areas, check for new messages from your ID that you didn't post, as well as replies to the same. If you find several such messages, post a notice that your password was stolen and that you were not responsible for messages posted between a specific date and the present.

✔ If you are on an online service that stores messages, check the folder or file for any unfamiliar messages. Keep an eye on your incoming e-mail for strange messages, and be prepared to explain that someone else was using your account.

✔ Change your password again.

Of course, the best approach is to take measures to ensure that nobody gets your password.

The Case of the Purloined Web Page

My friend, Chuck, found out the hard way that loaning your password, even to a family member, can be a bad idea.

Chuck and his family, who live in Indianapolis, were visiting relatives in Florida over the Christmas holidays. A brother-in-law asked to use Chuck's ISP account because the brother-in-law's ISP didn't provide Usenet access. Chuck agreed, and provided the usual warnings about not doing anything stupid with his account.

Some two weeks after Chuck's return from Florida, I happened to pay a visit to Chuck's Web site I was more than a little surprised to find a strange punk-rock page where I was accustomed to seeing pages dedicated to family and personal interests. This was definitely not Chuck!

Had the server somehow gone berserk, or had someone hacked into his account? I told Chuck about it immediately.

It didn't take Chuck long to solve the mystery. Someone had indeed replaced the home page, and a check of the server log revealed an entry from Florida on the day Chuck was traveling home. It all pointed to the brother-in-law with the borrowed password. When confronted, the brother-in-law admitted copying the new Web page from a stranger's site and replacing Chuck's home page with it. He assumed that Chuck would find out in a day or two—which of course was not the case. It was more than two weeks before anyone spotted the switch.

Fortunately, there was no real harm done. As Chuck put it, though, it was a good thing that the brother-in-law wasn't more technologically advanced. He might have done some things that were more difficult to undo.

Your Identity

The idea that someone knowing who you are could be dangerous to you may seem ridiculous, but it is a fact that online you need to guard your privacy carefully. Why? Because the more someone knows about you, the easier it is for them to reach out and touch you in the real world.

Do you have a listed phone number? Is your last name uncommon? Either way, it's relatively easy for someone to track you down if they know in which city you live. And you don't want to hand out detailed information as to where you work either.

Why is all this of such concern? Consider the possible consequences of any of the following happening:

✔ You may inadvertently offend someone, and they may seek "revenge" by harassing you. (Seemingly innocent remarks can be taken the wrong way. Plus, there are those online who look to harass others for "fun.")

✔ An online "friend" may not be what they seem.

✔ Your comments on a bulletin board are at odds with someone who decides that you need to be "taught a lesson."

Those are but a few scenarios; you can probably imagine more. (And yes, such things really happen; see the sidebar headed "Do These Things Really Happen?" later in this chapter.)

To protect your identity, keep these items in mind:

1. Don't give out your telephone number or address.

2. Avoid giving your full name to anyone online, even if you don't have an unusual last name.

3. Even if you get really chummy with a new online acquaintance, don't hand out information such as where you work or shop.

4. If you meet someone interested in romance, check them out as much as possible before an in-person meeting. Look for others online who know this person and find out as much as you can about them. Get his or her phone number—never give out your own!—and call from a pay telephone. And if you do meet, meet in a public place.

5. Finally, be a skeptic! Don't believe 100 percent of what anyone tells you, until it is proven.

Do These Things Really Happen? Some Cautionary Anecdotes...

Interestingly enough, even the news media can't quite exaggerate what happens on the Internet. I know, because over the past twenty years I've witnessed quite a bit of what you hear about in the news—and more than a few things you didn't hear about. Here's just a taste of some of the online oddities I've encountered, at first- or second-hand:

✔ Scores of instances of people misrepresenting or outright lying about themselves; the lawyer who wasn't, the M.D. likewise; women (and men) who were 60 pounds heavier and five years older than they claimed; and many others.

✔ The woman who answered an online personals ad, met the man, and decided he wasn't her type. A few days later, she came home from work to find him holding her son and a friend hostage. (Fortunately, this one had a happy ending.)

✔ The high school kid who used a stolen credit card number to hit online pornography sites. He thought he was anonymous and would never be found out—until I followed his trail for the police.

✔ "Disappearing" individuals who offer items for sale at great prices, with payment accepted online or at a PO box. The merchandise never materializes, and there's no way to track the thief.

✔ Instances of identity theft wherein people seeking revenge faked bulletin board postings, e-mail messages, and even photos of their victims.

✔ People impersonating celebrities online, until the real celebrities showed up.

✔ Adults who claimed to be teenagers, teenagers who claimed to be adults, and men who claimed to be women (though never a woman who claimed to be a man—in my experience).

At times, it would appear that some online inhabitants are not only stranger than we imagine, but also stranger than we *can* imagine!

Your Credit Card and Checking Account Numbers

As I wrote the preceding, I received a call from a police department requesting help with two separate incidents of stolen credit card numbers being used online to access pornographic sites. In one instance, a card statement was stolen from a mailbox; in the other, it appears that the credit card information was obtained online in a scam.

You may pay for your Internet service (via an ISP or an online service) with a credit card. This is fine. It is how most folks pay for their Internet service, and it is unlikely that someone will steal the credit card information you provided when you first signed up. However, there are all sorts of ways your credit card info can be lifted online.

You are on your own out in the real world, but here are some ways your card number can be lifted and used.

The most common approach used by thieves is to present themselves in e-mail (or, on occasion, in a realtime chat) as an employee of your ISP or online service. They will tell you that they are an employee of the ISP or online service, and that they need for you to give them your credit card number and expiration date for verification. Or, they may tell you that your account has been hacked into, or that there is some other problem with your online account, and ask for your credit card information. ISPs and online services make it a point *never* to do this, and many remind users that they do not do this. So, *do not give out your credit information online.* (See Chapters 1, 8, and 10 for related information.)

Online shopping is generally safe—when you deal with large, nationally recognized merchants. (Some—among them Amazon.com—even offer a guarantee of safety for their customers. If your financial or personal information is compromised because you gave it at their Web site, they will cover any loss.) Still, there have been a very few instances of credit card information being used without authorization by small online "merchants."

There have also been instances of fraud at Web sites and in e-mail wherein the supposed "merchant" takes your information and you never receive the item offered. The same thing sometimes happens with online auctions. Or, you receive the merchandise you ordered from a small operation, and it may not be as advertised—at which point you may discover that the merchant has disappeared.

Finally, there have been rare instances (two of which I know) in which improper installation or setup of software resulted in anyone who visited a merchant's Web site being able to see information—credit card numbers and expiration dates, and names and addresses—left by others.

The bottom line is this: Don't give your credit card information to someone who just asks, and avoid shady operations, or those that offer something too good to be true. If the outfit is run out of a PO box, and there's no telephone number, pass it by.

Similarly, do not give out checking account numbers online, in e-mail or otherwise.

Online Buying Tips

If possible, consummate your purchase by mail, telephone, or in person. I shop online to find items or compare prices but buy by mail or in person.

Never enter your credit card number at a site that isn't secure. Sites that offer secure systems say so up front. Your Web browser should be able to tell you if you are dealing with a secure server—Netscape and Microsoft's Internet Explorer even let you enable warnings that pop up if you are about to send information to a system that isn't secure. (The security involves encryption schemes that prevent anyone who may be intercepting communications from seeing your information "in clear.")

Look into the feasibility of using one or another of the *E-cash* online payment systems. These involve placing money on deposit with a real or virtual bank, then presenting a code as payment. The setup is basically a virtual debit card. You can limit your losses to the amount you have on deposit. In contrast, if your credit card number is stolen, your credit card might be maxed out long before you report the theft. (A starting point for more information on E-cash systems is the Web site of First Virtual Bank, at: http://www.netchex.com/index.html.)

Online Data Security

There is great concern among Internet users about the vulnerability of transmitted data. As you may know, data is transmitted over the Internet by being relayed through a number of computers along the way. Because of this, there is the possibility of data in transit being viewed at any of the relaying systems. How likely this is to happen is difficult to say, but the possibility does exist.

You can deal with this potential vulnerability in several ways. The first and simplest method is to avoid sending sensitive data over the Internet—including credit card numbers. This caution makes sense, even though the reported incidence of intercepting Internet data and e-mail "spying" is low.

Other approaches you can take are to use browser and Internet data-security features and, with e-mail and sensitive document transmissions, data encryption. (Data encryption is covered in detail in Chapter 7, and is discussed in Chapter 10 as well.)

Browser and Internet Data Security Features

As with other aspects of the Internet, security standards cover data encryption, and also keep data secure during transmission. Taking advantage of these features requires that the Web browser you use conform to specific security standards. Both Netscape and Microsoft Internet Explorer conform to prevailing security standards—*Secure Socket Layer* (SSL) and *Private Communication* (PCT).

Some of the most important security features are internal to browsers. These features include *security certificates* to authenticate your identity to a Web site, the warnings Netscape and Explorer offer when you start to send data to an unsecured Web site, and more. It's a good idea to leave these features active; even if they don't favorably affect your online activities now, they may in the future.

Web sites also can provide security if your browser supports the security protocols these sites use. Web site security features include security certificates that certify that they are what they represent themselves to be, and *secure sites*.

Secure Sites

A secure site protects the routes used by data moving to it, so that credit card numbers or other sensitive data cannot be viewed *en route*. You still have to trust the person running the site, of course—it's analogous to giving your credit card number via voice phone over a line that is guaranteed not to be bugged. But secure sites provide some assurance that no one but you and the person to whom you are giving sensitive information have that information.

Checking Security

There are a couple of ways to see whether a Web site you are visiting is secure. With Netscape, click the Security button on the button bar (or on the lock at the bottom left of the Netscape window). A dialog pops up to inform you whether any of the files you are requesting are secure, as shown in Figure 9.1. (When Netscape is receiving a secure document, the lock icon is displayed closed.)

Figure 9.1

Checking security with Netscape

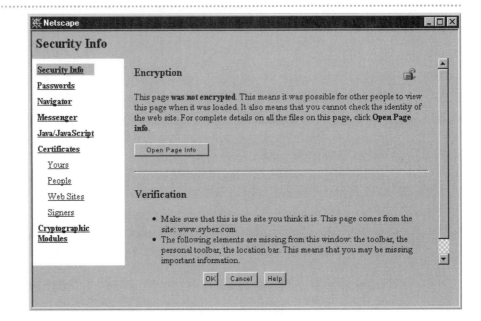

Microsoft Internet Explorer indicates that it is exchanging data with a secure site by displaying an icon that looks like a lock on the status bar.

Both browsers can warn you when you do something, like sending information via an online form, that might be a security risk. With Netscape, select on the Options menu, then click the General tab to enable or disable warnings about insecure sites. With Explorer, select Internet Options on the View menu, and press the Security tab.

Finally, if a URL begins with https:// rather than http:// it is on a secure server. Similarly, a Usenet Newsgroup URL that begins with snews: instead of news: is secure.

Download Security

As discussed in Chapter 8, computer viruses and Trojan horse programs can do a lot more than ruin your day. So it behooves you to consider both the nature and source of anything you download, from anywhere.

In general, follow these guidelines in deciding what to download:

- ✔ If a program or set of macros seems to offer something impossible, or at least too good to be true, pass it by.

- ✔ If a Web site or online service database tells you little or nothing about its files being checked for viruses, don't download anything from there.

- ✔ Look for comments about the file you wish to download.

- ✔ After you download a file (and/or during the download), scan it for viruses. (See Chapter 8.)

Online Privacy Offline

As far as someone spying on what you are doing online is concerned, the major threat is likely to be *offline*—from people snooping around your PC. So, you need to be concerned with the tracks you leave downloading, filing messages and other material, and the records that are kept by your Web browser.

Offline Download Security

What you download can tell someone quite a bit about what you are doing online. To prevent someone from seeing what you are downloading, first make sure that you always clear out or delete any download logs kept by your Internet or online service software. (With some software, such as AOL's, *not* scheduling software downloads will omit the logging.)

If a downloaded program comes in an archive or self-extracting archive with a number of files, you need to delete those files after you install the program in question. You must delete the original download, too, of course. To simplify this task, always download software into the same download folder. When you unpack and install a program, do the unpacking to a folder called \install. This will make it easy to find and delete all the installation files. (A few programs will delete their own installation files, but don't count on this.)

For files other than a program, move them from your download directory as soon as possible after downloading. I suggest that you create a holding folder (perhaps named /holding) for such files. (You can also store in this folder programs that you won't be installing right away.) Make the folder and its contents invisible (see Chapter 5 for details on how to do this), and you should be reasonably safe.

For additional security, you can either encrypt such stored files (see Chapter 7) or store them in a password-protected .ZIP file using WinZip (see Chapter 3).

Finding & Deleting Records of Online Activities

As you probably know, it is easy to track Web sites visited—and even individual keystrokes made—with the appropriate software. But much of the same can be accomplished simply by viewing Netscape's or MSIE's history file. These files show not only Web sites visited, but also specific pages' URLs, and even the content of a search or other data entry. If you are online, you can open any page listed by double-clicking on the URL.

Netscape's History List

Take a look for yourself. With Netscape open, press Ctrl-H, or select History on the Communicator menu. A window containing URLs and information about them will be displayed, like that shown in Figure 9.2.

To delete Netscape history items one at a time, highlight the desired items and press the Delete key, or click Select all on the Edit menu, then press the Delete key.

Figure 9.2

Netscape's History list provides lots of details about your Web browsing.

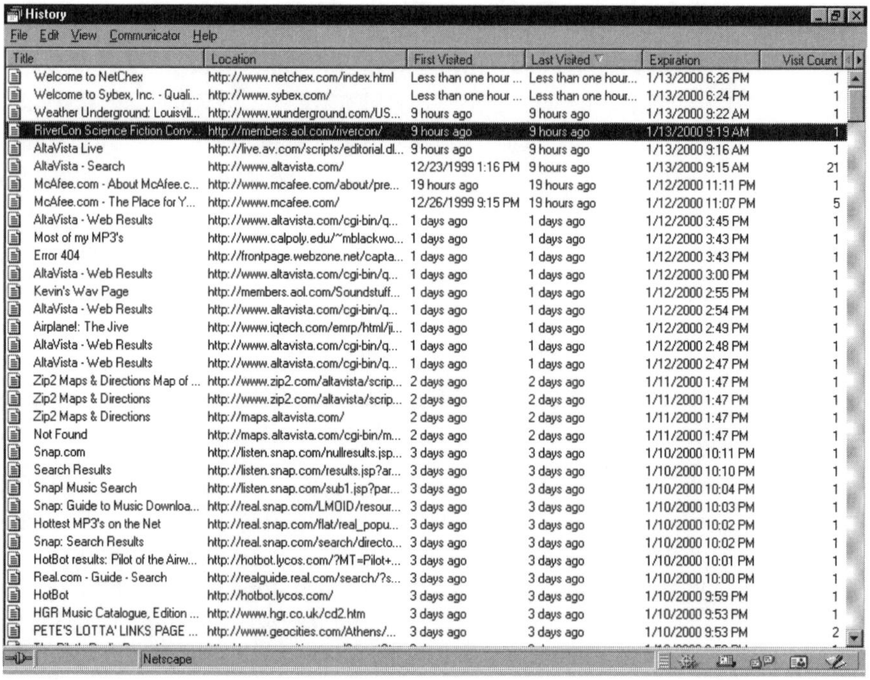

Title	Location	First Visited	Last Visited	Expiration	Visit Count
Welcome to NetChex	http://www.netchex.com/index.html	Less than one hour ...	Less than one hour...	1/13/2000 6:26 PM	1
Welcome to Sybex, Inc. - Quali...	http://www.sybex.com/	Less than one hour ...	Less than one hour...	1/13/2000 6:24 PM	1
Weather Underground: Louisvil...	http://www.wunderground.com/US...	9 hours ago	9 hours ago	1/13/2000 9:22 AM	1
RiverCon Science Fiction Conv...	http://members.aol.com/rivercon/	9 hours ago	9 hours ago	1/13/2000 9:19 AM	1
AltaVista Live	http://live.av.com/scripts/editorial.dl...	9 hours ago	9 hours ago	1/13/2000 9:16 AM	1
AltaVista - Search	http://www.altavista.com/	12/23/1999 1:16 PM	9 hours ago	1/13/2000 9:15 AM	21
McAfee.com - About McAfee.c...	http://www.mcafee.com/about/pre...	19 hours ago	19 hours ago	1/12/2000 11:11 PM	1
McAfee.com - The Place for Y...	http://www.mcafee.com/	12/26/1999 9:15 PM	19 hours ago	1/12/2000 11:07 PM	5
AltaVista - Web Results	http://www.altavista.com/cgi-bin/q...	1 days ago	1 days ago	1/12/2000 3:45 PM	1
Most of my MP3's	http://www.calpoly.edu/~mblackwo...	1 days ago	1 days ago	1/12/2000 3:43 PM	1
Error 404	http://frontpage.webzone.net/capta...	1 days ago	1 days ago	1/12/2000 3:43 PM	1
AltaVista - Web Results	http://www.altavista.com/cgi-bin/q...	1 days ago	1 days ago	1/12/2000 3:00 PM	1
Kevin's Wav Page	http://members.aol.com/Soundstuff...	1 days ago	1 days ago	1/12/2000 2:55 PM	1
AltaVista - Web Results	http://www.altavista.com/cgi-bin/q...	1 days ago	1 days ago	1/12/2000 2:54 PM	1
Airplane!: The Jive	http://www.iqtech.com/emrp/html/ji...	1 days ago	1 days ago	1/12/2000 2:49 PM	1
AltaVista - Web Results	http://www.altavista.com/cgi-bin/q...	1 days ago	1 days ago	1/12/2000 2:48 PM	1
AltaVista - Web Results	http://www.altavista.com/cgi-bin/q...	1 days ago	1 days ago	1/12/2000 2:47 PM	1
Zip2 Maps & Directions Map of ...	http://www.zip2.com/altavista/scrip...	2 days ago	2 days ago	1/11/2000 1:47 PM	1
Zip2 Maps & Directions	http://www.zip2.com/altavista/scrip...	2 days ago	2 days ago	1/11/2000 1:47 PM	1
Zip2 Maps & Directions	http://maps.altavista.com/	2 days ago	2 days ago	1/11/2000 1:47 PM	1
Not Found	http://maps.altavista.com/cgi-bin/m...	2 days ago	2 days ago	1/11/2000 1:47 PM	1
Snap.com	http://listen.snap.com/nullresults.jsp...	3 days ago	3 days ago	1/10/2000 10:11 PM	1
Search Results	http://listen.snap.com/results.jsp?ar...	3 days ago	3 days ago	1/10/2000 10:10 PM	1
Snap! Music Search	http://listen.snap.com/sub1.jsp?par...	3 days ago	3 days ago	1/10/2000 10:04 PM	1
Snap: Guide to Music Downloa...	http://real.snap.com/LMOID/resour...	3 days ago	3 days ago	1/10/2000 10:03 PM	1
Hottest MP3's on the Net	http://real.snap.com/flat/real_popu...	3 days ago	3 days ago	1/10/2000 10:02 PM	1
Snap: Search Results	http://real.snap.com/search/directo...	3 days ago	3 days ago	1/10/2000 10:02 PM	1
HotBot results: Pilot of the Airw...	http://hotbot.lycos.com/?MT=Pilot+...	3 days ago	3 days ago	1/10/2000 10:01 PM	1
Real.com - Guide - Search	http://realguide.real.com/search/?s...	3 days ago	3 days ago	1/10/2000 10:00 PM	1
HotBot	http://hotbot.lycos.com/	3 days ago	3 days ago	1/10/2000 9:59 PM	1
HGR Music Catalogue, Edition ...	http://www.hgr.co.uk/cd2.htm	3 days ago	3 days ago	1/10/2000 9:53 PM	1
PETE'S LOTTA' LINKS PAGE ...	http://www.geocities.com/Athens/...	3 days ago	3 days ago	1/10/2000 9:53 PM	2

Microsoft Internet Explorer's History List

MSIE's URL history is stored in folders by week, and by Web sites. Figure 9.3 shows this. With MSIE, pressing the History button on the menu bar displays a small window with a list of URLs visited. (You can also select Explorer Bar on the View menu, then select History, or type **Ctrl+H**.)

Figure 9.3

MSIE's History List provides sorted lists of the Web pages you visit.

You can delete individual URLs, but the quickest way is to delete entire weeks or Web site folders. Or, you can clear the history folder entirely by selecting Internet Options on MSIE's Edit menu, pressing the General tab, then pressing the Clear History button.

A Private Entrance

Internet users often enter URLs manually, either typing or pasting them in. There are two ways to do this, one of which leaves a trail, and one of which doesn't.

If you enter a URL in the location bar below the toolbar in Netscape or MSIE, the URL is recorded in a drop-down menu. These are shown in Figure 9.4. (A URL you visit is also entered if you open a link in a new window.)

Figure 9.4

Netscape's location field and MSIE's Address Bar provide records of where you have been on the Web.

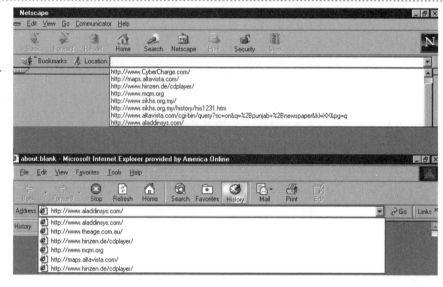

This information stays there until other entries make it scroll off. To open a page without having its URL recorded in this field, select Open page on Netscape's File menu, or Open on MSIE's file menu. Enter the URL in the dialog box. (Alternately, you can press Ctrl+O with either Netscape or MSIE.) Figure 9.5 shows both browsers' dialog boxes.

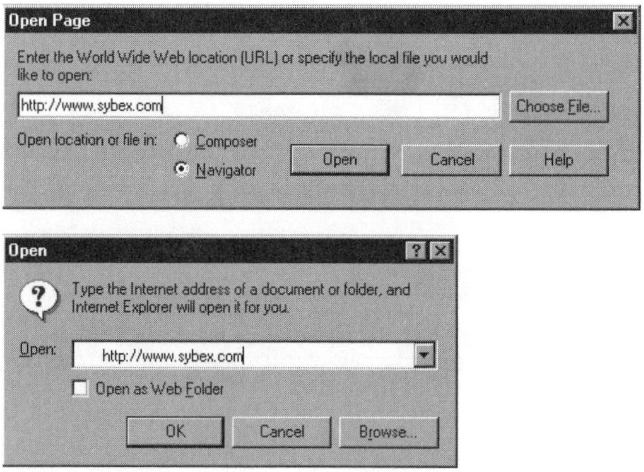

Figure 9.5

Entering a Web page address manually—and secretly

Clearing Netscape's Location Field

If there is information in Netscape's location field you want to get rid of, Netscape lets you clear it. To do this, select Preferences on Netscape's Edit menu, then click on Navigator. You will see the Preferences dialog box shown in Figure 9.6. Press the button labeled Clear Location Bar, and the location bar record of your travels will go away.

Figure 9.6

Clearing Netscape's location field

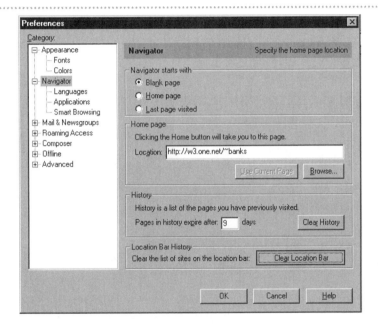

Hiding MSIE's Address Bar

You can hide MSIE's Address bar, right-clicking on the toolbar and then clicking the check mark labeled Address Bar. Figure 9.7 illustrates this.

Figure 9.7

Hiding MSIE's Address Bar

Checking Out the Stash

MSIE and Netscape stash caches of recent HTML pages and images on your hard drive. This speeds up Web access if you revisit pages. However, these files are accessible by anyone who knows the proper directories to search.

Such files are stored away in various subdirectories (the most obvious being a subdirectory called \CACHE), but you don't need to worry about where they are to delete them. All you need to do is clear the disk cache.

With Netscape, select Preferences on the Edit menu. Click the + sign next to the Advanced selection, then click Cache. Click on the button labeled Clear Disk Cache, as shown in Figure 9.8.

Figure 9.8
Clearing Netscape's disk cache

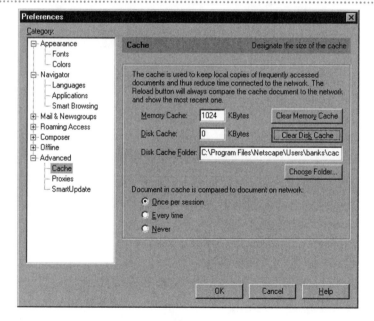

With MSIE, select Internet Options on the View menu, and click on the General tab. Press the button labeled Delete Files to delete the Web pages Explorer has saved (see Figure 9.9).

MSIE users will also need to clear out a folder used to store temporary Internet files. This file is in your Windows folder, on your main drive—normally drive C. Open Windows Explorer, and open C:\Windows\Temporary Internet Files, as shown in Figure 9.10.

Figure 9.9

Clearing MSIE's disk cache

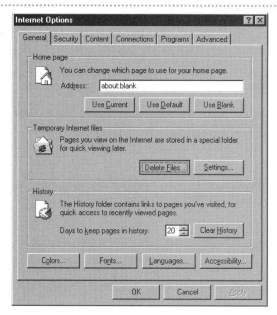

Figure 9.10

Clearing out temporary Internet files

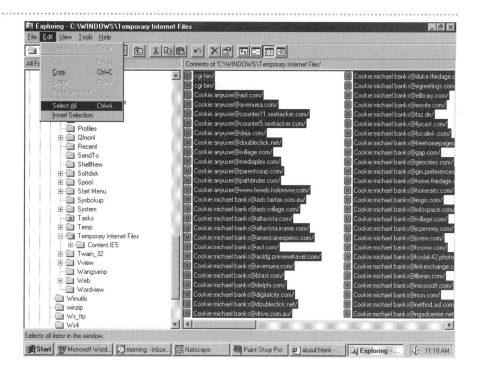

Open the Edit menu and click Select All. Then press the Delete key. Most files in the folder will be deleted, including some cookie files placed there by Web servers at sites you have visited.

Eliminating Cookies

Concerning cookies (the one-line information strings placed in the file `cookies.txt` created by your browser), you should know that even though you delete disk caches, these files will persist. Further, as you can see in Figure 9.10, cookies include the addresses of Web sites—which means that anyone can see the addresses of many of the sites you've visited. It is best to disable cookies with your browser so as to prevent cookies from being stored on your hard drive.

To disable cookies with Netscape, select Edit ➤ Preferences ➤ Advanced, then click the radio button labeled Disable cookies (Figure 9.11).

Figure 9.11
Disabling cookies with Netscape

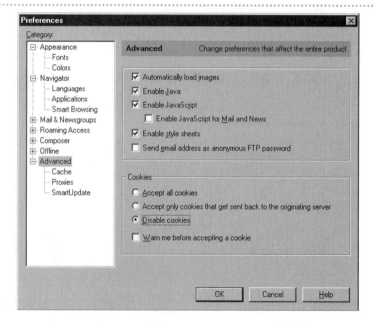

To disable cookies with MSIE, select Tools ➤ Internet Options ➤ Security, and then press the Custom Level button. The Security Settings dialog, shown in Figure 9.12, will appear.

Figure 9.12

Disabling cookies with MSIE

Bookmarks and Favorites Lists

Your bookmark files can tell quite a bit about what you are doing online, because frequently visited or favorite sites' URLs are stored in your bookmark file. You may wish to forego using bookmarks if you feel a list of them would give away things you don't want known.

Special Notes for AOL Users

AOL users may be intrigued to learn that much of their online life can be an open book to anyone who wants to prowl their AOL software and directories—without a password. We're not talking about Internet psychos invading your computer through your phone line, though. The people who can learn what you've been downloading, reading, and writing—as well as where you've been hanging out on the Web—may be in your home right now. All it takes is physical access to your computer. The tips following will help you keep your online business from prying eyes offline.

When Your Personal Filing Cabinet Isn't

If someone has access to your computer, they don't even have to log on to see some of what you've been doing. A quick look at the Personal Filing Cabinet associated with a screen name may tell you more about that person than you think. Press the Personal Filing Cabinet button on AOL's toolbar, and you can see a list of downloads, including messages with and without attachments, such as that shown in Figure 9.13. Right-click on any item, and you can learn where the file can be found—after which you can access it.

Figure 9.13

AOL's Personal Filing Cabinet may show quite a bit of info offline—and it doesn't require a password.

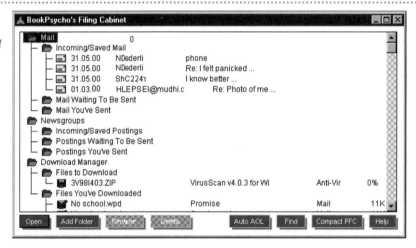

To prevent others from seeing what e-mail, files, and other things have been going on between you and AOL, you can either password-protect your Personal Filing Cabinet or delete your tracks from the Personal Filing Cabinet.

To password-protect your Personal Filing Cabinet, sign on to AOL and follow these steps:

1. Click the My AOL button on the toolbar and select Preferences.

2. Press the Password button.

3. Type your password in the Password box.

4. Click on the Personal Filing Cabinet check box.

If you must allow someone else to use a specific screen name, you can get rid of these telltale tracks entirely by deleting the items in your Personal Filing Cabinet after you log off. You will also want to delete or move items from the \DOWNLOAD subdirectory in your AOL directory. (Move or copy items you want to save to a different directory before you do any deleting.)

Don't Leave Tracks

If someone else has access to your screen name for whatever reason and you don't want them to know what you've been doing on AOL or the Internet, follow these steps to clear the online history trail that is normally kept in AOL's location bar:

1. Press the My AOL button on the toolbar and click Preferences.

2. Click the Toolbar button.

3. In the Toolbar Preferences box, check the History Trail box so that your online history trail will be cleared every time you log off.

Finally, to keep prying offline eyes from seeing where you've been on the Net, you'll need to delete the record of your Internet browsing that Internet Explorer keeps.

Open MSIE (separate from AOL) and delete the online history, thus:

1. Press the History button on MSIE's button bar.

2. In the window that appears to the left, open and delete the week-by-week collections of URLs you've visited.

Now you have a solid understanding of how to keep others from following your trail on the Internet. In a related vein, Chapter 10 takes a look at how to keep your e-mail private, online and off.

PC CONFIDENTIAL

CHAPTER 10

E-Mail Protection

- ✔ **E-mail and false threats to privacy**
- ✔ **Real e-mail risks online**
- ✔ **How you can compromise yourself in e-mail**
- ✔ **E-mail encryption and software**
- ✔ **Protecting your privacy from spammers**
- ✔ **E-mail risks offline**
- ✔ **Filing e-mail and protecting your filing system**

E-mail privacy takes its place among the most vital yet misunderstood elements of the Internet. Many of you reading this book have strong concerns—and fears— about private e-mail being read by others. That being the case, in this chapter I will identify privacy risks associated with e-mail and explain how to protect your privacy when sending, receiving, and storing e-mail.

E-Mail and False Threats to Privacy

You may be very concerned over the likelihood of your e-mail being intercepted and read by others. Many Internet users are. Actually, this is among the least likely things that can happen to you online, as you will see in the next section. For my part, I don't worry about interception with my own e-mail, primarily because I don't say things in e-mail messages that I wouldn't want anyone else to read. With regard to the actual transmission, all that concerns me is whether my messages arrive. Most of the mails I write would be fairly boring to a stranger.

Perhaps you have additional concerns. Maybe you are sending information in e-mail that you do not want anyone else to read, with good reason. If this is the case, the next section will be of interest to you.

So, *Can* Others Intercept My E-Mail?

The simple answer to the question posed by the header above is: "Yes." Can others intercept my e-mail easily? The simple answer this time is: "No." By and large, intercepting an e-mail message on the Internet requires quite a bit of effort and planning.

Data—including e-mail—is transmitted on the Internet in *packets*. This means that an e-mail message is often sent in several pieces. To further complicate things, not every packet is sent over the same virtual route as others. So, anyone who wants to intercept your e-mail must have considerable technical expertise, as well as access to computers and/or data lines that handle your messages. Then they must expend a lot of effort to track the packets, intercept, and reassemble them. This is sometimes referred to as *packet-sniffing*.

One thing that is a relief to realize is that, no matter how sensitive or intense or private the things you discuss in e-mail may be to you, they are probably of little or no consequence to other people. Someone might find passing entertainment in reading some of your mail, but that's about it.

The Case of the Eavesdropping Telephone Workers

A few years back, I worked installing switching equipment in telephone company central offices. A favorite pastime of at least one worker in every central office was to listen in on telephone calls. Whoever was listening to such calls often put them on a speaker, so everyone in the office could hear them. Without exception, the conversations that were broadcast were between people whom no one in the switching offices knew. And with rare exception, the conversations were fairly boring, which is true of the majority of e-mail (and regular mail) that is transmitted on a daily basis.

What About My Sysop? How Much Can System Operators See?

System operators—and others with the proper privileges—at many ISPs and online services may be watching you. In fact, it is possible to watch and record everything you do. Or, as the system administrator at one of my ISPs told me, "We can see literally every keystroke you make."

Of course, almost no system staff or administrators go to the trouble of watching people without good reason; they have too many other things to do. But it is possible. (Read Clifford Stoll's book *The Cuckoo's Egg* for revealing examples.)

The bottom line here is this: There isn't much you can do to prevent someone in the right position from intercepting your e-mail. You can keep the mail's content private, though, using techniques discussed in the following pages.

If you work for a business, large or small, or for a government agency, you may as well assume that your e-mail is being read. The Electronic Communications Privacy Act (ECPA) of 1986 exempts employers from liability in intercepting and reading e-mail (which is otherwise illegal). In other words, your employer can legally read any e-mail you send or receive using a company computer.

Real E-Mail Risks Online

Beyond someone actually being interested enough to go to all the trouble of intercepting and assembling en route the data packets that comprise your mail, e-mail poses two realistic dangers. These dangers have to do not with intercepting your messages, but instead with how recipients and senders handle e-mail.

The Adventure of the Crusading Chat-Room "Teacher"

In 1987, as was the case with online services in general, the Delphi online service was experiencing a growth spurt. This brought all sorts of new people online, and they naturally gravitated to the chat rooms (or conference rooms, as they were known on Delphi).

One person who stood out represented him- or herself (you never know in chat rooms) as a female teacher. "She" had a habit of cruising conference rooms and *lurking* (chat-room speak for listening in on conversations without participating). If the talk turned to sex, however, she would admonish the participants for talking about it in public.

The Teacher quickly became something of a fixture in the conference rooms. If you were in a chat room in the evening, you could count on a visit from the Teacher. The regulars shrugged and avoided references to sex when she was present. (There was a lot more tolerance in those days.)

Continued on next page

The Adventure of the Crusading Chat-Room "Teacher" (continued)

The Teacher didn't last long, however. As it turned out, this person had a Jekyll and Hyde personality. As the conference rooms thinned out every night around midnight, you would usually find The Teacher in a private conference with another Delphi member, not one of the regulars. No one had any idea what that was about, but judging from her behavior in public chats, we figured she was probably tutoring someone.

As it turned out, The Teacher wasn't tutoring—at least, not in the conventional sense. Her cover was blown after only a few weeks when she roped Rick, one of the regulars, into a solo chat. The next day, Rick sent several dozen of us an e-mail copy of the last couple minutes of their chat. That log revealed a private agenda quite at odds with The Teacher's public persona. After an evening of chastising those who were talking about sex in public, she (or he—again, you can't tell online) enjoyed slipping away to talk about sex in private—to be specific, to have a *hot chat* (more or less simulating sex by typing actions and reactions back and forth.)

We never saw The Teacher again after that. It appears that someone forwarded a copy of that e-mail message to her.

Indecent Exposure?

The first of several online dangers is simply described: A recipient could use private e-mail to share information about or from you with others—and without your knowledge (as happened in "The Case of the Crusading Chat-Room 'Teacher'"). Online, it is safe to assume that if you write something with entertainment value, it will be shared with others.

Given that it is very easy to forward e-mail to others, you either have to trust your recipients or refrain from putting information in e-mail that you wouldn't want shared. That goes double for potentially embarrassing messages.

Hold Your Temper

You can be compromised by someone turning your own e-mail against you, just as someone can use your Usenet or bulletin board postings against you. If you tend to fly off the handle and fire off outrageous comments to people you don't know (or even to those you do know), you may one day find one or two of your messages posted for the enjoyment of others.

There are people who cultivate the hobby of publicly sharing the more outrageously entertaining e-mail they receive, usually on a Web site. One such site is at `http://phobos.illtel.denver.co.us/pub/lamers/`. (Fortunately, the guy responsible for this page doesn't reveal the e-mail addresses of his correspondents.)

Don't Spam or Scam

You can also end up being one of the featured attractions at somebody's Web site by spamming. Where you spam doesn't matter; e-mail and Usenet spammers are hated equally by the majority of folks everywhere on the Net. So, if you're a budding entrepreneur who is tempted to seek early retirement by sending solicitations to the millions of "buyers" on the Net, you had better think twice. For examples of what can happen to you if you spam, take a look at this page:

   `http://ga.to/mmf/`

This site offers a list of notable spammers, with e-mail addresses. You'll find it very entertaining.

If you send a lot of e-mail to people you don't know, you might want to leave your real name out of the headers. This is because public postings can carry your e-mail address and, more importantly, you never really know how many times, and to whom, a message you send might be copied and forwarded—by accident or intent. On online services where it is possible (such as CompuServe and Delphi), you usually have to search out a Preferences, Mail Settings, or similar area, where you can specify the personal name to be included with your e-mail. This works with mail on the service itself, as well as e-mail to Internet addresses. If you use Pegasus, BeyondMail, Eudora, or the e-mail system included with Netscape or Microsoft's Internet Explorer, go into the Options or Setup area and delete your personal name. This way, you are in control of who knows your full name.

What Is Spam?

If you've been online more than a few months, you've probably experienced this: You log on to check your email, and new messages are waiting—a lot of new messages, in fact, and none from anyone you know. The subject headers shout at you: "Make Money While You Sleep," "Earn a Thousand Dollars Every Time the Phone Rings," or "Retire Next Week!"

These solicitations are called *spam*. (The name is a reference to an obscure Monty Python skit in which a group of Vikings singing "spam, spam, spam, spam" continually disrupts a diner giving his order. Spam is pretty much on the same level—useless verbiage without communication.) Spam overloads e-mail systems, annoys most people, and almost never results in the perpetrator selling anything. This lack of effectiveness is especially true because the overwhelming majority of spam consists of pitches for illegal pyramid scams or so-called multi-level or network marketing schemes that never work.

The Proper Address

The second way to get in trouble online has to do with how you handle your e-mail, both coming and going. One slip in addressing, and you set yourself up for embarrassment, or worse.

I've received more than my share of mis-sent e-mail messages. These have included apparent replies to questions about UFOs, communications from members of a secret group on an online service that was trying to force the management to dump a sysop, an RSVP to an invitation to the Governor of Ohio's inauguration, and several love letters not intended for me.

Love letters? Consider the Australian woman who ended up sending me copies of e-mail notes to two men she was dating. I live in the Midwestern United States and don't know this woman, had never written to her. Yet she somehow not only picked up my e-mail address, but also managed to bungle when adding it to her address book. Every time she sent mail to either of her two beaus, she sent the same mail to me.

The details were entertaining, to say the least—but I won't share them here. If, however, I were of a certain mindset, I just might share the details of this woman's torrid love affairs on a Web page.

The moral of the story is simple: Pay attention to the address when you send e-mail. Don't rely on your address book or your memory to get it right.

I've misaddressed mail a few times myself—usually because I was distracted and typed the e-mail address of someone I was thinking about or to whom I'd just sent mail, instead of the intended addressee. Other ways you can get into trouble with (mis)addressing e-mail include:

✔ Sending a reply to a group message to everyone else to whom the original mail was sent. This happens when you click Reply All instead of simply Reply to respond to a message that's been sent to you and others.

✔ Reading a forwarded message, then replying to the person who forwarded the message—rather than the person who originally composed it.

✔ Getting the address wrong because of similar characters. ROGER (with a capital O) or RØGER (with a zero) can be confusing. Each looks like the other. I managed to send mail several times to the wrong person because I read the TØØ (T-zero-zero) at the end of my friend Teena's address as TOO (with two capital Os). I was surprised when Teena didn't reply for several days, and even more surprised when I received a letter from a minister suggesting that I might not want the details of my personal life to go to a total stranger.

The Mystery of the Insecure Security Department

At one time or another in the 1980s I was on almost every online service in existence. Among the more interesting was a service called AT&T Mail. The most powerful and under-marketed e-mail service in history, AT&T Mail bristled with features of all sorts. Its online mailing lists, user directory, and list-management software were among its stronger features. As it turned out, they also served as a reminder to me and AT&T's security department that the greatest security software in the world is useless if nobody uses it properly.

I had been on the system perhaps two months when I started receiving e-mail obviously meant for someone else named Banks. I would get announcements of departmental meetings and training sessions within AT&T, company newsletters, and lots more. When I checked the AT&T directory, I found more than 30 people named Banks working for AT&T, including the Banks whose mail I was receiving.

Continued on next page

The Mystery of the Insecure Security Department
(continued)

In less than a minute of scanning the directory I could see the problem: My ID was banks, while his was banks preceded by an initial. The people who sent the errant mail had probably not bothered to check the directory. He was likely the only person named Banks that they knew in their particular segment of the company, and because user IDs on the system are assigned based on last names, they apparently all assumed that his address had to be banks.

I began forwarding the misdirected mail to its intended recipient, always with a copy and a note to the senders informing them that they should edit their mailing lists. Most people corrected the error, but some didn't. Worse, more and more people were making the same mistake. Apparently, some of the departments were sharing their mailing lists. Each time a list with my name was copied, the errors multiplied; it was almost as if my ID was a virus on the system, replicating through shared lists.

This went on for several years, peaking in 1989 when I received a message from AT&T corporate security. The message was an alert for employees traveling in Europe. It urged them to guard data on their laptop computers in France, and to take special care with e-mail, because the French Suarte (a government intelligence agency) were conducting industrial espionage.

I felt like I'd just come to the punch line of a long joke. I informed the security department of the gaffe. They studiously ignored the irony of the situation, but did start taking their own advice regarding e-mail.

This anecdote illustrates a couple of important points. First, it bears out the oft-cited maxim that computers do exactly what you tell them to do. Second, it proves that computers can multiply errors with the same efficiency with which they perform any other job.

Is Encryption the Answer? (And If Not, What's the Question?)

As you may already have gathered, the most important thing you can do regarding e-mail security is to pay attention. Pay attention to what you say in private e-mail, to whom you send e-mail, and to how you address your e-mail.

Beyond watching where you're sending e-mail, you would do well to encrypt outgoing e-mail of a sensitive nature if you feel there is any chance of someone intercepting your e-mail.

Keep in mind that staffers at your ISP or someone packet-sniffing are not the only threats to your e-mail. E-mail can also be intercepted by someone at the receiving end, perhaps a co-worker, friend, or relative of the recipient. Encryption can also protect you from those sorts of potential problems.

Encryption Software Revisited

If you haven't read it already (or, even if you have) you will find an extensive discussion of encryption, encryption technique, and encryption software in Chapter 7. I recommend using one of the encryption software packages discussed in Chapter 7. Among these, Norton Secret Stuff seems to offer the best combination of encryption strength and ease of use in e-mail applications. As also noted in Chapter 7, Norton Secret Stuff creates a program that contains an encrypted message or other encrypted file. The program will not run and re-create the encrypted file without the appropriate password.

In Figure 10.1, you can see an example of what a file encrypted with Norton Secret Stuff looks like. The top half of the illustration shows a portion of the encrypted version of the text file shown in the bottom half.

As you can see, there is little chance that someone can read the file from the encrypted version. And, since the program contained in the encrypted file will not provide the unencrypted version of the file, you have little to worry about if someone does get a copy of the encrypted message.

Of course, other programs offer other advantages. As noted in Chapter 7, PGP (Pretty Good Privacy) offers authenticating digital signatures for e-mail. This will be of interest to those who fear *identity theft*. (Identity theft occurs when someone masquerades as you. This can take the form of faking your address on e-mail—which a digital signature can discourage—in addition to other techniques.)

Figure 10.1

Encryption renders a text file totally unreadable by conventional means.

E-Mail Programs and Encryption

Some e-mail programs offer their own encryption, among them BeyondMail by Banyan (intended primarily for network use), and Pegasus (which offers add-on capability for PGP and certain other encryption programs).

Netscape's e-mail facility allows you to sign outgoing messages digitally using a VeriSign system provided with the browser. You can optionally encrypt messages to another user if the person to whom you are sending e-mail also has a digital certificate. The certificate must be purchased, and renewed annually. (A free trial is available.)

You can get additional information on digital certificates and Netscape from the Netscape browser itself. Click the Lock icon at the extreme lower-left of the browser or e-mail screen; then click the word Certificates. You will see the screen shown in Figure 10.2.

Figure 10.2

Netscape dialog with security certificate information

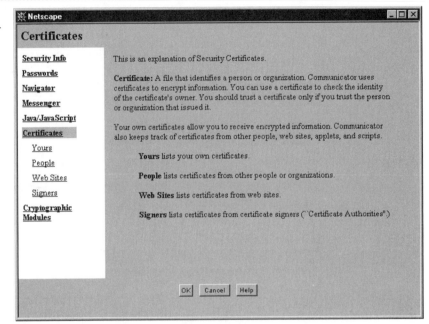

Click Yours ➤ People ➤ Web Sites ➤ Signers for specific information.

VeriSign also provides digital certificates for Microsoft Outlook and Microsoft Outlook Express. (For still more information, visit VeriSign's Web site at `http://www.verisign.com/`.)

Microsoft Internet Explorer also provides encryption if you obtain a digital certificate via VeriSign. (For MSIE users, there is a six-month free trial of the VeriSign service.) MSIE users can also get a certificate from GlobalSign, `http://www.globalsign.net/products/`.

MSIE will provide information about digital certificates via its Help system. Simply click Contents and Index on MSIE's Help menu. Enter **digital** in the text box and click List Topics. You will see the Help dialog shown in Figure 10.3.

Click Protecting Your Identity Over The Internet to read about digital certificates.

Figure 10.3

MSIE Help with digital certificates

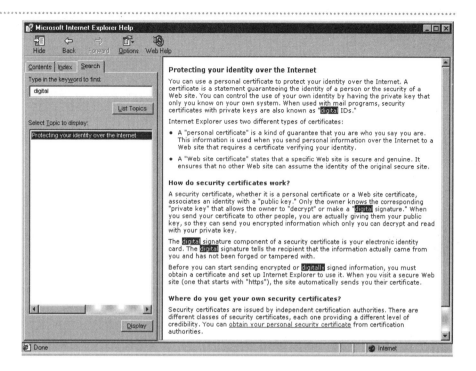

Protecting Your Privacy from Spammers

You may not realize it, but your e-mail address is a valuable privacy asset. It is also a valuable commodity to spammers and others who would like to trash your privacy with invasive, and at times harassing, messages for con games, scams, pornography, and the like.

Without getting into all the varieties of spam out there and the various ways its perpetrators try to disguise it, trust me when I tell you that you want to keep your e-mail address out of the hands (and off the lists) of spammers. Doing so requires that you follow a few simple instructions, as outlined in the following paragraphs.

Get an Alternate E-Mail Address

You should not put your e-mail address on public display. This means that you should not post in public using your address, nor should you use it to sign up for or access chat rooms. If you are going to post on public bulletin boards or Usenet, or use chat rooms, get a different address for that purpose only and don't bother with checking e-mail to it.

Keep your main or primary e-mail address for correspondence with friends and relatives, and/or for business correspondence, as appropriate.

If you use AOL, Prodigy, or another online service, or an ISP that offers multiple IDs, getting one is no problem. If you can't get an alternate ID for free and don't want to spend the money on a new ISP account, you can get free Web e-mail at any of a number of sites. Among them are these providers:

AltaVista:	`http://mail.altavista.com`
Excite Mail:	`http://mail.excite.com`
Hotmail:	`http://www.hotmail.com`
Net@ddress:	`http://www.netaddress.com`
Juno:	`http://www.juno.com`

(Juno also provides free dial-up access for e-mail.)

Stay off Lists

Keep your main e-mail address off lists. Do not sign up for updates at a Web site, and avoid e-mail discussion groups, unless you use a secondary or Web-based e-mail address.

If you use an ISP and the ISP has finger enabled, remove your address from the listings of users. (Your ISP's Web site will have instructions on how to do this.)

To check whether your ISP has finger enabled, enter your e-mail address at the URL below. If finger is enabled, you will see a listing with your name and other information.

`http://www.cs.indiana.edu:800/finger/gateway`

Keep a Low Profile with No Profile

Online services, Web sites, and many ISPs provide online facilities where you can list information about yourself—your interests, location, and so forth. These are called *profiles*. Such profiles are visible to anyone who cares to look at them, and spammers frequently use online profiles to add to their mailing lists. If you have a profile, delete it; if not, don't create one.

E-Mail Risks Offline

Offline, your only worries regarding e-mail are that someone will go through and/or delete your messages, which means you need to consider how you will protect saved messages from others. You have several options to protect your e-mail from prying eyes and destructive hands:

- ✔ Password-protect your e-mail program's inbox and outbox files (if the program accommodates this).

- ✔ Encrypt your e-mail program and its files.

- ✔ Print and save hard copies.

- ✔ Copy sensitive messages you wish to save to word processor files, password-protect and/or encrypt the files, and store them on floppy disks or CD-ROM.

Encryption is the best protection for copies of e-mail messages. You can password-protect your mail with your e-mail program's password setup, but as I've said before, there are ways around password protection. (Someone who knows you might be able to guess your password. Failing that, anyone who can get at the mail files can view them with a word processor or other program.) Printing and saving hard copies makes it almost too easy for someone to read what you're trying to protect. There is no password protection and no encryption with hard copies—all someone has to do is find your printouts.

Thus, you may want to encrypt your e-mail program and its files on your hard drive, for which I recommend Encrypted Magic Folders, Private File, or SecurePC, in that order. Alterntatively, you may want to bundle all the messages you want to save into a succession of word processor files—each file protected by encryption, for which I recommend Norton Secret Stuff or Private File (again, see Chapter 7), and storage on floppy disks.

That's the scoop on e-mail security and privacy. Now for one more trip into the realm of the Internet, as we take a look at some useful Internet-related software in Chapter 11. There, you will find software to help protect your privacy offline as well as online.

PC CONFIDENTIAL

CHAPTER 11

The Internet Revisited: Software Helpers

✔ **Cookies—what they are and how to manage them**

✔ **Anonymous surfing with a proxy server**

✔ **Software helpers for privacy online and off**

✔ **A few words on Internet monitoring programs**

This chapter takes a look at several additional elements of online safety and privacy. First, you'll get a close-up of browser cookies, which you will learn are loaded with more personal information than you may think.

Next, I'll show you how to surf anonymously using what is called a *proxy server*. Then we'll look at some useful programs for covering your tracks offline and protecting yourself online.

Finally, we'll get even more personal with monitoring programs—the kind that can tell someone literally everything you type, including passwords. I'll show you what they can do and how to find them.

When Cookies Aren't So Tasty

I mentioned *cookies* briefly in Chapter 9. Here, we'll take a detailed look at cookies, how they can affect you and your PC, and how to manage them.

What Are Cookies, and Why Are They on My Hard Drive?

A cookie is a line of information that a Web server puts in a file on your hard drive. It does this via your Web browser (which is why a cookie is sometimes called a *browser cookie*). Cookies usually consist of one line of information each. They are stored in a file called `cookies.txt` in one of your browser's sub-folders.

Cookies are used by Web servers (the computers that host Web sites) to put information on your hard drive. The types of information thus stored include, but are not limited to, user IDs and passwords, dates and times of visits to a Web site, pages viewed, and much more.

Some cookie applications benefit Web site visitors. For example, a user ID and password stored in the `cookies.txt` file can get you into a site that requires this information without your having to type it in every time. A Preferences listing for a Web site contains cookies that can customize the presentation of information. Cookies are also used to keep items in virtual shopping carts. (If you have ever visited a shopping site and ordered items, left without completing your order, then returned later to find your list of items intact, you can thank information stored in your `cookies.txt` file for "regenerating" the shopping list.) Likewise, these files might store records of what pages you've visited at a site, and then use this information to prompt the server to provide access to new pages and deny access to pages previously visited. Such a setup might be used to collect and store poll data, while prohibiting anyone from taking the poll twice.

The `cookies.txt` file is shown to any server that requests it. However, much of the information in a cookie is useful only to the server that placed the cookie, or to other servers with which the owner of the cookie-writing server elects to share cookie information.

The file `cookies.txt` is a standard 7-bit ASCII text file. You can open the file with a word processor. It will look something like this:

```
# Netscape HTTP Cookie File
# http://www.netscape.com/newsref/std/cookie_spec.html
# This is a generated file!  Do not edit.


.amazon.com TRUE    /    FALSE    2082787568  x-main  nIDfTAYzJDky5V6rp9
    K6UZsS915ULEq4
.amazon.com TRUE    /    FALSE    2082787240  ubid-main
    077-2649831-7662731
.egreetings.com TRUE    /    FALSE    1589544039  E-greetings
    zRH-NpVWp3-ZNbT11-hcK3-1-zvWOx3
.excite.com TRUE    /    FALSE    1609415891  popup   no
.egreetings.com TRUE    /    FALSE    2114510439  EGNauto 234719635
.amazon.de  TRUE    /    FALSE    2082754840  x-acbde eKQIfwnxuF
    7qtmM40x6VWAXh@Ih6Uo5H
www.shopping.com    FALSE   /store  FALSE    969519639    ShopperID
    BOC9PRNHEQS12LRS001PQJH9COU246UE
www.jcpenney.com    FALSE   /jcp    FALSE    1262325962
ShopperManager%2Fjcp    SHOPPERMANAGER%2FJCP=11BV2LKPSMUSH2GVH
    00J74GDH2G9H9EPOe82KcKCZaZOe82KcKCZaZT200BF9459B4BB67241C1FB9C5
    06B605E751F
banner.freeservers.com  FALSE   /r/ FALSE    953737814    CTEST   true
```

```
banner.freeservers.com  FALSE   /r/ FALSE   953737815   FSVIS_L 1999-09-24
banner.freeservers.com  FALSE   /r/ FALSE   953737815   FSVIS   1999-09
.usatoday.com   TRUE    /   FALSE   978307117   RMID    d132656538907180
.aaddzz.com TRUE    /   FALSE   94968486    ALTEMP|38284635|3891D0450055A86D
support.microsoft.com   TRUE    /   FALSE   978249519   Params
    S=F&HSL=0&FR=0&A=T&SD=GN&PSL=0&SPR=CHS&T=B&DU=C&T1=7d&TSL=0&FSL=
    0&LN=EN%2DUS&SG=&SU
ad1.impulsebuy.net  FALSE   /   FALSE   1072914778  IASIDX
    949250012-1421663-192.168.0.42
www.missingmoney.com    FALSE   /   FALSE   2137622210  CFTOKEN 90066
```

You will notice the sentence, "Do not edit," near the beginning of the file. Editing the file renders it useless. If you are using your cookie file to store passwords and other information having to do with how you use a Web site, you definitely do not want to edit this file. If you do, servers at the Web sites in question will not be able to read the information stored in the cookie file, and will therefore not fill it in for you automatically when you visit the site. If you do edit the file, however, you will still be able to access the site by entering your ID and password manually. As you have probably surmised, cookies.txt contains information about where you've been. Thus, you may wish to disable cookies entirely, lest a snoop at your PC decides to take a look at cookies.txt.

This example is a small portion of the cookies.txt file in my Netscape directory. The actual cookie itself is the line of information that follows each server's URL in the file. (You may note that a server can place more than one cookie in cookies.txt.)

The information following each URL is, for the most part, meaningless except to data-collecting programs on the servers at the Web sites listed (and, as noted earlier, to other servers that can share data placed by the servers in question).

However, the meaning of some of the data, such as user IDs and passwords for some sites, is obvious. Some listings include network addresses for ISPs I used while visiting these sites. Others, you may note, are for servers with which I did not connect directly, but which were contacted by sites I was visiting for data to display in that site's page. (The line for `ad1.impulsebuy.net` is an example of this. It caused an ad to be displayed on a page I was viewing, and recorded information about my visit and the ad displayed to me.)

The remainder of the data is either encoded with strings of letters and numerals that have significance to the sites that placed them there, or refers to elements or settings peculiar to a given site. The `FALSE/TRUE` strings, for instance, may indicate whether the visitor has been there before and has an ID at the site.

Cookies and Your Personal Information

Other applications for cookies are many and varied. Applications that may not be readily apparent involve collecting data *about* Web-site visitors—statistics for marketing or in support of a commercial Web site's advertising rates. This sort of data collection, which includes demographic information as well as information about which ads a visitor saw, what pages they accessed, products they ordered, and other sites they visited, is called *profiling*. It is normally anonymous—but not always, as you will see.

Profiling information consists of what is called non-personally-identifiable information. This can include your ISP address (to pinpoint the area of the country you are in), whether you use a commercial or education or government site to access the Internet (.com, .edu, or .gov, respectively), the type of computer and browser you use, and how you access and use the pages at a site.

As long as you don't mind freely giving information about your habits at a given Web site to the server at that site, you probably won't have any problem with cookies. If, however, you think that storing information about you on your own computer and retrieving that information to use when you visit a Web site more than once is an invasion of your privacy, your appetite for information cookies is probably minimal.

You probably won't care much for the idea of different Web sites trading cookies, either. This does happen. Plus, if you have given your personal information (name, address, telephone number) at one Web site, other sites may be able to share that information—along with information about what you viewed and did at that site. (An example of this is detailed in the sidebar titled "The Case of the Profiling Web Pages" coming up in a page or two.)

If you don't want cookies running rampant on your system for whatever reason, you will want to consider blocking or controlling them. You have several options for determining whose servers can place cookies on your system—or read them. There are do-it-yourself techniques that will block or limit cookies, and there is software that can do the same for you. Read on for details!

The Case of the Profiling Web Pages

The fix was in, and nobody had a clue. For all that Web marketing mavens swore that no one was collecting or sharing personal information about consumers visiting Web sites, thousands of Web surfers had their personal information—and their identities—compromised.

Early in 2000, it was revealed that certain Web sites that required information such as a visitor's real name, address, and telephone number (for purposes that might include ordering from online merchants) were sharing this information with other sites. The purpose? To identify Web surfers when they visited other sites where the personal info was shared.

As the story broke in *USA Today*, a major Web advertising coordinator on the Web called DoubleClick was sharing not only general demographic information about those visiting clients' Web sites, but also more personal info, such as names, home addresses, and telephone numbers.

In the wake of the news of the ad "personalization" (DoubleClick's *sobriquet* for what many considered an invasion of privacy), DoubleClick announced that it would allow those whose identifying personal info was being shared to "opt out" of its system.

This is but one example of how general, non-personal information on the Web is turned into readily identifiable information. How many other sites are doing this? There is no way to know. But there is a way to stop it on your end: Disable cookies—or at least be selective in which cookies you allow your browser to accept.

Do-It-Yourself Cookie Cutting

There are two approaches to stopping or blocking cookies. One is direct, and involves deleting the file `cookies.txt`. The other uses facilities provided by both Netscape and Microsoft Internet Explorer to stop or control cookies.

Kill the File?

One approach to handling cookies is to delete or edit the file named `cookies.txt` that your browser places on your hard drive. I don't recommend this because it is time-consuming, and you will have to delete or change it after every session browsing the Web.

Still, if you want to control cookies this way—or just want to take a look at what is in the file—it's a simple enough proposition. Depending on your PC's setup, the browser you are using, and the browser version, this file could be located in any of several directories; so you will have to find it first.

To find `cookies.txt`, use your system's search capabilities. Click Find on the Start menu, and then click Files or Folders. You will see the Find: All Files dialog box shown in Figure 11.1. (You can also get to this dialog by left-clicking an empty area of the Taskbar and pressing F3.)

Figure 11.1

Use Windows' built-in file finder to find your cookies file.

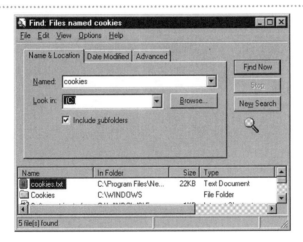

Enter **cookies.txt**, and click Find Now or press Enter to see the location of the `cookies.txt` file or files. You can delete or view the file from this dialog, using the right-click menu.

Blocking Cookie Access with Browser Settings

As explained and illustrated in Chapter 9, you can block cookies from your hard drive entirely, using settings provided by Netscape or MSIE. Here are the basics:

✔ With Netscape, select Edit ➢ Preferences ➢ Advanced; then click the radio button labeled Disable Cookies. (Refer to Figure 11.2.)

✔ With MSIE 4, select View ➤ Internet Options and press the Advanced tab. Use the radio buttons for Cookies.

✔ With MSIE 5, select Tools ➤ Internet Options ➤ Security, and then press the Custom Level button. (Refer to Figure 11.3.)

Controlling Cookies with Browser Settings

In addition to simply blocking cookies, you can use your browser settings to set varying levels of cookie control.

To do this with Netscape, select Edit ➤ Preferences ➤ Advanced. The Preferences dialog box (Figure 11.2) will be displayed.

Figure 11.2

Netscape's Preferences dialog

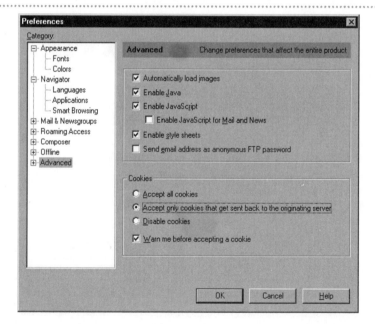

As you can see, in addition to blocking cookies, this dialog allows you to:

✔ Accept all cookies.

✔ Accept only cookies that get sent back to the originating server, which prevents information about your visit at one Web site from being immediately sent to a different Web site.

✔ Disable cookies (as described above).

✔ Warn me before accepting a cookie, which lets you choose if a cookie is to be written to your hard drive, whether you have set Accept all cookies, or Accept only cookies that get sent back to the originating server.

To access MSIE version 5's cookie settings, select Tools ➤ Internet Options ➤ Security; then press the Custom Level button to display the Security Settings dialog shown in Figure 11.3.

Figure 11.3

Cookie controls provided by MSIE

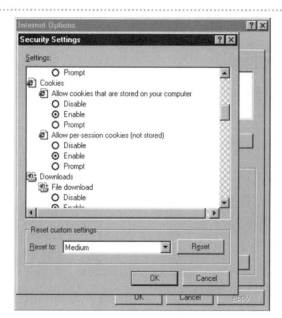

Scroll down in the dialog to the Cookies section. Here, you have the options of blocking, allowing all, or being prompted for cookies that are sent to your system at random intervals, and/or those cookies that are sent only the first time you go to a Web site.

Cookie Control Programs

Another option available for controlling cookies is to use a program designed for that purpose. There are a number available, including some good shareware programs. I'll highlight two in this section.

Cookie Crusher (included on the accompanying CD) is a shareware program that blocks or manages cookies, as you wish, in real time. If you wish, it allows you to look at each cookie that is sent to your system and decide if you will allow it to be written to your file. Figure 11.4 shows Cookie Crusher in action.

Another useful shareware program in this arena is Window Washer (also included on the accompanying CD). Window Washer does a total system cleanup of useless files, but can focus on Netscape or MSIE debris.

Figure 11.4

Cookie crusher, a cookie-management program

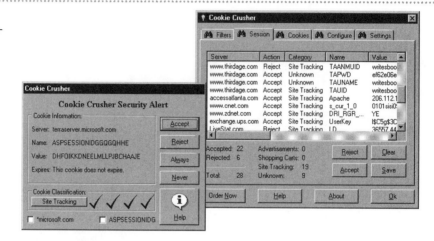

Of interest here is the fact that Window Washer allows you to specify the cookies you want to keep, as illustrated in Figure 11.5.

Figure 11.5

Window Washer cleans files of all sorts and provides useful options for Internet file cleaning.

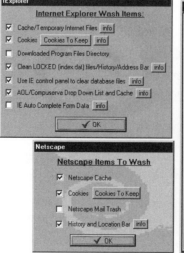
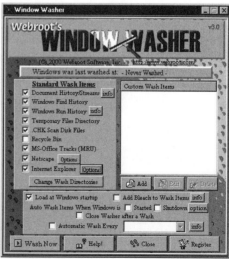

There is yet another way to avoid getting cookies on your system. As discussed in the following section, using a *proxy server* can prevent cookies being written to your system *and* provide additional benefits.

Surf Anonymously with a Proxy Server

Have you ever wanted to visit a Web site but wondered whether it might be recording your visit and any information it can gather about you? Perhaps you didn't want it known where you came from (as in the case of Web surfing from a company computer, and visiting a competitor's site). Or, maybe you are investigating a health problem and do not want anyone to know—least of all an insurance company whose researchers have access to the sites you visit in conjunction with your research.

Then, too, there is the potential that someone is tracking you *personally*, as in the case of the advertising operation discussed in the sidebar titled "The Case of the Profiling Web Pages." Or, what if you were visiting an Archdiocesan Web site and didn't want Father Mike, the Webmaster, to know that you had been visiting a "questionable" Web site?

Those and similar reasons aside, maybe you just don't like the idea of contributing to someone's marketing demographics. No matter what your reason(s) for wanting to be anonymous when visiting Web sites, you may wish to investigate using a *proxy server* when you surf the Web.

A proxy server is an agent or surrogate that shields you from being identified by the Web sites you visit. In conventional Web surfing, your system exchanges data with the Web site host, and the Web pages you request are transmitted to you. On the surface, the only data you appear to be sending is the URL you type in. Wrong! The remote system is often collecting all sorts of information from your computer, including—but not limited to—your ISP name, e-mail address, and the URL you visited previously.

To get an idea of what can be learned about you when you visit a Web site, visit this page: `http://privacy.net/anonymizer/`. Figure 11.6 shows a bit of what was revealed when I went to that URL.

This is only a portion of the information obtained. As you can see, all sorts of information about my PC is readily available to the Web site. So is a list of all the browser plug-ins (helper programs) I have. And more—including details of my ISP's exact location, who owns the network, the Web page I visited before I went to this URL, whether I have certain software active, and what sorts of files my system and browser will accept.

If you use a proxy server, none of this information gets through to the Web sites you visit. Nor are cookies written to your hard drive by any of the sites you visit.

Figure 11.6

Part of the information a Web site gets on every visitor

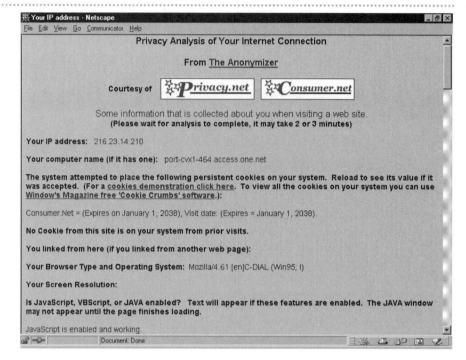

How Does a Proxy Server Work?

A proxy server stands between you and Web site hosts. Rather than your browser requesting pages from a server, the proxy server does it for you, then relays the pages to you. Every site you visit thinks it is being visited by the proxy server computer. *None* of your personal data is collected by the Web sites you visit. There is no way anyone can know even what part of the world you're in.

Many corporate Web servers use proxy servers to isolate themselves from other networks. The relationship of a proxy server to a corporate Web server in this application is similar to that of a proxy server to your Web browser. The proxy retrieves desired pages from the Web, then passes them on to the corporate server, without ever coming into contact with the servers from which pages are retrieved. Corporate Web servers usually filter or block access to certain types of Web sites, of course. Specific proxy servers are discussed in the following sections.

The Anonymizer: A Simple Proxy Server

One of the more popular of public-access, Web-based proxy servers in existence (and by far the easiest to use) is The Anonymizer (http://www.anonymizer.com/). Shown in Figure 11.7, The Anonymizer has a simple front end; go to the URL above, enter the URL you want to visit, and you're on your way—anonymously.

Figure 11.7

The Anonymizer, a proxy server

The Anonymizer also provides an extensive listing of links you can jump to anonymously. In addition to allowing you to surf Web pages anonymously, it can also be used to access FTP sites anonymously.

Once you enter the URL of a page, you will see the page you requested as hosted by The Anonymizer. Figure 11.8 shows how this looks, complete with a banner ad carried by The Anonymizer.

The Anonymizer is a commercial service, but you can use it for free. You will, however, have to wait approximately 30 seconds for each requested page to load, and you will see advertisements as well.

Figure 11.8

A Web page as viewed through the Anonymizer proxy server

Other Public Proxy Servers

You can find other commercial and free proxy servers at these URLs:

ByProxy: `http://www.besiex.org/ByProxy/index.html`

MagnusNet: `http://www.magusnet.com/proxy.html`

Proxymate: `http://1pwa.com:8000/`

Wiping Out Your Online Trail with Software Helpers

In addition to cookies, your bookmarks and temporary Internet files can give you away. This section discusses how to protect yourself in those areas.

Stop Giving Yourself Away with Your Bookmarks

If you've been on the Web more than a couple of times, you have probably accumulated a goodly number of bookmarks. These are stored in a `bookmarks.htm` file by Netscape and in a Favorites list by MSIE.

You can refrain from collecting bookmarks or just copy them into a file—which, of course, adds the risk of coming under snooper scrutiny. You can also write them down. Taking any of those routes, however, deprives you of the convenience of being able to click on a URL in a list and go there instantly.

Private Bookmarks

There is an alternative. You can use a clever program called Private Bookmarks, which is included on the accompanying CD. Private Bookmarks encrypts your bookmarks or favorites list so that no one but you can see the titles or URLs of Web pages they list. Figure 11.9 shows the program's front end.

Figure 11.9

Private Bookmarks encrypts, hides, and organizes your bookmark or favorites lists.

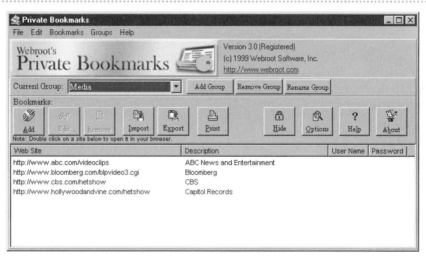

As the controls imply, Private Bookmarks performs a number of useful functions. The primary functions are encrypting and hiding bookmark and favorites lists. Private Bookmarks also imports and exports lists, and lets you organize them into groups and print hard copies. Adding and removing URLs is simple.

This shareware program works with Netscape, MSIE, and AOL running with any version of Windows.

Get Rid of Telltale Files

One of the most difficult things to do in securing your PC is to get rid of all of the bits Internet flotsam and jetsam left on your system every time you log on. These bits include entire Web pages, graphics, URLs, temporary files, Java and ActiveX programs, fragments of incoming and outgoing e-mail messages, cookies, and more.

You learned quite a lot about the tracks that Web browsing and e-mailing leave on your system in Chapter 9. But there's still more—and some of it is difficult to find.

Fortunately, it's not difficult to get rid of—with the appropriate software. There are programs that can clean out the Internet junk for you. Most can also clear out other junk, such as those .TMP files discussed back in Chapter 6.

Norton CleanSweep and Quarterdeck's Remove-It, also discussed in Chapter 6, are two products in this category. Another is Window Washer, mentioned earlier in this chapter.

Window Washer lets you specify what sorts of files should be kept before you let it clean your disk. Window Washer also offers the option of rewriting over deleted file space multiple times to prevent an unerase program from recovering the files you've deleted—a feature offered by Norton CleanSweep, as well.

Two Specialized Internet Safety Helpers

Safety while you're on the Internet is of course a vital concern. Two programs that help in this area are McAfee's Guard Dog and Norton Internet Security 2000. Both guard against virus and Trojan horse programs that might come in with Java applets or ActiveX controls.

These programs can also block or control browser cookies. Norton Internet Security 2000 goes a step further in guarding against threats in IRC chats and blocking ads, as well as setting up parental controls to limit children's Web access.

Both programs are discussed in more detail in Chapter 6.

A Few Words on Internet Monitoring Programs

When you think of Internet blocking and monitoring software, you probably think of protecting children from some of the Web's more lascivious content and logging what they are doing online.

This is not the only application for such programs. Many can be used to record what goes on in your PC offline as well as online. In effect, they are "bugs," which can tell someone everything you do—even what security measures you take! They even show passwords that you enter, online or off.

All of this can be done with or without your knowledge. One such program—a version of which is marketed to businesses that have employees on PCs—is Cyber Patrol (`http://www.microsys.com/business/`). In addition to being able to log Internet activity, it also has a facility for logging offline activity. Another is 007 Stealth Activity Monitor (SAM), which is designed to log anything and everything on your PC (and is included on the accompanying CD). Both of these are covered in Chapter 12, but you should be aware that such programs can also be installed without your knowing it.

How is that? Well, your work PC can be accessed by others, of course, and there is no way you can block such an installation. As for your home PC, someone can bypass the password protection by using a floppy disk with DOS system files to boot your computer. (This includes power-on passwords, detailed in Chapter 3.)

To prevent anyone bypassing a power-on password on your system, you must disable booting from floppy disk (normally drive A). First, access your system's settings at boot-up. You can usually do this by pressing F1 or another designated key as your system is starting up. (You will see a message telling you which key to press when you first turn your computer on.) From there, look for a setting such as Boot Options and follow the prompts until you find an enable/disable setting for Boot From Floppy, Check Drive A, or something similar.

How Do I Know If I'm Bugged?

No matter what the circumstances of installation, Internet monitoring programs can be hidden from view. Certainly, almost all are designed to run in the background, invisible to the user.

You may be able to see a snoop program on your Start ➤ Programs menu. Then again, you may not. Some monitoring programs are designed so they don't show up on the Programs menu. Neither do they create desktop shortcuts when installed.

The lack of obvious evidence of a monitoring system on your PC means you have to go looking. (Note that this refers primarily to non-networked PCs. If you use a networked PC, the odds are slim that any snoop software will be put on your local drive.)

Looking for a hidden program involves mostly reversing some of the things you've already learned to do in hiding programs and other files. The first place to look is on the Start menu's Documents list (Start ➤ Documents). You may find that a snoop has been viewing a file that logs what you've been doing.

Next, start Windows Explorer—and be sure to enable it to view hidden files. Then, look in these folders for new program files or folders:

✔ The main or root directories of your hard drives (normally, C:\ and D:\)

✔ Program Files

✔ Windows

✔ Windows/System

You should also look in the Recycle Bin for evidence of snooping, such as deleted log files.

If an archiving program, such as Aladdin Expander, PKZIP, or WinZip, is on your system, start it, and take a look at its File menu. You may find that the snoop had to unzip a program's files to install it and, even though they deleted the original .ZIP file, they left tracks on your archiving program's File menu.

A program installation may also leave tracks in your system's AUTOEXEC.BAT and CONFIG.SYS files. You don't necessarily have to examine the files' content, much or all of which may be meaningless. Instead, check their properties with Windows Explorer. (Go to drive C's main directory; then right-click the file in question.) If the date is very recent, it may be that someone has modified the settings with a program installation. The file WIN.INI, located in your \WINDOWS directory, should also be checked.

If you do find that you have been bugged, you can try uninstalling the monitoring program. If this turns out to require a password, you can simply delete some of the program files from Windows Explorer. This should render the program inoperable. Be certain that you have the correct program files, of course! It's simplest if the program has its own directory.

Failing any of the above, you can confront the suspected perpetrator. At that point, you're on your own, however.

The Case of the Hacking Ex-Husband

I recently heard about the case of a woman who had been divorced for several months, but whose ex-husband continued following her activities closely. Just how closely she had no idea, until he telephoned one day to tell her in detail what she had said in a rather risqué online chat—and who had e-mailed photos of themselves to her.

She contacted the local police department, who, in turn, contacted me. I spent a couple of hours with her PC, eventually locating a stealth program (not one of those mentioned here) that was grabbing specific types of files and e-mailing them to the ex-husband.

As it turned out, he had installed the program before their divorce and activated it during a visit. It wasn't impossible to find—even though it had deleted itself after e-mailing a number of stolen files.

There are two lessons here. The first is that you really need to keep an eye on who gets their hands on your PC. The second is that sometimes it may not be safe to store on your PC anything that may be compromising.

I hope that you are now fully prepared to keep your sensitive files and activities safe, both online and off. Still, it won't hurt for you to get acquainted with a few of the tools available to the dedicated snoop. Whether you feel your privacy is at risk at home or at work, you need get an idea of the weapons available to the other side in the war on privacy—which you will do when you read Chapter 12.

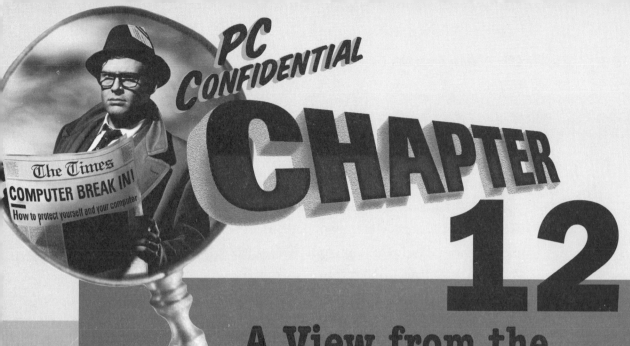

PC CONFIDENTIAL

CHAPTER 12

A View from the Other Side

- ✔ Password crackers
- ✔ A solution for e-mail insecurity
- ✔ Stealth logging programs
- ✔ High-tech spying with TEMPEST
- ✔ Hacking and other things out of your control

The Times
COMPUTER BREAK IN!
How to protect yourself and your computer

In this chapter, we'll focus on the *other* side of PC security: the tricks and software tools that might be used to invade your privacy. We'll also examine a few of the software tools used for more nefarious purposes, and see how to protect yourself against those invasions.

Passwords are the foundation of good PC security. The chapter opens, therefore, with useful information on password cracking and how to thwart it. Then, it's on to logging and other stealth programs (the dangers of which were illustrated in Chapter 11). E-mail security and insecurity are next up, with a focus on Web-based e-mail services.

From there we move into the more esoteric realms of TEMPEST surveillance and hacking.

Password Security and Insecurity

Password protection is vital. We use passwords with our PCs, to log on to ISPs or online services, to log on to a PC as a user, and so forth.

With passwords being so vital, it is no surprise that programs have been developed to crack password protection. Depending on your goal, this type of software can be used for security or for snooping purposes.

Obviously, a snoop would like to know your passwords. It would make following your trail a snap. Just as obviously, you don't want your passwords to be found out—but they may be, under various circumstances or with the help of certain tools.

The bottom line is this: Anyone can get your passwords. All that's required is access to your computer and/or your online accounts, persistence, patience, time, and the right knowledge or tools.

Given this possibility, it is important that you not only guard your passwords by not writing them down or sharing them, but also that you make it as difficult as possible for someone to guess your passwords

With that in mind, let's take a look at how someone who wants your password might go after it.

Human Password Hacking

I've mentioned this before, but it bears repeating: Do not create passwords based on something of a personal nature. Passwords based on the names, birthdates, or other personal information of your relatives, significant other, pets, lover, children, and the like are too easily guessed by anyone who knows you even a little.

Likewise, passwords based on your personal interests, or perhaps the names of sports teams or writers or actors can be guessed. They may be easy for you to remember—but they will be almost as easy for someone to guess.

On numerous occasions, and much to their horror, I have shown friends how easy it is to guess their passwords. You have a dog named Sophie? How about **sophie1** as your password… or **sophierun**… or **sophiedog**? Your child's birthday is March 17, 1997? How about **970317** as your password?

You get the idea: Given a little knowledge, anyone can extrapolate several possible passwords. One of them (or a variation thereof) is likely to be the password you are using. Thus, the password you ought to be using should have nothing to do with anything related to you.

This sort of password may not be easy to remember. However, you will find that after three or four uses, the password will be lodged in your memory.

You should also change your password regularly—at least every four to six weeks. This way, if someone does get your password, it won't be of use for long.

Never keep the password you are assigned by an ISP, online service, or Web page. Often such passwords are based on your name or the date you signed up, and thus may be easy to figure out by someone else using the same online system.

The longer a password is, the better. Long passwords are more difficult to guess than short ones. Mixing letters and numerals is a good idea, too. Plus, if your system recognizes upper- and lowercase letters, use them.

Software Password Hacking

As you might imagine, programmers have been developing software to break passwords for some time—and it's not always to break into someone's system. There are situations in which a user may forget a password and need to break their own password.

For example, Windows allows you to store frequently used passwords, like the password for your dial-up Internet connection or your Outlook Express mail. If you store your passwords, you may forget them after a time. What if you need to use the password with another program or on another computer?

There are programs that will show you the password behind that row of asterisks. (The row of asterisks being the "stars" that appear in place of the characters you type in for your password.) One such program is 007 Password Recovery, shown in Figure 12.1.

Figure 12.1
007 Password Recovery will show you what's behind that row of asterisks in a Windows Password field.

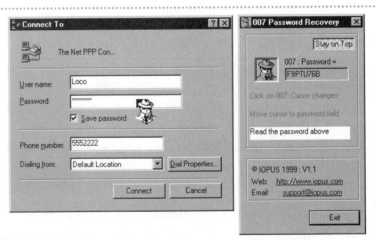

This program, which you can find on the accompanying CD to this book, displays the password behind the asterisks. All you have to do is start the program, click and hold on the image of the spy, and drag the altered cursor to the password field.

007 Password Recovery works well with most password screens you will encounter in Windows, including Web site password screens. But it will not work with applications

that do not store the password "behind" the asterisks, such as the Windows NT User Manager.

There are other, more powerful password hacking programs that can be used to break into PC system passwords, application and file passwords, and online passwords. Your best defense against these is to not let anyone use your PC; this way, no one can install and use such programs.

A Solution for E-Mail Insecurity

As established in Chapter 10, e-mail can leave tracks on your system. If you are really concerned about e-mail privacy, you may wish to take your mail operations completely off your system. This can be done either by signing up for an online service or using Web-based e-mail.

Online services are discreet entities, separate from, yet connected to, the Internet, as discussed in Chapter 9, and actually predate the Internet. Online services are hosted on mainframe or mini-computers, and offer a number of "value-added" services you can't get from your ISP or the Web. Among these services are powerful specialized e-mail systems, chat rooms with features you won't find on the Web (like sound), forums hosted by nationally known companies or individuals, shopping capabilities, specialized databases that cannot be accessed from the Web, and more.

Online services cost about the same per month as ISP access (though most offer some premium services for which there is an extra charge), and still provide access to Internet e-mail, the Web, and Usenet Newsgroups through their front-end programs or your own browser.

For more information on online services, visit the following Web sites:

✔ AOL: `http://www.aol.com`

✔ CompuServe: `http://www.compuserve.com`

✔ DELPHI: `http://www.delphi.com`

✔ Prodigy: `http://www.prodigy.com`

These online services normally require special software on your PC, but the software is free. (CompuServe and DELPHI can be accessed with any terminal program, such as Windows Terminal or HyperTerminal, or programs like ProComm.) You can access them directly via dial-up numbers worldwide, or over an Internet connection (using the aforementioned special software or terminal programs).

Web-based e-mail services, detailed in Chapter 10, provide e-mail access from any PC. All you need to get your e-mail is access to the Web.

It is worth noting that online services are very reliable, while Web-based e-mail services can encounter overloads or periods of outage. Still, Web-based e-mail services are *free*. And some provide free ISP service.

Either way you go, you can keep your e-mail online and avoid risking e-mail tracks on your PC. You will have to clean up your system from time to time, though. This is best done with one of the cleanup programs discussed in Chapter 11, although you can take care of much of the housekeeping yourself, per my advice in Chapter 9. If you use an online service, you should not download e-mail or attached files, nor should you write new or reply messages offline. (The download prohibition holds for Web-based e-mail services, too.)

Stealth Logging Programs

As you saw in Chapter 11, anyone can bug your computer without your knowledge, using a stealth program. This kind of program records and stores information about how a computer is used for later access. Information recorded and stored may include:

- ✔ The date and time that a user logged on and off a PC (if multiple users are enabled)
- ✔ When programs were started and closed
- ✔ When files were accessed
- ✔ When files were modified and saved
- ✔ URLs visited on the Web
- ✔ Files downloaded
- ✔ Files deleted
- ✔ Passwords entered, on the computer and on the Web
- ✔ Every command keystroke you make

The data may be stored on your system in a hidden folder or file, or e-mailed to someone without your knowledge.

One such program is 007 Stealth Activity Monitor (SAM). SAM is designed to monitor everything someone does on a PC. As shown in Figure 12.2, SAM will log exact keystrokes, the paths (folders) of programs, and more. It can even show when hidden programs were accessed.

Figure 12.2

Some 007 Stealth Activity
Monitor settings

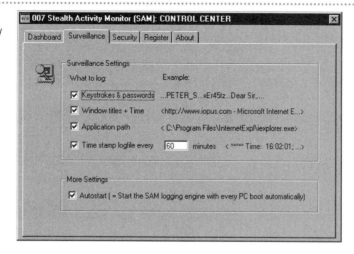

Figure 12.3 shows a sample SAM log file. As you can see, the file lists what program was run when, Web site visits, passwords used online and offline, and switches between application windows.

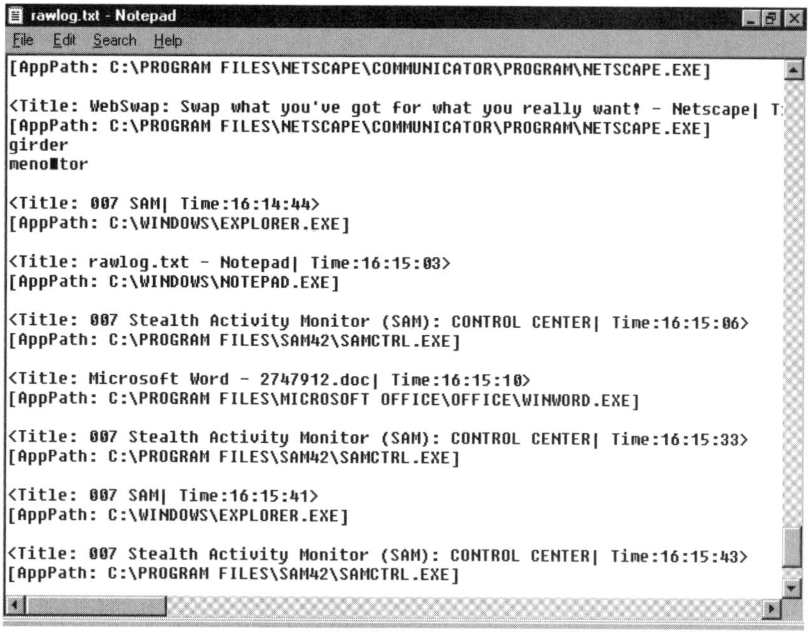

Figure 12.3

SAM log file

SAM has a more advanced cousin, also included on the enclosed CD, that will secretly e-mail reports to a specified address. This program, called STARR (for Stealth Activity Recorder & Reporter), is a bit more detailed in its collection of user data.

Another program of this type is WinGuardian. Billed as a user monitoring utility, it is comprehensive in its surveillance. You can see a log of activities, keystrokes, and even screen shots, as illustrated in Figure 12.4.

Figure 12.4

WinGuardian activity reports

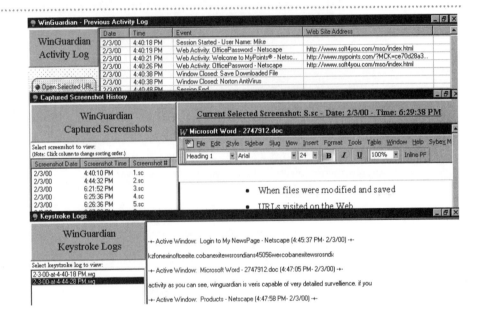

WinGuardian is also capable of compiling separate exported reports on various types of activities.

What If I *Am* Bugged?

If you can, imagine that one of these programs has been installed on your system. What can you do?

First, look to see if there are any new programs on your Start menu or Taskbar. Check for Desktop shortcuts as well. If you are proficient in the use of Windows Explorer, spend some time looking in your \Program Files directory for program folders you don't recognize. Remember that you can see the date a program was installed by checking the date of creation on the folder's Properties dialog. (To do this, right-click the filename, then click Properties on the menu displayed.)

If you find a suspicious folder, open it and double-click any `readme.txt` or similar files to read what the program is about. Or, you can run any .EXE file in the folder.

If the program still puzzles you, delete the folder from Windows Explorer. *But do not empty it from the Recycle Bin*; you may later realize that it is something you need but did not recognize.

At the same time, think hard about who may have had access to your computer.

If you are on a networked system at your office, you will have to assume that the system administrator can log everything you do (which is true). But it may still pay to search for unwanted programs.

Prevention Is Still the Best Cure

In order for you to be bugged, someone would have access to your PC to install, set up, and use the bugging program. This could happen through hands-on access, or, in a rare instance, via an e-mail attachment that contains a Trojan horse program.

If you cannot control who has physical access to your PC, either place password protection on the system (see Chapter 3) or physically disable your PC (see Chapter 2) when you are away.

You can avoid e-mail attachments and Trojan horse programs by not downloading and running programs attached to e-mail messages. Trojan horse programs can also come from programs on disk, so you need to take care with programs given to you by someone else.

High-Tech Spying with TEMPEST

You may have heard of a technique TEMPEST. TEMPEST allows electronic eavesdropping on your PC. With TEMPEST, someone can see what is on your computer monitor from a distance, without tapping a phone line.

TEMPEST is possible because all electrical and electronic devices emit some electromagnetic radiation, pretty much the same as radio transmitters. Depending on their strength and nature, such emissions can travel great distances, although they grow weaker with distance.

Tuned to the appropriate frequency, it is possible for specialized equipment to receive electromagnetic emissions from a PC monitor. It is also possible to use those emissions to recreate what is on the monitor that emitted them. Figure 12.5 is a simplified illustration of how this takes place.

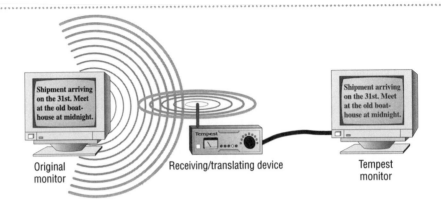

Figure 12.5
TEMPEST monitoring

The only way to prevent someone spying on you with TEMPEST is to shield your monitor with what is called a *Faraday cage*. This is a system of steel wires and/or rods that absorbs a monitor's radiation.

While you will probably never have to deal with TEMPEST surveillance, you should know that it is possible. On the other hand, it may come to pass that, within a few years, the specialized equipment required to receive and interpret PC monitor emissions will become relatively commonplace. If that comes to pass, let us hope that the shielding devices are equally commonplace.

Hacking and Other Things Out of Your Control

No matter what precautions you take, there are some elements of snooping that are probably out of your control. These include various kinds of hacking and things like packet-sniffing (as discussed in Chapter 11).

Mostly, hacking is related to online activities. Hackers may try to detect or guess your password to your ISP, online service, or to a Web page. There isn't a lot you can do about this beyond using a cryptic password and changing your password regularly.

You can best protect yourself from Trojan horse programs as already discussed:

✔ Do not download and run programs attached to e-mail.

✔ Check out any program you are given on disk carefully.

✔ Be sure of your source when downloading programs from the Internet.

✔ Use Norton Anti-Virus or McAfee VirusScan software to monitor all e-mail and downloads.

If you have sensitive data to store or send via e-mail or on a disk, encrypt it. Make certain any recipient of such data understands the encryption used, possesses the necessary password or key, and also understands the sensitive nature of the data.

Beyond all this, I caution you to keep up with what's new in viruses, hacking, employee monitoring, and other threats. These Web sites can keep you informed about online and offline issues:

✔ Anonymity on the Internet: `http://www.dis.org/erehwon/anonymity.html`

✔ CyberTimes (New York Times technology news online): `http://www.cybertimes.net/yr/mo/day/tech/indexcyber.html`

✔ Cypherpunks: `ftp://ftp.csua.berkeley.edu/pub/cypherpunks/Home.html`

✔ Electronic Privacy Information Center (EPIC): `http://www.epic.org/`

✔ The Privacy Page: `http://www.privacy.org`

Now it's time to take a look at some things you *can* control by way of reviewing and expanding on what's gone before. Chapter 13 will show you some additional ways to apply what you have learned and introduce a few more tools and tricks for protecting your privacy.

PC CONFIDENTIAL

CHAPTER 13

Reviews, Recourses, and Resources

- ✔ **When someone gets your password(s)**
- ✔ **Getting a new computer?**
- ✔ **Fooling the Web**
- ✔ **When breaking up is hard to do**
- ✔ **More privacy tools**
- ✔ **Electronic privacy resources**

This chapter is in part a review, and in part a fresh look at useful information and applications. Here, you can examine your options if someone gets or guesses your password and look at some things you need to do when you get a new PC.

You'll also revisit the Web, and I'll show you how to use some things you've learned (and some things you haven't yet learned) to fool all those Web sites that are aching to get personal information from you. In a related vein, I'll also show you how to keep your information out of online directories—and how to get it off the Web if it's already there. We'll wind up with a look at privacy resources, online and off.

Someone Got Your Password(s)?

What if someone guesses or finds your password? As noted in earlier chapters, this could be disastrous, because your password gives people access to anything you do or *might* do online. That's a lot of territory!

Password Recovery

The first indication you may have that someone has your password is that your password doesn't work—in which case the culprit may have changed it. In this case you will have to find out what that new password is before you can access your own computer. To do so, you may be able to use a password cracking/retrieval program like 007 Password Recovery (included on the accompanying CD).

Online Password Recovery

If this doesn't work or is impractical, you may find it necessary to get outside help to undo the passwords. If ISP, online service, or Web site passwords are involved, contact the customer service people immediately, explain what has happened, and ask for a new password or account. These entities can set new passwords for your account.

File and Program Password Recovery

If another kind of password is involved, you need to log in to whatever program or file is involved, and change the password. If you can't get into the program or file, there are a couple of options. One is to try to outguess whomever stole your password. If you have a suspect or suspects in mind, you can try whatever sorts of words you think they might use for a password.

If that doesn't work, you can then try opening the file with an application other than the one used to create it and attempt to copy out the contents. Your most likely choices are Notepad or the DOS EDIT program. (See Chapter 6 for more information on EDIT and how to use it.) You will more likely than not have to wade through quite a bit of useless binary data to get at the "literal" data you want.

Password Recovery Programs   Your next option is to go for a password-recovery program (also known as password crackers). There are a number of specialized shareware programs available for specialized password cracking. Among these are programs that recover or go around passwords for .ZIP or other archives, as well as files created by Lotus, Word, Outlook, MS Money, Excel, and other applications.

Several such programs are available from Elcomsoft, at `http://www.elcomsoft.com`. You can also search out addition shareware of this type by visiting Download.com and Shareware.com (at `http://www.download.com` and `http://www.shareware.com`, respectively), and searching with the keywords **password recovery** and **password crack**.

Your Final Option for Files   If the password for a program or file has been changed and you cannot guess it or crack it, I suggest deleting the file so that it cannot be accessed by the culprit again. Do this from Windows Explorer or DOS.

Windows or System Passwords

As noted elsewhere, you can get around a Windows or system password by booting from a system disk. (A system disk is a floppy disk that has been prepared with DOS system and startup files on it.)

Power-On Passwords

If someone has changed your power-on password (see Chapter 3), you will have to try to guess the password or find an expert who can remove the password for you.

At Work

If your password is compromised at work, there should be a plan of action in place. If there is no such plan of action, follow these steps:

✔ Change your password (if you can).

✔ Contact the system administrator.

✔ Search for new, altered, or missing files on your system.

You might also want to send a note to everyone on the network that your password was compromised, and to please disregard any out-of-character e-mail from you.

At Home

If your password is compromised at home, change it immediately (again, if you can). Next:

✔ Check for new, altered, or missing files.

✔ Change all the passwords on your system, and online.

✔ Send e-mail to everyone you know explaining the situation and asking them to ignore any weird e-mail from you.

If necessary, set up a reminder program to remind you to change your password every 30 days.

Prevention Is Still the Best Cure

With any luck, you won't have to worry with any of the preceding because you will have been changing your password on a regular basis.

Getting a New Computer?

Sooner or later you will replace your PC—or it may be replaced for you. This may happen because of a change in your workplace, or because you have to swap out a PC or hard drive of your own that is under warranty. Or, perhaps you will simply want to upgrade to the latest and fastest system for your home or home office.

No matter what the reason, there are certain considerations involved in maintaining your privacy when you get a new PC. These have to do not with your new PC, but with your old one.

Unless you sell or give your old computer to a specific person (and perhaps not even then), you will have no idea where it's going or who will be using it. Donate the PC to an organization or watch your old office computer being taken off to auction—it doesn't matter either way. Anything you leave on your hard drive is going with it.

Since you don't know who will have their hands on your old PC after it's gone, it's best to assume that someone who can dig up old and deleted files will be using it. Always take appropriate steps to minimize the chance of information getting into the wrong hands, as described over the next few pages.

Take What's Yours

The first thing you'll want to do is copy your personal files—documents, images, data files, and programs—onto whatever media is appropriate. (Remember: You can copy entire folders if you wish.) Or, you might e-mail the files to another e-mail address.

To speed up the copying process, use the Move selection in Windows Explorer to get your files onto floppies or other removable disks. This deletes files after it copies them. Accessing the Move selection requires that you right-click the file name(s), then drag them to the destination disk/folder. Once you've done this, release the right mouse button. A menu will appear offering several choices, among them Move Here. If your e-mail program is set to save copies of outgoing messages, remember that it also saves attachments. Either disable the feature that saves outgoing messages or be sure to delete copies of outgoing messages.

Clean It Up

Once you have copied all the files and folders you want, delete them (if you haven't used the Move option.)

Also, run a program that cleans out useless files, such as McAfee Uninstaller (included with McAfee Office 2000) or Norton CleanSweep 2000. This will delete files not needed by the PC and its applications—while the same time getting rid of Internet and temporary files that have information about you and your activities.

Once you've deleted useless files and those you've copied, there's one more step you must take: Wipe the deleted disk space completely using one of the commercial tools designed for that purpose. Either Norton Wipeinfo (which comes with Norton Utilities 2000) or McAfee Office 2000. This ensures that no one will be able to retrieve your deleted files.

Passwords, Anyone?

If you have any system passwords set, change them to something you won't use again elsewhere. You should do this because your password file may be retained by Windows and can be accessed with the proper software tool. This way, you won't be leaving behind clues to passwords you might have active elsewhere.

Fooling the Web

In Chapters 9 and 11, you saw how easy it can be for information about you to get out on the Web. I advised you then about keeping your name and personal information off the Web by not interacting with Web sites or filling out online profiles, and so forth.

More and more online advertisers, stores, and other entities, however, are making it attractive to interact on the Web with online sweepstakes, discounts, points systems, and other incentives. Of course it remains true that if do want to sign up for things, take surveys, enter contests, and/or shop online, you are going to have to provide personal information.

You can use a variety of techniques to buffer your contact with the Web and minimize the personal information you do provide. You can employ proxy servers (discussed in Chapter 11) and you can provide false information (perhaps 555-1212 for your telephone number and similarly generic responses for other information requested).

You can also create throwaway e-mail addresses at Web e-mail sites (discussed in Chapter 9) so that no strangers can access your regular e-mail address.

If you post in Usenet Newsgroups or on any kind of public bulletin board online, remember that the walls have ears—and memories! Anything you post can be copied, stored, and shared and may be placed in a publicly accessible online database, as is the case with Usenet postings (see `http://www.dejanews.com`). Thus, it is probably a good idea to use a throwaway e-mail address to post in public. (This also goes for Listservs and other mailing lists in which your comments may be passed on.)

Whatever kind of e-mail address you use, remember to take your full name out of the From and Reply-To headers. This way, no one can identify you as you from the source of your mail or postings, unless of course they know you well.

When you sign up for a throwaway e-mail address, do not give your real name. And remember to exclude your name and address from the e-mail service's directory!

Beyond this, there is a relatively new kind of service on the Web that holds your non-personal demographic information in trust and shares it with other partner Web sites. The bottom line is that you are requested to answer online questionnaires less frequently, and you get more customized Web content.

How you feel about this is your business. But if you want to check out one such site, visit the nCognito Web site at `http://www.ncognito.com`.

A Few Notes on Web E-Mail Directories

Web e-mail directories are useful tools if you need to find someone's e-mail address or want yours to be found. If you don't want your e-mail address to be found, e-mail directories can be a nuisance. People you don't want to hear from can contact you, as can spammers.

Keeping Your Name Out of E-Mail Directories

To keep your name and e-mail address out of Web e-mail directories, take these steps:

✔ Use a throwaway e-mail address with your name removed from the headers when you make public or mailing list postings.

✔ Use a made-up e-mail address—or your throwaway address—when you sign up for Web sites. The throwaway address is probably going to be necessary to sign up at many Web sites that will require you to reply with a confirmation message from the e-mail address you provide.

✔ Do not give your real name when you sign up for Web sites.

Getting Your Name Out of E-Mail Directories

Are your e-mail address and name already in an online e-mail directory? They may well
be. Most new Internet users are unaware of how many places their names and addresses
can be harvested and end up posting in public or giving out their names and addresses in
other ways.

You can give up the e-mail address(es) listed in directories, but you don't have to
do this. Most of the time, all you need to do is ask that your name be removed from a
directory.

To have your name removed, go to each e-mail directory and either select a link that
lets you request removal or write to the Customer Service, Webmaster, or other address
listed as a contact for the site. *You may have to request removal two or even three times*, but
you can get removed.

Here's a list of Web e-mail directories. You may find it useful to visit each to check
whether you are listed:

AnyWho:	`http://www.anywho.com`
Bigfoot:	`http://www.bigfoot.com`
Internet Address Finder:	`http://www.iaf.net`
Infospace:	`http://www.infospace.com`
Switchboard:	`http://www.switchboard.com`
Lycos Who Where:	`http://www.whowhere.com`
World E-Mail Directory:	`http://www.worldemail.com`
Yahoo's People Finder:	`http://www.four11.com`

When Breaking Up Is Hard to Do

You may recall "The Case of the Hacking Ex-Husband" in Chapter 11. This sort of thing
happens all too frequently when a relationship goes bad. Unfortunately, there is little you
can do to change someone's thoughts or emotions, but you can plan to protect yourself
with any or all of the following actions before and after the relationship ends:

✔ Guard access to your PC. Use the techniques discussed in Chapters 2, 3, and 4
to keep others from using your PC when you are away from it.

✔ If you share a PC, insist on different user profiles, with passwords.

✔ Protect your files and applications with passwords and encryption.

✔ Consider using a password-protected (and invisible) logging program to keep track of what others do with your PC (discussed in Chapter 12).

If someone with whom you have shared a PC does end your relationship, one of you is going to end up with the PC. If you give up the PC, take care to remove all of your personal files and run a cleanup program to get rid of unused files that may have information about you, as described earlier in this chapter. Remember to use a utility to wipe the deleted data space, too.

If you are keeping the PC, check it carefully for stealth programs (discussed in Chapter 12). Also check for viruses. If the PC is very old, consider replacing it as the least-complicated option.

More Privacy Tools

As concern about PC and online privacy grows, so do the tools for testing and reinforcing PC privacy. This section discusses several of interest.

Anonymous Remailers

Anonymous remailers are sites that allow you to send and receive e-mail without revealing your e-mail address to correspondents. E-mail is still forwarded directly to whatever e-mail address you provide when you sign up with a remailing service. Here are two of the higher-profile services of this type:

Integrity Remailer: `http://www.remailer.integrity.org`

Mixmaster: `http://www.gilc.org/speech/anonymous/remailer.html`

There are quite a few of these on the Web, but many come and go. If you find that you cannot reach either of those listed above, try using the phrase **anonymous remailer** with a search engine.

Check Your Surfing Privacy

This site (also discussed in Chapter 11) will show you some (but not all) of the information that a Web server can collect about you.

URL: `http://privacy.net/anonymizer`

The Enonymous Advisor

The Enonymous Advisor provides a free, downloadable software tool that allows you to create anonymous Web-surfing profiles. This prevents Web sites from getting information about you from your browser. An online tool, the Enonymous Advisor rates the privacy levels of Web sites. An example is shown in Figure 13.1.

This tool also provides privacy ratings for a Web site as you surf. To check out a site's rating or download the program, visit `http://www.enonymous.com`.

Figure 13.1

The Enonymous Advisor rates privacy of Web sites.

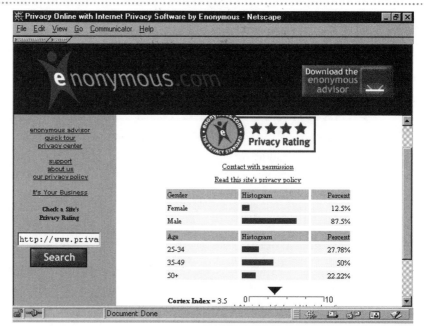

Fortify for Netscape

Fortify is an online tool for checking the strength of encryption provided by your browser. It also offers a free downloadable tool for strengthening browser encryption.

Fortify's URL is `https://www.fortify.net/cgi-bin/ssl`.

Freedom

Freedom is the name of a program that works with your browser to protect you from information-gathering servers using encryption, blocking (data requests and cookies), and more. It helps block spam and privatizes your e-mail, chat, telnet, and FTP activities.

This is a commercial program. At $49.95, it is worth checking out. Visit `http://www.freedomnet.com`.

PrivacyScan

This service searches more than 1600 commercial and government databases to find out what personal information is stored away about *you*. Currently, the report is $29.

PrivacyScan's URL is `http://www.privacyscan.com`.

Proxy Servers

As described in Chapter 11, proxy servers allow you to surf the Web without any information about yourself being picked up. Proxy servers are like a "front" for you. To any Web servers you visit while using a proxy server, it looks as though the proxy server is visiting.

The Anonymizer's URL is `http://www.anonymizer.com`.

Lucent ProxyMate: `http://lpwa.com:8000`.

ProxyMate's welcome screen is shown in Figure 13.2.

Search Engines

I have mentioned search engines a few times now. As you may know, Internet search engines (which are essentially searchable catalogs or listings of sites on the Web) are the best way to get at information you need quickly.

Figure 13.2

Lucent's ProxyMate

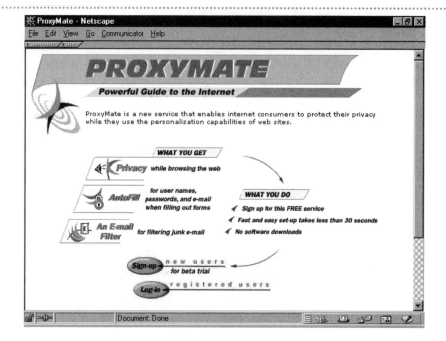

In case you are new to the Web or otherwise unfamiliar with search engines, here's a list of the more popular ones:

AltaVista:	http://www.altavista.com
Ask Jeeves:	http://www.askjeeves.com
Excite:	http://www.excite.com
Infoseek:	http://www.infoseek.com
LookSmart:	http://www.looksmart.com
Lycos:	http://www.lycos.com
Search.com:	http://www.search.com
SNAP:	http://www.snap.com
Webcrawler:	http://www.webcrawler.com
Yahoo:	http://www.yahoo.com

Privacy Resources

As you might imagine, you aren't the only person concerned with how PCs at work, home, and online may be used to intrude on your privacy. Nearly every PC user has some concern about these issues; hence this book and a number of pro-privacy organizations, listed here.

Anonymity on the Internet

Offers a seemingly endless number links to excellent privacy information sources and resources, along with useful information.

URL: http://www.dis.org/erehwon/anonymity.html

Center for Democracy and Technology (CDT)

An organization that is backed by the computer/Internet industries, CDT is among the best privacy resources on the Web.

URL: http://www.cdt.org

Cypherpunks

Cypherpunks is an organization dedicated to privacy supported by encryption.

URL: ftp://ftp.csua.berkeley.edu/pub/cypherpunks/Home.html

Electronic Frontier Foundation (EFF)

Founded in 1990, the EFF is devoted to free speech, privacy, and individual rights online.

URL: http://www.eff.org

Electronic Privacy Information Center (EPIC)

EPIC has a wealth of information and resources online. The organization's main thrust is to preserve privacy through government regulation.

URL: http://www.epic.org

The Privacy Page

URL: http://www.privacy.org

Privacy Rights Clearinghouse (PRC)

This organization promotes common sense and straightforward approaches to preserving individual privacy. Lots of good information and advice.

URL: `http://www.privacyrights.org`

PrivacyTimes

PrivacyTimes is an industry newsletter that offers quite a bit of information of use to consumers. Figure 13.3 shows some recent headline stories.

Check out *PrivacyTimes* at `http://www.privacytimes.com`

Figure 13.3

PrivacyTimes newsletter

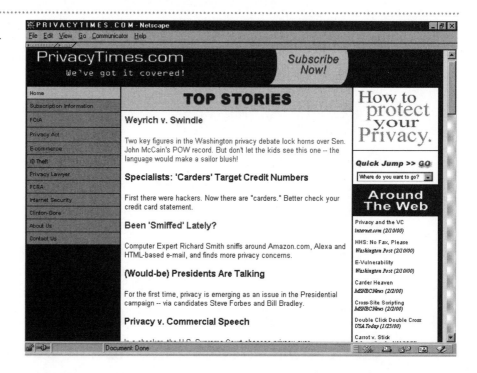

There are still more privacy tools, techniques, and resources available both online and off. What you have seen in this book, however, is representative of the entire spectrum. Combine what you have learned here with your own approaches to preserving your privacy and you can rest assured that you are secure.

The following appendices contain useful information and references. Beyond these and the information I've already given you, I urge you to take whatever measures are required to keep your privacy intact. Giving up even a little privacy only encourages them to take more!

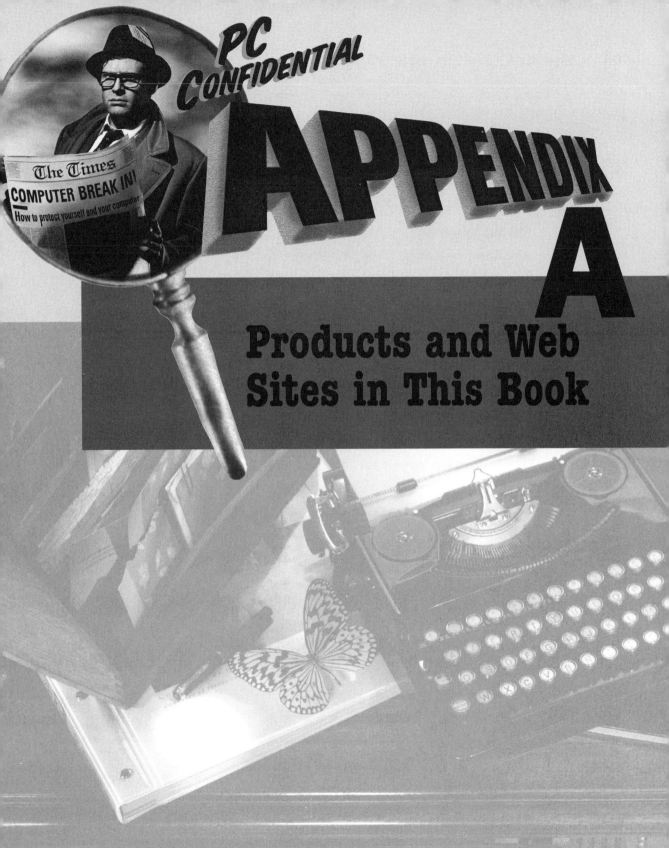

PC CONFIDENTIAL

APPENDIX A

Products and Web Sites in This Book

007 Password Recovery and 007 Stealth Activity Monitor (SAM)
IOPUS Software: `http://www.iopus.com`

Aladdin Expander
Aladdin Systems: `http://www.aladdinsys.com`

The Anonymizer
The Anonymizer: `http://www.anonymizer.com`

AutoShutdown
Barefoot Productions: `http://www.barefootinc.com`

Black Magic
Download and other information available via a search at: `http://www.download.com`

Cookie Crusher
The Limit Software, Inc.: `http://www.thelimitsoft.com`

Cyber Patrol
The Learning Company: `http://www.microsys.com/business`

Digital Certificates
GlobalSign: `http://www.globalsign.net/products`
VeriSign: `http://www.verisign.com`

Dr Solomon's Anti-Virus
Dr Solomon's On-Line: `http://www.drsolomons.com`

E-Cash
First Virtual Bank: `http://www.netchex.com/index.html`

Elcomsoft
Application-specific password recovery programs: `http://www.elcomsoft.com`

E-Mail Directories
AnyWho: `http://www.anywho.com`
Bigfoot: `http://www.bigfoot.com`

E-Mail Directories (*continued*)

Internet Address Finder: `http://www.iaf.net`

Infospace: `http://www.infospace.com`

Switchboard: `http://www.switchboard.com`

Lycos Who Where: `http://www.whowhere.com`

World E-Mail Directory: `http://www.worldemail.com`

Yahoo's People Finder: `http://www.four11.com`

E-Mail Programs

BeyondMail: `http://www.banyan.com`

Eudora: `http://www.eudora.com`

Pegasus: `http://www.pegasus.usa.com`

Encrypted Magic Folders (EMF)

PC-Magic Software: `http://www.pc-magic.com`

Enonymous

Privacy-rating Web site and software tool: `http://www.enonymous.com`

Finger Server

Finger Gateway with Faces: `http://www.cs.indiana.edu:800/finger/gateway`

Fortify

An online tool for testing the strength of encryption provided by browsers:
`https://www.fortify.net/cgi-bin/ssl`

Freedom

Commercial program that blocks Web servers from getting information from your browser and system: `http://www.freedomnet.com`

McAfee Guard Dog, Office 2000, and VirusScan

McAfee: `http://www.mcafee.com`

McAfee Guard Dog: `http://www.mcafee.com/products/default.asp`

McAfee Office 2000: `http://store.mcafee.com/product.asp?productID=89`

McAfee VirusScan Deluxe: `http://www.mcafee.com/centers/anti-virus`

Microsoft Internet Explorer

The Internet Explorer Home Page: `http://www.microsoft.com/windows/ie/default.htm`

Miscellaneous

Anti-Spam Tips: `http://kryten.eng.monash.edu.au/gspam.html`

Coalition Against Unsolicited E-Mail (CAUCE): `http://www.cauce.org/`

Lamers on the Net: `http://phobos.illtel.denver.co.us/pub/lamers`

The Make-Money-Fast Hall of Shame: `http://ga.to/mmf`

Information about Cookies: `http://www.cookiecentral.com`

Electronic Communications Privacy Act text: `http://www.lawresearch.com/v2/Ctprivacy.htm`

Netscape NetWatch (Enables you to control what types of pages are viewed with your *Netscape* browser only. This page provides complete information, site rating information, and interactive setup.): `http://home.netscape.com/communicator/netwatch`

nCognito

Web tool for anonymous but interactive surfing: `http://www.ncognito.com`

Netscape

Netscape NetCenter Download and Upgrade Page: `home.netscape.com/computing/download/index.html`

Norton Computing Products from Symantec: AntiVirus 2000, CleanSweep, Internet Security 2000, Secret Stuff, SystemWorks 2000, Unerase, and Norton Utilities 2000/Norton Utilities 8

Symantec Worldwide Home Page: `http://www.symantec.com`

Norton AntiVirus 2000: `http://www.symantec.com/nav/nav_9xnt`

Norton CleanSweep: `http://www.symantec.com/sabu/qdeck/ncs`

Norton Internet Security 2000: `http://www.nortonweb.com/nis/1033/index_nc.html`

Norton Secret Stuff: `http://www.symantec.com/press/n970213a.html`

Norton SystemWorks 2000: `http://www.symantec.com/sabu/sysworks/index.html`

Norton Computing Products from Symantec: AntiVirus 2000, CleanSweep, Internet Security 2000, Secret Stuff, SystemWorks 2000, Unerase, and Norton Utilities 2000/Norton Utilities 8 (*continued*)

Norton Unerase: http://www.symantec.com/nu/index.html

Norton Utilities 2000: http://www.symantec.com/nu/index.html

Norton Utilities 8: http://www.symantec.com/nu/index.html

Online Services

AOL: http://www.aol.com

CompuServe: http://www.compuserve.com

DELPHI: http://www.delphi.com

Prodigy: http://www.prodigy.com

PKZIP

PKWARE, Inc.: http://www.pkware.com

Pretty Good Privacy (PGP)

PGP Home: http://www.pgp.com

Download site: http://web.mit.edu/network/pgp.html

PGP Front Ends: http://home.earthlink.net/~rjswan/pgp
or http://web.mit.edu/network/pgp.html

Privacy Resources

Anonymity on the Internet: http://www.dis.org/erehwon/anonymity.html

Center for Democracy and Technology (CDT): http://www.cdt.org

CyberTimes (New York Times technology news online): http://www.cybertimes.net/yr/mo/day/tech/indexcyber.html

Cypherpunks: ftp://ftp.csua.berkeley.edu/pub/cypherpunks/Home.html

Electronic Frontier Foundation (EFF): http://www.eff.org

Electronic Privacy Information Center (EPIC): http://www.epic.org

The Privacy Page: http://www.privacy.org

Privacy Rights Clearinghouse (PRC): http://www.privacyrights.org

Your ISP Address: http://privacy.net/anonymizer

Privacy Scan

A service that searches more than two dozen online databases for information about you: http://www.privacyscan.com

Private Bookmarks

Webroot.Com Software: http://www.webroot.com

Private File

Aladdin Systems: http://www.aladdinsys.com/privatefile

Proxy Servers

Anonymizer: http://www.anonymizer.com

ByProxy: http://www.besiex.org/ByProxy/index.html

MagnusNet: http://www.magusnet.com/proxy.html

Proxymate: http://lpwa.com:8000

Public Key Servers

BAL's PGP Public Key Server: http://www-swiss.ai.mit.edu/~bal/pks-commands.html

University of Paderborn PGP Public Key Server: http://www-math.uni-paderborn.de/pgp/pks-toplev.html

Public Key Server Commands: http://bs.mit.edu:8001/pks-toplev.html

Quarterdeck Remove-It

Quarterdeck Products/Symantec: http://www.symantec.com/sabu/qdeck/removeit-98/main98.html

Quarterdeck Zip-It

Quarterdeck Products/Symantec: http://www.symantec.com/sabu/qdeck/zip-it/main.html

Remailers

Integrity Remailer: http://www.remailer.integrity.org

Mixmaster: http://www.gilc.org/speech/anonymous/remailer.html

Search Engines

AltaVista: http://www.altavista.com

Ask Jeeves: http://www.askjeeves.com

Excite: http://www.excite.com

Infoseek: http://www.infoseek.com

LookSmart: http://www.looksmart.com

Lycos: http://www.lycos.com

Search.com: http://www.search.com

SNAP: http://www.snap.com

Webcrawler: http://www.webcrawler.com

Yahoo: http://www.yahoo.com

ScreenLock

iJEN Software: http://www.screenlock.com

SecurePC

RSA Data Security: http://www.rsasecurity.com

Security 98

LC Technology International: http://www.lc-tech.com

Shareware Download and Information Sources

C|NET's Download Site: http://www.download.com

C|NET's Shareware.com: http://shareware.cnet.com

Stealth Activity Recorder & Reporter (STARR)

IOPUS Software: http://www.iopus.com

TEMPEST Surveillance

Unofficial TEMPEST Information Page: http://www.eskimo.com/~joelm/tempest.html

Usenet Newsgroup Information and Access

AltaVista Search Engine: http://www.altavista.com

Deja News Search: http://www.deja.com/home_ps.shtml

Virus Myths

The Computer Virus Myths Home Page: http://kumite.com/myths

McAfee Virus Information Library/Hoaxes: http://vil.mcafee.com/hoax.asp

Symantec's AntiVirus Research Center: http://www.symantec.com/avcenter

Web-Based E-Mail Services

AltaVista: http://mail.altavista.com

Excite Mail: http://mail.excite.com

Hotmail: http://www.hotmail.com

Juno: http://www.juno.com
(Juno also provides free dialup access for e-mail.)

USA.Net/Net@ddress: http://www.netaddress.com

WinCode

WinSite Shareware Downloads: http://www.winsite.com/info/pc/win3/util/wincode.zip

Windows Task Lock

Posum Software Security Technologies: http://www.posum.com

WinGuardian and Window Washer

Webroot.Com Software: http://www.webroot.com

WinGuard Impact

Rely Software: http://relysoftware.u41.com

WinZip

Nico Mak Computing: http://www.winzip.com

PC CONFIDENTIAL

APPENDIX B

Glossary of Terms

A

Analog signal   A signal that varies as it travels between two states (changes in frequencies, voltage levels, or phase angles). An example is an old-style (non-digital) radio volume control that allows you to set the volume anywhere between high and low. Telephone lines also use analog signals, as do most broadcasting systems. An analog system is one that uses variations in amplitude (strength or fullness) or frequency to carry information.

Applet   A program that is sent to your computer and run via your *Web browser*. The program may be written in a special language such as ActiveX, Java, or JavaScript. Applets normally support functions at a Web site.

Archive   A type of file that contains one or more other files, usually in a compressed form. Archiving is used to efficiently store groups of files, and to store files in less space. Archive types for PCs include .ARC, .ARJ, and .ZIP. Most archives can be password-protected.

ASCII   Acronym for *American Standard Code for Information Interchange*. ASCII is a standard numeric code used by most computers for transmitting data. There are 128 standard ASCII code numbers (0–127), each of which is assigned to an alphanumeric character, control character, or special character.

ASCII download   A download format that transfers only 7-bit ASCII characters.

Attachment   A file or program that is sent along with an e-mail message.

Attribute   A value or characteristic assigned to a file. File attributes can include *Hidden* or *Read-only* and can be set in Windows using Windows Explorer.

B

Baud rate   A measure of how often a signal in a communications channel makes a transition between states (changes in frequencies, voltage levels, or phase angles)—i.e., a measure of the number of signal events per second. Baud rate is not necessarily equivalent to bits per second (or speed); depending on the communications system, one transition of state can transmit 1 bit, or more or less than 1 bit.

Binary   A system of counting that uses only two digits: 1 and 0. Referring to a system that uses two states (off/on, high/low, 1/0, negative/positive, etc.) to represent information.

Binary file   A file that is stored in binary format, using binary digits, as opposed to ASCII format. Often used to refer to files stored in 8-bit ASCII format, as well.

Bit   Contraction of BInary digiT. The smallest unit of computer information; its value is either 0 or 1.

Bits per second (bps)   (Also known as *bps* or *bit rate*.) A measure of the rate of data transmission expressed as the number of data bits sent in 1 second. This is not necessarily the same as *baud rate* (q.v.). Neither does it represent the number of *characters* sent per second, as each character is composed of more than 1 bit.

BBS   (Also *Bulletin Board System*.) A dial-up system that is normally based on PCs or networked PCs and operated by small groups or individuals.

Board   Slang term for *Bulletin Board System*. Also, an area on a Web site or online service where public messages are posted.

Browser   (Also *Web browser*.) A specialized program that communicates with the Internet and retrieves files from Web sites. Browser functions also include interpreting and displaying *HTML* code on *Web pages*, along with graphics and other sorts of data. A browser may also be used to handle *e-mail* and *Usenet Newsgroup* messaging.

Bulletin Board System   (See *BBS*)

Byte   (Also, *character*, *data word*, or *word*.) A group of bits handled by a computer as a discreet unit; a computer data character. A byte is usually composed of 7 or 8 *bits*.

C

Capture   To store the text or other material that a remote system on your computer is displaying.

Character   (Also *data word*, *word*.) A letter, number, space, punctuation mark, symbol, or control character; any piece of information that can be stored in 1 byte. A representation of this information coded in binary digits.

Character set   Those characters that can be displayed, printed, stored, and/or transmitted by a particular computer or type of computer.

Characters per second   (Also *cps*.) A measurement of the number of characters transmitted each second, based on the *bps* (bits per second) rate and the length of the characters being sent.

Chat   An interactive, real-time conversation system in which users type and read. Sometimes referred to as a CB simulator or conference system.

Cluster   A small area on a computer disk devoted to storing a certain quantity of data. Several clusters may comprise a *sector*, and sectors are grouped on *tracks* on the disk.

CMOS settings   A general term for all the hardware settings on a PC that can be altered, such as time, memory size, disk types, and so on. These settings are usually accessed by pressing a key, as directed on the screen, when a PC is first starting. Most PCs provide a means of password-protecting the system at *power-on* in the CMOS settings.

Command   An instruction or set of instructions that tells a program to perform a specified function or operation. Commands are either typed or selected from a menu.

Communications software   Dedicated software whose job is to enable and facilitate data communications. Also known as *terminal software*.

Configuration   The specific, customized arrangement of hardware, or the parameter selections and operating setup of communications software.

Control character   A non-printing character generated by holding down the Control key and a letter key on a computer keyboard. Control characters are used on many systems to issue commands. In hardware, software, and system documentation, control characters are usually referred to as *Control-X* but may sometimes be denoted as *CTRL-X* or *^X*.

Control key   A special key on your computer keyboard marked CONTROL, CTRL, Ctrl, or <CTRL>. The Control key is designated as Control, CONTROL, CTRL, or ^ in computer software and hardware documentation. The Control key is used in conjunction with other keys to transmit special characters as commands.

Cookie   A line of information that a Web server puts in a file on your hard drive. The cookie contains information about your past visits to a Web site, as well as other information, such as a user ID and password.

D

Data   Information of any type. Addresses are data; so are names, or groups of numbers. (*Data* is actually the plural of the Latin *datum*, but common usage has *data* for both singular and plural forms.)

Database   (Also *data base*.) An online database is an organized collection of related data stored in the form of binary and/or ASCII files. Databases are usually organized into various topics and may contain text, data, and program files. The files may be searchable by various key words and may be downloaded.

Data bits   The number of all bits sent for a single character that represent the character itself, not counting parity or stop bits; normally 7 or 8 bits. A communications setting.

Decode   To translate or convert an encoded or encrypted message to "clear" text.

Default   A setting, instruction, or data used by program if no value is entered by the user.

Defragmentation   A process of rearranging data stored on a floppy disk or hard drive so that it can be accessed faster.

Delete/Erase   To remove a file's location listing and other information from a computer disk's directory track so that the computer system no longer "sees" the file and new data can be written where the deleted or erased file resides. Note that this does not remove the data from the disk, which means it can be recovered.

Dial up   (Also *dialup*, *dial-up* [adj.].) The process of calling one computer with another via telephone.

Dial-up system   Any *ISP* or *online service* that is accessible via voice-grade telephone lines.

Digital   Referring to or using the binary system, particularly in storing, handling, and transmitting data.

Digital Computer   Digital computers handle data as strings of *binary numbers* that are digital counterparts of numbers in the *ASCII* code, which numbers in turn represent certain *characters*. Some computers may use a modified ASCII set, with an additional 128 characters, called *8-bit* ASCII. (8-bit ASCII is sometimes referred to as EBCIDIC, an acronym for Extended Binary Coded Decimal Interchange Code.)

Digital signal A discontinuous signal identified by specific levels or values, typically *on* or *off*, or 1 or 0. An electrical signal in which information is coded as a series of pulses or transitions.

Directory Synonym for *folder* on a PC disk.

Download To receive data from another computer via connection to the Internet or online service, or via direct connection by telephone line or other connecting cables.

Electronic mail (e-mail) Often referred to as e-mail, electronic mail is an online message system used to deliver messages from one online user to another. E-mail files are usually private (i.e., accessible by the sender and recipient only). Most e-mail systems can handle both ASCII text files and binary files as *attachments*.

E

Encode To alter a message or other document following a prescribed pattern of encryption.

Encryption A means of altering a message or other document so as to render its content unrecognizable by a process of *encoding* the message content.

F

File A collection of data stored as a discreet unit on a disk or online. A file may consist of text in ASCII format, or text, data, or programs in binary format.

File name (Also *filename*.) The identifying label given to a file. File names for PCs commonly consist of a name of up to eight letters or digits, followed by a period, followed by an *extension* of up to three letters or digits. For example: `name.ext`. Extended file names, like `new glossary.doc`, can also be used by PCs.

Folder A collection of related files stored on a hard drive. Synonym for *directory* on a PC disk.

Freeware Software that is distributed freely, and for which no payment is required.

FTP   Acronym for *File Transfer Protocol*, which is the general term for the method used to transfer (*upload* or *download*) files between a PC and a Web server over the Internet.

H

Hardware   The individual or collective physical components of a computer system, including but not limited to the keyboard, monitor, CD-ROM drive, printer, modem, and other attached or removable devices.

Hidden   An *attribute* that renders a file or folder invisible to applications and file- or folder-viewing commands.

Host system   A relative term of reference designating the system you are using. Usually, the system receiving a call from another system (also called the *remote system*).

HTML   Acronym for *HyperText Markup Language*. HTML is a system of coding or tagging text files so as to display the text in a specific manner (font type and size, positioning, and so forth). *Web browsers* interpret the HTML codes and display material on Web pages appropriately. HTML is also used to provide *hyperlinks* to other Web pages and sites, to graphic images, to files for download, and more.

Hyperlink   A line of text, a graphic, or a region on a graphic or Web page that provides a link to a resource—either another Web page, a file, or a program. Hyperlinks are marked with HTML code, and lead to a specific *URL*.

I

ID   (Also *identifier, user ID, username.*) The name or "handle" by which you identify yourself to an online service, ISP, or Web site. Various information is tied to your online ID, such as your *password*, screen display parameters, and more. An ID may be a number, a name, or a series of letters and numbers.

Input   A command, value, or other data provided to a program or database by a computer user or another outside source. Normally, information entered at a prompt.

Internet   The worldwide network of interlinked computer systems and the data they contain. This includes Web pages, e-mail, public message–posting systems like *Usenet Newsgroups*, and the physical hardware and communications links that tie the computer systems together. Note that the the Web, Usenet, and e-mail are not themselves alone "the Internet." Nor do online services like AOL constitute the Internet. Rather, the Internet is all of these combined.

ISP   Acronym for *Information Service Provider*. An ISP provides individuals and businesses with links to the Internet. Typically, an ISP also handles e-mail for its clients and may host *Web pages* as well as information about each user. *Online services* also function as ISPs for many users.

K

Kilobyte   (Also *K*.) A unit of computer memory, normally referring to the number of bytes in RAM or the size of a file, equal to 1024 bytes.

L

Local System   A relative term of reference, usually indicating the computer system you are using or a computer making a call to another computer (which in turn is called the remote system).

M

Megabyte   (Also *MB*.) A unit of computer memory equal to 1024 kilobytes. Usually refers to the number of bytes in RAM or the size of a file.

Modem   (From *MOdulate-DEModulate* device.) A device used to translate binary signals from a computer into tone signals for transmission via telephone line, and vice versa.

N

Newsgroups   (See *Usenet Newsgroups*.)

O

Offline   A state in which a computer system is not connected with another computer.

Online   Connected with another computer; the opposite of *offline*.

Online service   A commercial service that provides any or all of the following services for a fee: communication, database, information storage and retrieval, and other services. Sometimes referred to as *networks* (or erroneously as *BBSs* or the *Internet*), online services host multiple users and are connected to the Internet via e-mail, Web access, and Usenet. Examples of online services include AOL (America Online), CompuServe, Delphi, and the Prodigy service.

Output   Information sent from a computer to its screen, a printer, a disk file, or another computer.

P

Packet   A transmitted data unit composed of a set or variable number of *characters* along with information as to their origin, route, and destination. Computer data files are transmitted in such packets via *packet-switching networks*.

Packet-switching network   (Also *PSN*.) A data communications service that transmits data from one computer system to another in the form of *packets*. Most packet-switching networks provide a nationwide system of local telephone numbers (called *nodes*) to enable users to access online services and elements of the Internet without incurring long-distance charges. SprintNet, and Tymnet are packet-switching networks, as are AOLnet and the CompuServe Network.

Parameters   Settings selected by a computer user, and/or included in a program, used as established values or defaults in program operation.

Password   A string of letters and/or numbers used to verify the identity or access level of a user calling an ISP, online service, or BBS. Passwords are also used to identify users of some Web sites. The use of a password prevents unauthorized use of an online *ID*, or unauthorized use of a PC. Ideally, passwords are known only to those who set them.

Post   To place a message on a public bulletin board or message database.

Power-on password   (Also *boot password*, *startup password*.) A password set within a PC's *CMOS settings* that blocks a PC from loading its operating system.

Private key   In *public key encryption*, data that serves as a guide for a specialized program to how to decrypt a message or other document that has been encrypted using a *public key* and the same program. Private keys are never made public but are reserved for the use of people receiving messages encrypted with their public key.

Profile   On some ISPs, BBSs, Web sites, and online services, a set of *default parameters* that the *host system* uses to communicate with your computer. A profile may contain information about display parameters (screen width and lines, color), prompt/menu displays, and other elements.

Another sort of online profile contains information about an individual *user*, such as name, location, areas of interest, and so forth. Both types of profiles are normally changeable by the user.

Program   A set of instructions that tell a computer how to perform a defined task or tasks, and which process commands and input.

Public key   In *public key encryption*, data that serves as a guide to a specialized encryption program as to how a message or other document is encrypted. Once encrypted, it can be decrypted only with the same program and a *private key*. A public key is usually made available on the Web for the use of anyone who wants to send a coded document to the person who posted it.

Public key encryption   An encryption method whereby anyone using an e-mail recipient's public key can encrypt a message that only the recipient's private key can decipher.

R

Read-only   An *attribute* that prevents a file from being altered by an application.

Remote system   A relative term of reference designating the system you are not using; normally the system receiving the call (also called the *host system*), as opposed to the computer making the call.

S

Sector   An area of a computer disk that stores all or part of the data in a file. Sectors are sometimes composed of smaller data-storage units called *clusters* and are placed on *tracks* on the disk.

Shareware   Software that is freely distributed on a "try before you buy" basis. If you like the software and continue to use it, you are expected to pay a fee to the software's creator or publisher.

Sign on   (Also *login, logon.*) The process or event of connecting with and identifying your computer to another computer system, or to a Web site. Signing on typically involves providing a user ID and password when requested.

Spam   Internet slang for unsolicited commercial e-mail, which typically consists of scams, come-ons, and cons.

String   A series of letters, numbers, or symbols to be input or output as data. Strings that cannot be used as numeric operands and whose values do not vary are *character strings.* `Franklin Robert Adams`, `555-1969`, and `3-21-51` are all character strings. Strings with set numeric values are *numeric strings*. `451.50` and `910234` are numeric strings.

Sysop   Shorthand for *SYStem OPerator.* The person who operates an ISP or BBS, or who operates a specific area of an online service or Web site. Where local area networks (LANs) are involved, the title is usually "system administrator."

System   A term used to refer to any computer (and its peripherals)—particularly a computer that is connected with another computer, whether as a host or as an originating system.

T

Telecommunications   Data communication over telephone lines via computers and associated devices.

Telecomputing   In general, using a personal computer to communicate with other computers.

Temporary files   Files created by a computer system or programs in support of various tasks required by a program. These are sometimes removed when the program has finished with them, but not always. Temporary files often provide a detailed guide to what someone has been doing with a computer.

Text   Any message or file composed of standard *ASCII characters*.

Text file   A file that is in ASCII format as opposed to *binary* format.

Track   A region of a computer disk on which data is stored, usually organized into subareas called *sectors*, which in turn may contain smaller areas of data called *clusters*.

Trojan horse   A program that is presented as having a certain function, but which actually has a hidden function, usually destructive.

U

Undelete/Unerase   A process of recovering data that has been *deleted* from a computer disk.

Upload   To send data to another computer, via an Internet connection, online service, or via direct-connection by telephone line or other connecting cables.

URL   Acronym for *Uniform Resource Locator*. URLs are the "addresses" that your browser uses to connect with Web sites and Web pages. An example of a typical URL is http://www.sybex.com.

Usenet Newsgroups   A system of public message bulletin boards accessed via the Internet. There are more than 50,000 Newsgroups available, each devoted to a specific topic.

User   A term applied to someone who dials up, or uses, the Internet, a BBS or online service. Also, any computer user in general.

V

Virus   A program or macro whose function is usually destructive or disruptive to a computer system. There are endless variations (with over 50,000 known), but the end result is the same—disruption or destruction of your computer operations.

W

Web page Typically, a document formatted with *HTML*, and containing *hyperlinks* (also known as *links*) to other Web pages at that site, or anywhere else on the Web. The Web page may also contain graphics, and links to activate programs on your system, download files, and/or perform other operations.

Web site A collection of *Web pages*, graphics and other data files hosted by a computer connected to the Internet. The computer that hosts the site is referred to as the *server*.

Wipe To completely remove all traces of a deleted file by writing over the disk space the file once occupied.

World Wide Web (Also *WWW*, *Web*.) The collection of *Web sites* and *Web pages* available via an Internet link.

Index

Note to the Reader: Throughout this index **boldfaced** page numbers indicate primary discussions of a topic. *Italicized* page numbers indicate illustrations.

A

ActiveX controls, **119–122**, *120–121*
activity monitors, 202–203, *203*
activity records on Internet, **150–151**, *150–151*
Address bar, 153, *153*
addresses
    for e-mail, **167–170**, **173–174**, 215
    giving out, 143
Aladdin Expander program, 62–63, *64*
algorithms, 102
AltaVista search engine, 220
alteration
    of files, **35–36**, *36*
    of folders, **37**
    of information, 5
alternate e-mail addresses, **173–174**
alternate e-mail IDs, 174
alternate folders, **54**
analog signals, 81, 232
anonymity, online, 139
Anonymity on the Internet site, 207, 221
Anonymizer proxy server, **189–190**, *189–190*
anonymous remailers, **217**
anonymous Web-surfing profiles, 218
anti-virus software, **127–132**, *128–132*
AntiVirus Research Center, 133
AnyWho e-mail directory, 216
AOL online service
    debut of, 137
    privacy on, **157–159**, *158*
    saving data on, 61

applets
    defined, 232
    viruses from, **118–123**, *120–121*, *123*
applications
    hiding, **73–75**
    passwords for, **27**
    renaming, **74–75**
.ARC format, 62
Archive attribute, 70
archives, **61–65**, *62–64*
    defined, 232
    for hiding files, 75
    packing and unpacking, **66**
    passwords for, **76**
    self-extracting, **102–103**
    storing, **65–66**
    in WinZip program, **46–47**
.ARJ format, 62
ASCII code, **83–84**, 232
ASCII downloads, 232
AskJeeves search engine, 220
at-risk information, **2–3**
attachments
    defined, 232
    viruses from, **124**
attributes
    defined, 232
    for hiding files, **69–72**, *70*
    for read-only files, 35–37
auctions, online, 145
Auto Hide option, 34
AUTOEXEC.BAT file, 194
AutoShutdown program, 47

B

backups for disasters, **16–17**
batteries for CMOS settings, 37
baud rate, 232
BBSs (bulletin board services), 137
    defined, 233
    posting on, 214
BeyondMail program, 171
BigFoot directory, 216
binary data, **81–84**
binary digits, 80–82
binary files, 100, 233
binary numbers, 81, 233
bits, 82, 233
bits per second (BPS), 233
Black Magic program, 43, *44*
boards, 233
bookmarks, 157, **191–192**, *191*
bookmarks.htm file, 191
Boot From Floppy, Check Drive A option, 42
Boot Options, 42
boot-up passwords, 39
BPS (bits per second), 233
browsers
    bookmarks and favorites lists in, 157
    caches in, **154–156**, *154–155*
    cookies in. *See* cookies
    defined, 233
    information left on, 8
    and secure servers, 146
    security in, **147–148**, *148*
bulletin board services (BBSs), 137
    defined, 233
    posting on, 214
buying tips, online, **146**
ByProxy proxy server, 190
bytes, 82, 84, 233

C

cables, disconnecting, 19
caches in browsers, **154–156**, *154–155*
capturing data, 233
case-sensitivity of passwords, 56
CD-ROM
    storing data on, **60**
    viruses on, 125
CDT (Center for Democracy and Technology), 221
certificates
    with browsers, 147
    for e-mail, 171–172
Change Password dialog box, 38, *38*
changing passwords, 199
character sets, 234
character substitution, 99
characters, 81, 84, 233
characters per second (CPS), 234
chat systems
    addresses for, 173
    defined, 234
checking account numbers on Internet, **145–146**
ciphers, 101–102
cleaning up
    Internet files, **192**
    temporary files, **94–96**, *96*
Clear Disk Cache option, 154
clear documents, 98
Clear History option, 151
Clear Location Bar option, 153
clearing Documents menu, **21–22**, *22–23*, **28**, *29*
clusters, 85, 234
CMOS settings
    defined, 234
    for passwords, 37, 42

codes in encryption, 98, 101
commands, 234
commercial databases, searching, 219
communications software, 234
compromised data, **5–7**
CompuServe online service
    debut of, 137
    saving data on, 61
computer formats, **80–81**
    ASCII, **83–84**
    binary data, **81–83**
computer passwords, **27**
Computer Virus Myths Home Page, 133
CONFIG.SYS file, 194
configuration, 234
Connect To dialog box, 40, *40*
control characters, 234
Control key, 234
control viruses, **116**
Cookie Crusher program, 185–186, *186*
cookies, **156**, *156–157*
    controlling, **185–187**, *186*
    defined, 234
    personal information in, **181–182**
    purpose of, 178–181
    stopping and blocking, **182–187**, *183–186*
cookies.txt file, 156, 178–183
copying files, 56, 58, **213**
corruption and archiving, 66
CPS (characters per second), 234
crackers, **138**, 211
Create Shortcut dialog box, 32
Create Shortcut(s) Here option, 39
credit cards, **145–146**
Custom Level button
    for cookies, 156, 184–185
    for disabling Java, 120
Cyber Patrol program, 47, *48*, 193
CyberTimes site, 207
Cypherpunks site, 207, 221

D

data, 235
data bits, 235
data formats, **80–81**
    ASCII, **83–84**
    binary data, **81–83**
data theft viruses, **116**
data transmission, encryption for, **105**
databases
    defined, 235
    searching, 219
deceptive filenames and extensions, **53–54**
deciphering, 101
decoding, 98, 235
decryption programs, 101
default extensions, 54
default folders, 54
defaults, 235
defragmentation
    benefits of, 85
    defined, 235
DEL command, 30
Delete option
    for icons, 31
    for Start menu items, 33
Delete Files option, 154
deleted files and text, **6**
    on disk drives, **86–88**, *86*
    in word processor files, **89–92**, *90*
deleting
    attributes, 71
    caches, **154–156**, *154–155*
    defined, 235
    files, **15**, **30**, 95
    folders, **37**
    Internet activity records, **150–151**, *150–151*
    shortcuts, **31**, *31*
    Start menu selections, **31–33**, *32–33*
deletions, backups for, **16–17**

desktop shortcuts
  creating, 32
  removing and renaming, **31**, *31*
destroyer viruses, **116**
destruction of information, **5–7**
dial-up passwords, **40**, *40*
dial up process, 235
dial-up systems, 235
digital certificates
  with browsers, 147
  for e-mail, 171–172
digital computers, 235
digital format, 80–81
digital signals, 236
digital signatures, 108
digital systems, 235
directories
  disk
    defined, 236
    on floppy disks, 17
    passwords for, **27**
  e-mail, **215–216**
directory tracks, 85, *85*, 242
Disable cookies option, 156, 183
Disable Java option, 121
disabling
  Java, **120–122**, *120–121*
  unattended PCs, **18–20**, *19*
disasters, backups for, **16–17**
discussion groups, 174
disk drives
  archives on, **65**
  cleaning up files on, **94–96**, *96*, **192**
  data storage on, 14, 18, **85**, *85*
  deleted files on, **86–88**, *86*
  shared, **125**
disks, floppy
  data storage on, 14, 18, **58**
  rescue disks, 16
  subdirectories on, 17

Display option, 38
Display Properties dialog box, 38, *38*
disposing of old computers, **213–214**
.DLL extension, 53
Do Not Move Files To The Recycle Bin option,
  15, 30
Documents menu, **21–22**, *22–23*, **28**, *29*
DOS
  deleting files in, 30
  full-screen mode, 19, *19*
  getting to, 20
DoubleClick, 182
Download.com site, 43
downloads
  defined, 236
  guidelines for, **148–150**
  logs for, 149
  viruses from, **124**
Dr Solomon's Anti-Virus program, **128**

E

E-cash online payment systems, 146
e-mail
  addresses for, **167–170**, **173–174**, 215
  anonymous remailers for, **217**
  defined, 236
  directories for, **215–216**
  encryption for, **105**, **170–172**, *171–173*, 175
  exposure of, **165–166**
  interception of, **162–163**
  offline risks in, **175**
  saving data in, 61
  security for, **201–202**
  spam, **173–174**
  system operator viewing of, **163–164**
  viruses from, **124**
  vulnerability of, **14**
Econymous Adviser, 218, *218*

ECPA (Electronic Communications Privacy
    Act), 105, 164
Edit menu
    Copy command, 92
    Preferences command, 120
    Select All command, 92, 156
EDIT program, **91–92**
editing Start menu items, **33**, *34*
Electronic Communications Privacy Act
    (ECPA), 105, 164
Electronic Frontier Foundation (EFF), 221
electronic mail. *See* e-mail
Electronic Privacy Information Center (EPIC)
    site, 207, 221
EMF (Encrypted Magic Folders) program, **106**,
    106, 175
employers and e-mail privacy, 164
Empty Recycle Bin option, 15, 30
emptying Recycle Bin, **15**, *15–16*, **30**
Enable Java option, 120
Enable JavaScript option, 120
encoding, 98, 236
Encrypted Magic Folders (EMF) program, **106**,
    106, 175
encryption, **98–99**, 207
    applications for, **104–105**
    decrypting, **101**
    defined, 236
    for e-mail, 105, **170–172**, *171–173*, 175
    in file transmissions, **100**
    formats for, **102–104**, *104*
    process of, **99–101**
    in secure servers, 146
    software for, **106–110**, *106–109*
    strength of, 219
entering URLs, **151–153**, *152–153*
EPIC (Electronic Privacy Information Center)
    site, 207, 221
erasing. *See* deleting

Excite search engine, 220
extensions
    deceptive, **53–54**
    default, 54
extracting archives, 66

F

Faraday cages, 206
Favorites lists, 157, 191
File menu, 21
    Empty Recycle Bin command, 15, 30
    Open page command, 152
    Properties command, 30
    recently used file lists on, **50–52**, *51*
    Save As command, 54–56
File Properties dialog box, 20, 70, *70*
File-Transfer Protocol (FTP), 60, 237
filenames
    deceptive, **53–54**
    defined, 236
files
    alteration of, **35–36**, *36*
    attributes for, 35–37, **69–72**, *70*
    copying, 56, 58, **213**
    defined, 236
    deleted, **6**
        on disk drives, **86–88**, *86*
        in word processor files, **89–92**, *90*
    deleting, **15**, **30**, 95
    encrypting. *See* encryption
    hiding. *See* hiding
    passwords for, **27**, **56–57**, *57*
    read-only, 35–36, **54–56**, *55*, 69
    recently used file lists, **50–52**, *51–52*
    temporary, **93–96**, *94*
    tracks left in, **20–22**, *21–23*
Find: All Files dialog box, 183, *183*

finding
    cookies.txt, 183
    Internet activity records, **150–151**, *150–151*
    temporary files, **94–96**, *96*
First Aid utility, 129
First Virtual Bank site, 146
flame wars, 138
floppy disks
    rescue disks, 16
    saving data to, 14, 18, **58**
    subdirectories on, 17
folders
    altering and deleting, **37**
    attributes for, **71**, *71*
    defined, 236
    misdirection with, **54**
    passwords for, **27**
fonts in word processor files, 89
Fortify tool, 219
forwarded messages, 168
fraud on Internet, 145
free e-mail, 174
Freedom program, 219
freeware, 63, 236
FTP (File-Transfer Protocol), 60, 237
full-screen DOS mode, 19, *19*

G

General tab
    for attributes, 37
    for caches, 154
    for history list, 151
    for network passwords, 41
    for recently used file lists, 51–52, *52*
    for secure sites, 148
Global tab, 15, *16*, 30
Good Times virus, 132
government databases, searching, 219

graphics
    archiving, 61
    in word processor files, 89
Guard Dog program, **122**, 192

H

hackers, **138**
hacking, **206–207**
hard drives
    archives on, **65**
    cleaning up files on, **94–96**, *96*, **192**
    data storage on, **85**, *85*
    deleted files on, **86–88**, *86*
    shared, **125**
hardware, 237
hashing, 102, 108
heat, media damage from, 60
Hidden attribute, 37, 70, 72, 237
Hide Files Of These Types option, 72
hiding
    files, **68–69**
        archives for, **75–76**
        cautions in, **76–78**, *77*
        file attributes for, **69–72**, *70*
        folder attributes for, **71**, *71*
        Windows Explorer options for, **72**, *73*
    programs, **73–75**
    Taskbar, **34**, *35*
history lists, **150–151**, *150–151*
History option, 151
History Trail option, 159
hoaxes, virus, **132–133**
host systems, 237
hot key combinations, 44–45
HTML (Hypertext Markup Language), 237
https protocol, 148
humidity, media damage from, 60
hyperlinks, 237
Hypertext Markup Language (HTML), 237

I

icons, removing and renaming, **31**, *31*
identity
    on Internet, **143**
    theft of, 170
IDs
    in cookies, 180
    defined, 237
    viruses for stealing, 116
information
    destruction of, **5–7**
    protection strategies for, **8–9**
    value of, **3–4**
    vulnerability of, **4–5**
Information Service Providers (ISPs), 238
Infoseek search engine, 220
Infospace directory, 216
.INI files, 96
input, 237
Integrity Remailer service, 217
interception of e-mail, **162–163**
Internet
    AOL, **157–159**, *158*
    bookmarks for, 157, **191–192**, *191*
    caches for, **154–156**, *154–155*
    cleaning up files from, **192**
    cookies for. *See* cookies
    credit cards and checking account numbers
        on, **145–146**
    data security on, **146–148**, *148*
    defined, 238
    download security on, **148–150**
    e-mail directories on, **215–216**
    entrances to, **151–153**, *152–153*
    favorites lists for, 157
    history of, **137–139**
    identity on, **143**
    monitoring programs for, **193–195**
    passwords on, **139–142**
    personal information on, **214–215**

    proxy servers for, **187–190**, *188–190*
    records of activities on, **150–151**, *150–151*
    risks on, **136–137**
    software helpers for, **190–192**, *191*
Internet Address Finder directory, 216
Internet Explorer
    address bar in, 153, *153*
    caches in, **154–156**, *154–155*
    certificates in, 172, *173*
    cookies in, **156**, *157*, 184–185, *185*
    disabling Java in, **120–122**, *121*
    history lists in, **151**, *151*
    and secure servers, 146, 148
Internet Options dialog box, 120–122, *121*
invisible files, 68–69
ISPs (Information Service Providers), 238

J

Java language, **119–122**, *120–121*
JavaScript language, **119–122**, *120–121*

K

K (kilobytes), 84, 238
keyboards, disconnecting, 19
keys in encryption, 100–101, **103–104**, *104*

L

labeling floppy disks, 58
laptops, encryption for, 105
last accessed file date, 20
layers in PCs, 26, *26*
letters in ASCII code, 84
links
    hyperlinks, 237
    in word processor files, 89

lists, **174**
literal characters in word processor files, 90
local systems, 238
location bar, **159**
location considerations in security, 12
location field in Netscape, **153**, *153*
locking workstations, 39
logging
    offline activity, 193
    stealth, **202–205**, *203–204*
long passwords, 200
LookSmart search engine, 220
Lycos search engine, 220
Lycos Who Where directory, 216

M

macro viruses, **118**
MagnusNet proxy server, 190
mail. *See* e-mail
MB (megabytes), 238
McAfee Guard Dog program, **122**, 199
McAfee Office 2000 program, 88, 214
McAfee Uninstaller program, 214
McAfee Virus Information Library/Hoaxes site,
    133
McAfee VirusScan Deluxe program, **129**, *129*
McAfee VirusScan online subscription service,
    128, *128*
megabytes (MB), 238
Microsoft Internet Explorer
    address bar in, 153, *153*
    caches in, **154–156**, *154–155*
    certificates in, 172, *173*
    cookies in, **156**, *157*, 184–185, *185*
    disabling Java in, **120–122**, *121*
    history lists in, **151**, *151*
    and secure servers, 146, 148
MIME format, 100

misdirection
    with alternate folders, **54**
    with deceptive filenames and extensions,
        53–54
misleading disk labels, 17
misrepresentation on Internet, 144
Mixmaster service, 217
modems
    data transmission by, 100
    defined, 238
monitoring
    Internet, **193–195**
    PC activity, 202–203, *203*
monitors
    disconnecting cables to, 19
    monitoring, **12–13**
    turning off, 19
more command, 92
mouse cables, 19
moving files, 56
multiple passwords, **76**
multiple user profiles, **39–40**

N

names
    files, 53–54
    programs, **74–75**
    shortcuts, **31**, *31*
    Start menu items, **33**, *34*
nCognito site, 215
Netscape browser
    caches in, **154**, *154*
    certificates in, 171, *172*
    cookies in, **156**, *156*, 183–184, *184*
    disabling Java in, **120**, *120*
    history lists in, **150**, *150*
    location field in, **153**, *153*
    and secure servers, 146–148, *148*

networks
    file storage on, 17
    passwords on, **41**, *41*
New option for shortcuts, 32
newsgroups, 214, 238, 242
non-printing characters in word processor files, 89
Norton AntiVirus 2000 program, **130–132**, *130–132*
Norton CleanSweep program, **95–96**, *96*, 214
Norton Internet Security 2000 program, **122–123**, *123*, 192
Norton Secret Stuff program, **106–107**, *107*, 170, 175
Norton Unerase utility, 86
Norton Utilities 8 program, 47
Norton Utilities 2000 program, 47, 88
Norton Wipeinfo program, 214
NSS (Norton Secret Stuff) program, **106–107**, *107*, 170, 175
numerals in ASCII code, 84

O

off-system storage and archiving, **17–18**, **57–58**
    archiving process for, **61–66**, *62–64*
    CD-ROM storage, **60**
    floppy disk storage, **58**
    online, **60–61**
    tape backup drives, 59
    ZIP drives, **59**
offline privacy issues
    activity logging, 193
    e-mail, **175**
    Internet
        downloads, **149–150**
        records of activities, **150–151**, *150–151*
offline status, 239
Oil Change utility, 129
old computers, disposal of, **213–214**

online auctions, 145
online buying tips, **146**
online password recovery, **210–211**
online services, 137
    defined, 239
    for e-mail, 201–202
online status, 239
online storage, **60–61**
online threats, **7–8**
Open dialog box, 152
Open Page dialog box, 152
Open With dialog box, 53
Options dialog box
    for default extensions, 54
    for default folders, 54
    for hiding files, 72, *73*
    for recently used file lists, 51, *52*
output, 239

P

packet-sniffing, 163
packet-switching networks, 239
packets, 162–163, 239
packing archives, **66**
parameters, 239
Password Properties dialog box, 39–40
Password Protected option, 38
password-protection programs, 18
007 Password Recovery program, 200–201, *200*, 210
Password To Modify field, 56
Password To Open field, 56
passwords, **27**
    for archives, **76**
    bypassing, 211
    CMOS settings for, 37, 42
    commercial programs for, **47–48**, *48*
    compromised, **141–142**

in cookies, 180
defined, 239
dial-up, **40**, *40*
for e-mail, 105, 175
for files, **56–57**, *57*
good and bad, 77
hacking, **199–200**, *200*
on Internet, **139–142**
for multiple user profiles, **39–40**
network, **41**, *41*
for Personal Filing Cabinet, 158
power-on, **42**
recovering, **210–212**
screen saver, **38–39**, *38*
in SecurePC, 110
security of, **198–201**, *200*
for shared computers, 217
shareware programs for, **43–46**, *44–46*
vaults for, 78
viruses for stealing, 116
in Windows, **37–42**, *38*, *40–41*, 211
PCT (Private Communication) standard, 147
Pegasus program, 171
people as privacy threat, 7–8
Personal Filing Cabinet, **158–159**, *158*
personal information
in cookies, **181–182**
on Internet, **214–215**
PGP (Pretty Good Privacy) program, **108–109**, *108*
PGP for PCs program, **109**
PKZIP program, 46, 62
plain-text documents, 98
Play Animations option, 121
plug-ins, 63
posting messages, 240
power-on passwords, **42**
defined, 240
recovering, 212
PRC (Privacy Rights Clearinghouse), 222

Preferences dialog box
for caches, 154
for cookies, 156, *156*, 184, *184*
for disabling Java, 120, *120*
for location field, 153, *153*
Pretty Good Privacy (PGP) program, **108–109**, *108*
printing, **13–14**
privacy
protection strategies for, **8–9**
resources for, **221–222**
Privacy Page, 207, 221
PrivacyScan program, 219
PrivacyTimes newsletter, **222**, *222*
Private Bookmarks program, **191–192**, *191*
Private Communication (PCT) standard, 147
Private File program, 48, **109–110**, *109*, 175
private Internet entrances, **151–153**, *152–153*
private key encryption, **103–104**, *104*
private keys, 240
products list, **224–230**
profiles, 174
anonymous, 218
defined, 240
passwords for, **39–40**
for shared computers, 217
profiling, cookies for, 181
programs
defined, 240
hiding, **73–75**
passwords for, 27
renaming, **74–75**
Properties dialog box
for file access time, 20–22, *21*
for file attributes, 35–37, 70
for folder attributes, 71
for network passwords, 41
Properties option, 20
Protecting Your Identity Over The Internet
topic, 172, *173*

protection
   layers in, **26–27**, *26*
   strategies for, **8–9**
proxy servers, **187**, *188*, 219, *220*
   Anonymizer, **189–190**, *189–190*
   operation of, **188**
ProxyMate proxy server, 190, 219, *220*
public domain software, 123
public key encryption, **103–104**, *104*, 240
public key servers, 103–104
public keys, 240
punctuation in ASCII code, 84

R

Read-only attribute
   defined, 240
   for files, 35–36, **54–56**, *55*, 69
   for folders, 37
Read-Only Recommended option, 55
Recently Used File List option, 52
recently used file lists, **50–52**, *51–52*
records of Internet activity, **150–151**, *150–151*
recovering
   files, 6
   passwords, **210–212**
Recycle Bin, emptying, **15**, *15–16*, **30**
Recycle Bin Properties dialog box, 15, *16*
registration fees for shareware, 43
remailers, anonymous, **217**
remote systems, 240
Remove-It program, 88, **96**
removing
   attributes, 71
   caches, **154–156**, *154–155*
   files, **15**, **30**, 95
   folders, **37**
   Internet activity records, **150–151**, *150–151*
   shortcuts, **31**, *31*
   Start menu selections, **31–33**, *32–33*

Rename option
   for files, 53
   for icons, 31
renaming
   files, **53–54**
   programs, **74–75**
   shortcuts, **31**, *31*
   Start menu items, **33**, *34*
rescue disks, 16
resources, privacy, **221–222**
revealed information, cost of, **4–5**
risk sensitive information, **2–3**
Run dialog box, 32

S

007 SAM (Stealth Activity Monitor), 202–203, *203*
Save dialog box, 55–56, *55*, *57*
Save As dialog box, 55
Save Password option, 40
.SCR files, 39
Screen Saver tab, 38
screen savers
   passwords in, **38–39**, *38*
   in ScreenLock, 44, *45*
ScreenLock program, **43–45**, *44–45*
Search.com search engine, 220
search engines, **219–220**
searching
   for cookies.txt, 183
   for Internet activity records, **150–151**, *150–151*
   for temporary files, **94–96**, *96*
sectors, 85, *85*
   defined, 241
   zeroing-out, 87
secure online systems, 146
secure sites, **147**
Secure Socket Layer (SSL), 147

SecurePC program, **110**, 175
security
    for e-mail, **201–202**
    on Internet, **146–149**, *148*
    of passwords, **198–201**, *200*
Security 98 for Win95/98 program, 48
Security button, 147
security certificates, 147
Security Settings dialog box
    for cookies, 156, 185, *185*
    for Java, 121, *121*
Security tab
    for Java, 120
    for secure sites, 148
self-extracting archives, **102–103**
self-replicating viruses, **116**
servers, files on, 17
Settings dialog box, 54
Settings menu, Taskbar command, 28, 31, 34
Shareware.com site, 43
shareware programs
    defined, 241
    for passwords, **43–46**, *44–46*
    viruses from, 123
sharing
    computers, **216–217**
    disks, viruses from, **125**
    files, viruses from, **124**
    word processor files, **93**
Sharing tab, 41
shopping carts, 179
shortcuts
    creating, 32, 39
    removing and renaming, **31**, *31*
shutting down, precautions in, **23–24**
sign ons, 241
signature files, 108
SNAP search engine, 220
software helpers for Internet, **190–192**, *191*

Source online service, 137
spam, **166–167**, **173–174**, 241
spying, **205–206**, *206*
SSL (Secure Socket Layer), 147
STARR (Stealth Activity Recorder & Reporter)
    program, 204
Start menu
    editing and renaming items on, **33**, *34*
    removing selections on, **31–33**, *32–33*
    Settings command, 38
Start menu folder, 33
Start Menu Program tabs, 22, *23*, 28, *29*,
    31–33, *32*
007 Stealth Activity Monitor (SAM), 202–203,
    203
Stealth Activity Recorder & Reporter (STARR)
    program, 204
stealth logging programs, **202–205**, *203–204*
storage, off-system. *See* off-system storage and
    archiving
strings, 80, 241
subdirectories, 17
substitution in encryption, 99, 101
surveillance, 206
Switchboard directory, 216
sysops, 241
System attribute, 70
system disks, 16
system passwords, bypassing, 211
systems, 241

T

tape backup drives, 59
Taskbar, hiding, **34**, *35*
Taskbar Options tab, 34, *35*
Taskbar Properties dialog box, 22, 32–34
telecommunications, 241
telecommuting, 241

telephone numbers, giving out, 143
TEMPEST monitoring, **205–206**, *206*
temporary files, **93**, *94*
  cleaning out and finding, **94–96**, *96*
  defined, 242
text, 242
text files, 242
text formats in word processor files, 89
throwaway e-mail addresses, 215
tilde (~) symbol, 94
.TMP files, 94
tokens in encryption, 99
Toolbar Preferences option, 159
tracks
  disk, 85, *85*, 242
  left in files, **20–22**, *21–23*
trash, emptying, **15**, *15–16*, **30**
Trojan horse programs, 7, **112–113**, 206
  defined, 242
  example, **117**
turning off computers, **23**
TYPE command, 92

U

unattended PCs
  disabling, **18–20**, *19*
  file tracks in, **20–22**, *21–23*
undeleting, 242
Undo text, **92**
unencryption, 101
unerase utilities, 86–87
unerasing, 242
unpacking archives, **66**
unzipping archives, **66**
uploading, 242
URLs
  defined, 242
  entering, **151–153**, *152–153*

Usenet newsgroups
  defined, 242
  posting on, 214
user IDs
  in cookies, 180
  viruses for stealing, 116
user profiles
  passwords for, **39–40**
  for shared computers, 217
users, 242
UUENCODE format, 100

V

value of information, **3–4**
vandals. *See* viruses
VeriSign system, 171–172
View menu
  Internet Options command, 154
  Options command, 72
  Stop Animations command, 120
virtual drives, 69
virtual shopping carts, 179
viruses, 7, **112**
  anti-virus software for, **127–132**, *128–132*
  applet, **118–123**, *120–121*, *123*
  defined, 242
  hoaxes, **132–133**
  interference from, **118**
  macro, **118**
  operation of, **115–118**
  origination of, **113–114**
  precautions for, **114**
  protection from, **125–127**
  reasons for, **115**
  sources of, **123–125**
VirusScan Deluxe program, **129**, *129*
VirusScan online subscription service, **128**, *128*
vulnerability of information, **4–5**

W

Web browsers
bookmarks and favorites lists in, 157
caches in, **154–156**, *154–155*
cookies in. *See* cookies
defined, 233
information left on, 8
and secure servers, 146
security in, **147–148**, *148*
Web pages, 243
Web sites
defined, 243
list of, **224–230**
Webcrawler search engine, 220
Who Where directory, 216
Window Washer program, 186, *186*, 192
Windows, password systems in, **27**, **37–42**, *38*,
40–41, 211
Windows Task Lock program, 45, *46*
WinGuardian program, 45, 204, *204*
WinZip program, 62, 75
archived files in, **46–47**
password protection in, **46**
wiping files, 243
word processor files, **88**
contents of, **89**

deleted text in, **89–92**, *90*
sharing, **93**
work disks, off-system, **17–18**
workstations, locking, 39
World E-Mail Directory, 216
World Wide Web (WWW), 137, 243
writing down passwords, 140
WS_FTP program, 60
Wugnet.com site, 43
WWW (World Wide Web), 137, 243

Y

Yahoo search engine, 220
Yahoo's People Finder directory, 216

Z

zeroing-out sectors, 87
Zimmerman, Phillip, 108
ZIP drives, **59**
.ZIP format, 46–47, 62, 75
Zip-It program, 62–63, *64*
zipping archives, **66**

SYBEX BOOKS ON THE WEB

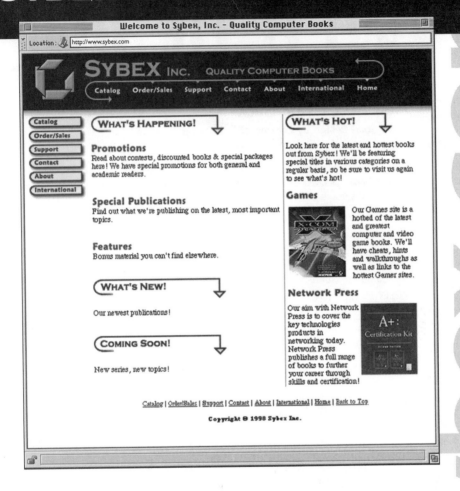

At the dynamic and informative Sybex Web site, you can:

- view our complete online catalog
- preview a book you're interested in
- access special book content
- order books online at special discount prices
- learn about Sybex

www.sybex.com

SYBEX Inc. • 1151 Marina Village Parkway, Alameda, CA 94501 • 510-523-8233

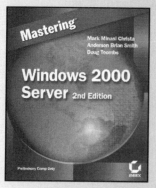

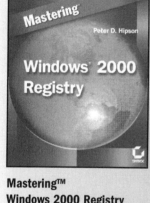
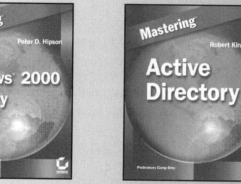

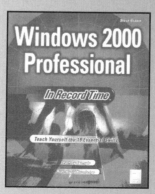

What's on the CD

✓ 007 Password Recovery

Recover the passwords hidden behind the *****
in Windows and Web site password screens.

✓ 007 Sam (Stealth Activity Monitor)

Unbeknownst to the PC user, SAM monitors
every move they make. Exact keystrokes, paths of
hidden programs, and more information are all
logged for later retrieval.

✓ 007 STARR (Stealth Activity Recorder & Reporter)

SAM's more advanced cousin. Compiles even
more detailed information and secretly e-mails
reports to a specified address.

✓ AutoShutdown

Takes care of shutdown housekeeping so you can
leave your PC quickly and safely if necessary. It
also provides password protection on startup.

✓ Black Magic

Simple but powerful password protection for your
Windows desktop. In addition to password protecting your system, Black Magic logs attempts at
getting past the password—which may provide
clues as to who was trying.

✓ Cookie Crusher

Blocks or manages cookies in real time as you surf
the Web. You can view each cookie sent to your
system and decide if you will allow it to be written.

✓ Fastcode32

Decodes (and encodes) MIME and other Web-
encoded data.

✓ Private Bookmarks

Encrypts and hides your Web browser bookmarks or favorites list so that no one but you
can see the titles or URLs of Web pages they
list. Also organizes bookmarks and favorites.

✓ Screenlock

Secures access to your PC with password
protection on multiple levels. Provides question-
and-answer password generation, and records
failed login attempts.

✓ Window Washer

Performs a total system cleanup of useless files
of any type, or focuses on Netscape files. A great
tool for cleaning out traces of your online and
offline activities.

✓ WinGuardian

A monitor utility that serves as an alternative to
filtering, WinGuardian runs completely hidden
and monitors almost everything. It keeps track of
the programs a user runs, logs text typed into a
program, logs all web sites visited, and even cap-
tures screenshots at specified intervals.

✓ WinZip

A popular file-compression and archiving program for Windows that offers a useful password-
protection scheme. You can set up an archive so
that any files added to it are password-protected
and cannot be removed or copied from the archive
without the password you have set.